***Front cover:*** Bishop Auckland Market Place in about :
AEC single-decker, fleet number **EA24** (**PW 8213**), whic
full-width canopy. The bus was working the short Bishop Auckland Town Service,
then numbered 29, which in June 1932 was renumbered 9 and is still run, by
Arriva, as these words are being written in 2001. *(Robert Grieves Collection)*

***Endpapers:*** United in the landscape: West End, Bedlington, in the summer of
1938 or 1939 is devoid of traffic apart from one small open car (possibly a Clyno)
and two United buses. Nineteen-twenty-nine's petrol-engined Bristol B, fleet
number **B69** (**VF 5169**), and Bristol H **BHO32** (**HN 9762**), dating from 1934 and
having recently been fitted with a Gardner five-cylinder oil engine, await their
departure times in this quiet, possibly Sunday, scene. As at 1st February 1938,
both these vehicles were allocated to Ashington depot. *(Robert Grieves Collection)*

# United Automobile Services Limited

## Part One
## The Fleet - 1912 to 1941

## Alan Townsin & John Banks

*Title page:* United's fleet in the 1930s had a strong Leyland presence. After the large batch of Bristol B types in 1929, the new ownership of United at first directed choice away from that firm as suppliers and it would be 1933 before the next new Bristols arrived. In the meantime, 1930 saw a batch of fifty TS3 Tigers fitted with United's own bodywork. Nineteen were left with the new Eastern Counties Omnibus Company in 1931; the remaining 31 served United well in the North-East. This view of AT102 (VF 7666) was taken for the lady who was the first conductress in Berwick. She worked for Scottish Motor Traction and was going home on the United Tiger. At that time, United did not issue such quality uniforms. The vehicle was working the lengthy service from Newcastle to Edinburgh, then numbered 12, an identity it retained for over 35 years until in 1965 its variations were renumbered 504, 505, 506 and 507 in the Scottish Omnibuses revised route-numbering scheme. *(Courtesy Mrs C Voase)*

*Above:* Fleet number AA197 (PW 3009), a solid-tyred AEC, entered the fleet in July 1924. It was numbered A197 when built, receiving its AA-class reclassification in 1926. The top part of the body could be lifted off for summer touring work, when a folding canvas hood would be fitted at the back. In those days before jig-built interchangeability, the two registration numbers ensured that the correct top was put back afterwards and that the number was illuminated on winter nights. This picture was taken at Lowestoft after the bus had been overhauled and repainted and was one of a series used in a booklet designed to publicise the advertising spaces on United buses. Advertising the advertising, one might say. *(United)*

# United Automobile Services Limited

## Part One
## The Fleet - 1912 to 1941

## Alan Townsin & John Banks

with additional material by Philip Battersby
and John D Watson

# Venture *publications*

# Table of Contents

# Foreword
# by Fred Kennington

In asking me to contribute this foreword the authors have bestowed something special. When I joined United in 1949, it was to a 1,000-bus fleet serving much of north-eastern England. It had grown to that from small beginnings in Lowestoft in 1912. Within 16 years of its inception there its buses had reached Edinburgh. It is a remarkable tribute to the pioneers, led by Ernest Boyd Hutchinson, that that should have been achieved.

Now that the United name has gone in the quest for progress, it is vital that its history be recorded before the details are lost forever. All credit is due to those whose research and dedication have made this record possible.

As well as recording that history, the book is a tribute to the many men and women who served the Company so well during the more than 80 years of its existence. For transport enthusiasts countrywide it is an invaluable work of reference. Those with connections to United's area will read it with affection.

*Stockport, Cheshire*
*March 2001*

# Introduction & Acknowledgements

The idea of publishing an illustrated history of United Automobile Services Limited has been long gestating. Outside London, the Company was perhaps the biggest of them all if its territory at all stages of its history is considered. At various times United buses and coaches operated in East Anglia and the Midlands as well as in the North-East of England. At one period its operating territories reached from Suffolk almost to the border between England and Scotland. Later, following the withdrawal operationally from East Anglia, the Company's slogan "from Bridlington to Berwick" said it all. That was still very much among the biggest operating areas to have been under the control of one company. To that can be added United's involvement, either as sole operator or jointly with others, in express services from London to Newcastle, from Newcastle to Edinburgh and Glasgow, and from the Tyne and Tees areas across to Leeds, Manchester and Liverpool.

The fleet was vast, too, as befitted such an operation. Over the decades, from its humble beginnings with a pair each of Scottish Halleys and English Commers in 1912 to its disappearance from the scene in 1998, almost every type of passenger vehicle was represented in it, from crude, solid-tyred lorry-buses, through tiny 14-seaters and all sorts and sizes of more or less full-sized single- and double-deckers to the most luxurious and exotic coaches. Variety was one thing: sheer numbers was another. Apart from the many hundreds of new AECs, ADCs, Daimlers, Leylands and Bristols; the dozens of Whites and Chevrolets; the handfuls of Guys; there were somewhere around a thousand second-hand vehicles which were acquired when competing bus and coach concerns were taken over. These latter saw examples of ADC, AEC, AJS, Albion, All-American, Atlas, Austin, BAT, Bean, Beardmore, Bedford, Berliet, Bristol, Brockway, Chevrolet, Commer, Crossley, Daimler, Dennis, Dodge, Ford, Garner, Gilford, GMC, Graham, Graham-Dodge, Guy, Karrier, Laffley, Lancia, Leyland, Maudslay, Minerva, Morris, Morris-Commercial, Palladium, Renault, Reo, Straker-Squire, Thornycroft, Tilling-Stevens, W & G Du Cros and Willys-Overland enter the United fleet, mostly in the late 1920s and through the following decade, although operators were being taken over into the 1990s.

If the Engineer's Department had much, therefore, with which to contend on the vehicle side, the administrators were no less busy. Some of the latter were themselves "taken over" (one of United's leading characters, Charles Dickinson, for example, came to the Company from the Amos, Proud, of Choppington, concern in 1928). Coping with various changes of ownership and status must not have been easy for the incumbents of the various managerial chairs when, in 1929, United came under LNER, and then Tilling, control and its founder and guiding light, Ernest Boyd Hutchinson, did not remain; nor when, in 1948, the Company became state-owned as part of the British Transport Commission; nor in 1969 when the National Bus Company took control; nor in the 1980s when much of United's responsibilities were lost to Northumbria Motor Services and to East Yorkshire Motor Services and the rump of United passed into private ownership; nor in the 1990s which saw further partition and the decision of the Cowie Group, by then the owners of what remained, to suppress the UNITED name in favour of subsuming it into the corporate ARRIVA image.

The Traffic side, too, ought not to be forgotten. With, at various times and in the areas outlined above, stage carriage services to plan, for which to obtain licences from authority, to cost effectively, and to adequately supervise, they were not exactly under-employed.

All this amounts to a large and complicated story, which has been studied and researched for many years by many people, notable among them the members of the Provincial Historical Research Group (United Circuit) of The Omnibus Society.

For many years the multi-part fleet history of the Company, published by the PSV Circle, was the main source of information. This was a monumental undertaking whose compilers deserve every credit and the thanks of all enthusiasts. It would be idle to deny, however, and I think that its creators would agree, that the years have brought to light inaccuracies, mainly through access to archive material that was not available at the time the fleet history was compiled.

One or two attempts to publish in book form the History of United, including one put out by the Company to mark its 75th Anniversary, were hampered by space restrictions and other problems, leaving the need for a definitive history as urgent as ever.

When planning this publication, it was realised at the very outset that - were every single facet of the vast operation to be dealt with at length in a single volume - the project would be so vast as to require many years in the preparation and would at the end of it all produce a volume so bulky as to be commercially unviable.

The solution has been to split the story into natural segments. It is intended that this first volume will be followed by others, the whole telling the tale from 1912 up to the Company's demise in 1998.

Each member of The Omnibus Society's United Circuit was approached and asked to contribute items on his special area/s of interest and knowledge. Alan Townsin has responded most nobly by providing the fascinating story of United's fleet from the outset to the end of the prewar period (represented by the eventual delivery of the last of the 1940 single-deckers) in a *tour de force* of descriptive writing which tells a story in a fashion very far removed from the "prose fleet lists" which often pass for company histories. Alan is a native of the North-East and United was "his" fleet. There is nobody better qualified to be its historian.

Alan is keen to give credit to the benefit gained from the input of, in particular, John D Watson and Philip Battersby, whose breadth of knowledge and painstaking research are without parallel. Much of Philip's and John's work has been done following long hours in the Durham County Record Office, which holds the United papers. Research among such material can be generally regarded as producing a true picture (although even official records are by no means error-free) and where earlier, unsupported, information clashes with the Durham material, the latter has been preferred.

Maurice Doggett, David Grisenthwaite, Alan Lewis and Arthur Staddon have also read Alan's manuscripts and offered a number of comments which have gladly been incorporated. Philip Groves has acted as coordinator for the project; without his skill in keeping track of the dozens of sets of draft pages passing back and forth, there would have assuredly been no book to publish. We shall hear more of Philip: he was a member of United's management in the 1950s and 1960s and will be contributing to a later volume.

The writer of this introduction (not a member of the United Circuit) has been in love with the United fleet for forty years (more, if childhood and youthful bus spotting is counted) and thus has been delighted to act as editor and producer for the book, as well as to have researched the availability of pictures, made a selection and provided captions. The illustrations have largely come from his and the Philip Battersby collections, with invaluable additional items from other sources individually acknowledged, where known, throughout the book. Many of the pictures used originated as United officials. The writer was responsible, in 1966, for setting up United's picture collection in albums and providing captions. In return he was allowed to make copies of the photographs and it is from this source that most of the United officials have come; for it is believed that, sadly, the United photograph albums have not survived into the new Millennium.

It is always invidious to name names. One could not have left any of the above unmentioned; but, in truth, dozens if not hundreds of enthusiasts, photographers, former employees and correspondents have contributed in greater or lesser ways over the years to what we are able to bring together in this volume. Obviously, lack of space precludes mentioning everybody individually: anybody who feels left out has the team's apology and can be assured that his contribution over the years has been vastly appreciated and that he is thanked most warmly.

Mention must also be made of Robert Buckley and the United Enthusiasts Club, to which most of this book's contributors belong, which has for many years published historical material in its monthly newsletter, and has thus constantly expanded the boundaries of our knowledge.

A large and dedicated team, then, for a large and complicated story: a story whose lack has been felt for a long time and which is now - better late than never - offered as a memorial to one of the finest and proudest passenger undertakings to have served the British travelling public.

*John Banks*
*Romiley, Cheshire*
*July 2001*

Leyland Tiger AT115 (VF 7679), another of the 1930 batch, at Grantham during a lunch stop on the London service circa 1934. *(G H F Atkins)*

United Automobile Services Ltd was registered in London on 4th April 1912. Ernest Boyd Hutchinson, aged 29, listed simply as "traffic expert", although he had a background in electrical engineering and railways, was one of the directors and was to be the leading light in the business through its formative years up to 1929. He had obtained the backing of his father, Captain Walter Ernest Hutchinson, a retired marine superintendent for the British India Steam Navigation Co Ltd, and various friends, some possibly connected through his father. It is noteworthy that Captain Hutchinson and his son, E B Hutchinson, had started a small motor service in Stirling in 1906, indicating the father's direct involvement in this earlier venture which, even if short-lived, had not put them off trying a further similar venture.

Oddly, EBH's name was preceded on the Memorandum of Association by that of Andrew Miller Alexander, civil engineer, about whom little is known, though he had become Chairman by September 1914 and remained so until after the 1914-18 War. There were three directors initially, the above two gentlemen being joined by John Arnold, electrical engineer. Arnold died in November 1913, and was replaced by William James Bussey, Trinity pilot. The initial authorised capital was £3,000.

"United" might seem an odd choice of name for a concern that was not a merger of existing businesses. However, the objects were unusually broadly drawn: they included the buying, sale, manufacture, letting on hire and dealing in motor cabs, omnibuses, cars, carriages, vans, cycles, ships, launches, boats, etc., whether propelled by petrol, steam, electricity, gas, etc., as well as the carrying on of the business of proprietors of the above, plus dealing in parts, acting as garage keepers and coach builders, generation of electricity, even the construction of roads, tramways, bridges etc. This doubtless reflected lawyers' fondness for covering all foreseeable circumstances but "Automobile Services" seems to have been meant in a very broad way, and hence "United" may have been chosen to underline this. The word "Automobile" was used fairly widely at that time, another noteworthy instance relating to the bus industry being what was founded as British Automobile Development Co Ltd in 1905 as a motor-bus offshoot to the British Electric Traction Co Ltd, then running a series of tramway systems - its unfortunate initials led to the former's name changing to British Automobile Traction Co Ltd in 1912; its successors were to play a major part in the United story from 1929.

Indeed, UAS did engage in activities beyond bus operation, such as the sale of various makes of motor vehicles as well as bodybuilding, and the motor trader aspect was conducted on quite a substantial scale in the 1918-29 period. A tourist office was run for a time and local steamer trips operated, using hired vessels.

The choice of location for United's first operations, based in Lowestoft, well-known as a fishing port on the coast of East Anglia but far from major centres of industry, and the initial modest service begun in May 1912, running a few miles southwards along the coast as far as Kessingland and Southwold, gave no hint of "the grand design" that gradually took shape in later years. The choice of route soon showed sound judgement of the local traffic potential but few could have guessed how far this modest business would grow. At first the vehicles ran from existing stables in Mill Road and Hutchinson's office was in the back bedroom of a small terraced house in Morton Road.

The first two vehicles were Halley 28/32hp open-sided 27-seat single-deckers, supplied new by their manufacturers. They were made at Halley's works in Yoker, on the outskirts of Glasgow, the registration numbers, V 1501 and 1502, being issued to Halley by Lanarkshire County Council. They were numbered 1 and 2 in United's fleet, photographic evidence denying reports that V 1502 was No. 1. It is noteworthy that V 1503 was also a Halley with bodywork of very similar style but was a smaller 25hp model with fewer seats - it was sold to an operator in the Tomintoul area. Sides with panels or doors up to waist height had become usual by that date, even for charabanc bodies, and the style of body, later usually described as a "toastrack", may have been intended to cater largely for tourist traffic - the roof was rigid, with canvas side screens which could be rolled down.

Halley vehicles of that period were basically conventional in design, with four-cylinder petrol engines, as could then generally be taken for granted for buses or charabancs, although from 1919 Halley was among the first to offer six-cylinder models. In view of the earlier Hutchinson venture, the choice of a Scottish make is not too surprising - in addition, E B Hutchinson had worked for a railway company in Scotland and his wife, Eleanor Beatrice, was a Glasgow lady - it has been said that the choice of make was influenced by connections she had. These two vehicles are reported to have been driven by Glaswegian drivers when placed in service, one being named Alex Rowan.

In July 1912, two Commer vehicles, which seem likely to have been WP2 models, with bodywork

United's early fleet is not easy to sort out. A large, expanding operator's activities in the years before the First World War can be expected to be less than clear: records, even when they were kept, have often not survived or are inaccessible to researchers. And, of course, matters were sometimes simply not documented at all in those pioneering days. It is generally accepted, however, that United's first two motor buses in 1912 were 27-seat charabancs from the Scottish manufacturer Halley registered locally, before delivery south to United, as V 1501 and V 1502. These are now firmly believed to have been the Company's fleet numbers 1 and 2.

For decades researchers were misled by the picture *(below left)* of V 1502. It was published by United in a 1921 commemorative brochure with the caption "The *first* Car owned by the Company" (author's italics), thus giving rise to the belief that it must have been United's fleet No. 1. A copy of the original of the picture *(above)*, in which the fleet number 2 is clearly visible on the bonnet side, tells a different story. Perhaps United, not having a picture of V 1501 to use in its brochure, doctored this official Halley Motors photograph by removing the fleet number and claiming it as "the first".

Number 2 (V 1502) was later moved to Bishop Auckland *(below right)*, where it was photographed outside the depot in Morland Street. In a later view *(>> opposite page upper)*, No. 2 is in the charge of a youthful crew working on the Bishop Auckland to Durham service. The oil lamps, missing in the previous picture, and not always carried in those early days, were back and the registration number had been moved to a plate fixed to the roof. In the Bishop Auckland views it can be seen that a partition had been fitted behind the front row of seating. This photograph was taken for the crew of the vehicle; it is noteworthy throughout the early period of the bus industry in Great Britain just how many such pictures were taken and when the photographer included all of the vehicle, as here, some quite splendid portraits resulted. *(Jim Wilkinson Collection; Philip Battersby Collection; John Banks Collection)*

*>> Opposite page lower:* Repeat orders for Halleys were not placed and the Company turned to the Commer marque. The first two were registered in London. This is No. 4 (LF 9072), new in July 1912. *(Philip Battersby Collection)*

8

Early types of cars, 1912 Charabanc.

Here is the other 1912 Commer, No. 3 (LF 9071), from a rather battered contemporary print. Originally fitted with a charabanc body as on LF 9072, it later received a single-deck body which had more than a hint of LGOC practice about it. In fact, it looks like a General double-deck body with the upper deck removed. It is not known whether the charabanc body was reused, but it may have gone onto a Daimler chassis registered AH 0193 *(see page 16). (Senior Transport Archive)*

seating 28, of broadly similar nature but panelled up to waist height and having side doors, were added to the fleet for a further service running from Lowestoft. These Commers were Nos 3 and 4, registered in London as LF 9071/2. Commer, more correctly Commer Car at that date, was the marque name of Commercial Cars Ltd, of Luton. The Linley gearbox had been a standard on vehicles of this make from the beginning of production in 1906 - it gave an early form of preselective facility, with control lever on the steering column, using a system of spring-loaded dog clutches to engage the gears when the loading on them was released by using the clutch. At that date Commer's WP range of bus chassis used chain drive to the rear wheels, then still common and also found on the Halley, though the Commer chains were enclosed in a casing and this can be seen in various pictures of United examples.

An entry in a United rule book showing the procedure for ordering urgent spares by telegram is addressed to Commer, referring to "chassis WP2, 108" and gives a front wheel hub as the part required. It is known that greasing hubs twice a week and checking wheel bearings for slackness weekly was part of the operating routine for the vehicles of this make, itself suggesting a design weakness; there is some evidence suggesting that

the model may have been prone to failures in this area.

It had been realised that the demand for the Lowestoft services would dwindle as the local holidaymaking season ended at the end of August, even though they were successful enough to embarrass the Great Eastern Railway, which had operated motor buses in the area since 1904. When the local council granted licences for United to operate buses from Lowestoft to Southwold, the Great Eastern gave notice that its local services would be withdrawn, as indeed they were in January 1913, which opened the door to expansion of the local service network. It seems that an agreement of some kind, perhaps merely an exchange of letters, may have been reached with GER, as the United fleet moved to the GER's former garage in Denmark Road, which was rented by Mr Hutchinson; part of the building still exists.

### A venture in the north

In the early days of the motor bus, operators often sought new territory for expansion but the decision to open a new branch at Bishop Auckland, County Durham, 250 miles north of Lowestoft, seems remarkable in its boldness, unless there was some reason related to personal connections leading to

*Above:* United's first four buses had been registered in Scotland and London - respectively the home of the chassis builder Halley and United's first registered address. Later in 1912 Norfolk County Council numbers made their first appearance, as on No. 6 (AH 0121), another Commer. The bodywork, by Liversidge, of Old Kent Road, London, SE, was an improvement on the charabanc style which preceded it, having a triple-doorway layout. In this view, AH 0121 was brand new and lacked headlamps, although brackets for them were there. The domed roof outline was rare at that date. The picture was used in a press advertisement. *(Alan Lewis Collection)*

*Below:* Number 9 (AH 0128) was one of the 1913 Commers. It had a destination board for Bishop Auckland. *(United)*

This view of No. 12 (AH 0132), another of the 1913 Commers with Liversidge bodywork, in Bishop Auckland heading for Durham is the earliest available of a United bus actually moving rather than posed while stationary. The narrow, steep road, which the bus was descending, is thought to be the main road out of Bishop Auckland to Durham until 1928 when the direct road from the Market Place was built. *(United)*

the move there. Perhaps it is too fanciful to wonder whether E B Hutchinson might have had any notion at so early a stage of building a huge operation extending over much of the ground between these distant areas. In later years it was explained that part of the reasoning was based on the year-round demand for transport in coal-mining and industrial areas; even on that basis, the reason for choosing that particular district remains a matter for speculation. Samuel Adams of Bishop Auckland was appointed a director, but apparently not before the move to the north.

Whatever the reason, it was to prove a sound choice. "Notes on the history of United Automobile Services Ltd", issued by the company in 1962 and revised in 1976, indicates that at the beginning of operations in Bishop Auckland in 1912, the two Halleys were garaged at Stable Yard, North Bondgate, in the town centre. It is not clear when United first had its own garage in the locality though a local directory for 1914 quotes an address in Cockton Hill, about a mile to the south of the town centre and a personal reminiscence by a Mr Pigg implies that it was already there when his

family moved nearby in April 1913. He quotes the Chief Engineer as a Mr Smith - not to be confused with B V Smith who held that post from 1924 - and immediately below Mr Hutchinson was Mr Harriott.

The original garage there was probably quite small, but there are references to two parcels of land being acquired in 1914-16 and what became No. 1 garage erected in Morland Street, evidently soon followed by No. 2; part of these premises was used for the manufacture of aircraft wings during the war when the fleet would have been depleted, and indeed this activity may have facilitated the erection of the buildings.

A further garage, No. 3, was brought into use nearby in about 1920, after which Nos 1 and 2 became at least in part the company's bus overhaul works in the north. This role was to continue and expand until the Darlington works came into operation in 1933, when they were vacated. Further premises were taken in the town in 1918-20 for use as a showroom and a service and repair depot, adding to Bishop Auckland's overall importance in the United story. The first United bus service in the north, begun in October 1912, ran to Durham via

Spennymoor, one of the Halleys operating on the service that winter. The photograph of Halley V 1502, carrying a destination board reading "Durham", was taken outside Cockton Hill No. 1 garage and hence thought to be at some date after 1916 or so. The style of bodywork seems very unsuitable for service-bus work in a northern climate, save in exceptional summer weather. The livery chosen was grey, which seems to have been fairly popular in that period, probably because it was thought not to show up the dirt vehicles collected when country roads were rarely tarred. A little later a blue waistband was added. At first no fleetname was carried, and although it has been reported that the Lowestoft-based business at first operated under the fleetname "Grey Cars", by 1913 in Bishop Auckland the vehicles simply carried small lettering reading "United Automobile Services Ltd, Great Eastern Garage, Lowestoft".

Four more vehicles, of which three at least were further Commers, were added to the fleet by the end of 1912, evidently taking the fleet numbers 5 to 8. This time they received registration numbers more local to the Lowestoft base, yet not having the BJ mark then current for East Suffolk, in which area Lowestoft and the East Anglian services thus far operated were situated. Instead, the vehicles received Norfolk registration numbers, setting a precedent that was to remain standard practice for the entire period that the operational headquarters remained in Lowestoft. It seems that the choice was made because the Norfolk County Council motor taxation office in Norwich was more readily accessible from Lowestoft than the East Suffolk office in Ipswich. Some operators with extensive operating areas registered some of their vehicles on a more local basis but this principle was not favoured by United, even though there were soon more buses at work in County Durham than in the Lowestoft area. Nos 5 and 6 of the Commers placed in service in late 1912 were registered AH 0120/1 - Norfolk County Council was unusual in issuing numbers prefixed by a zero for vehicles classified as Heavy Motor Cars and this was to continue as a characterisic of most United buses until 1920; the system ceased as a result of the provisions of the Roads Act, 1920, which came into effect from 1921. Commer chassis were again favoured for single-deck additions to the fleet in 1913, believed to number eight. Mr Pigg recalls Commers Nos 6, 8, 9, 10 and 12 operating from Bishop Auckland and that they had two doors on the left-hand side (originally three; wartime pictures show the rearmost out of use), describing the internal arrangement as "a passage along the left side of the vehicle, and seats to hold four passengers on the right." They also had an external step running along the left side, which he recalled giving rise to a tragic accident. Young children living near the Cockton Hill depot would sit on this when a bus was stationary so to have a ride when it moved off. On one occasion, a boy fell off as the bus gathered speed and was run over by the rear wheel - he was taken to the nearby hospital but died.

Mr Pigg also describes the operation of the Commer gearboxes, which had three speeds, preset by the driver "setting a lever which ran horizontally through a semi-circle under the steering wheel" and wrote that "on steep hills, the second or so which elapsed on changing from second gear into bottom gear by the driver pushing the clutch down used to startle some passengers." No doubt the bus would lose speed and the engine speed probably rose, giving an impression that something was amiss, yet the driver would seem not to be taking any action, waiting for the spring-loaded dog clutch to engage the lower gear as the loading came off the gears previously in use - with what would have needed to be widely spaced ratios, this may well have taken quite a bit more than a second.

Some, including the first of the 1913 deliveries, No. 9 (AH 0128), are said to have had enclosed 34-seat bus bodies by Liversidge, the size suggesting they would be WP2 13ft 8ins wheelbase or possibly WP1 models of the 13ft 9ins wheelbase version of that model. This concern is believed to have been J Liversidge & Sons Ltd, of 561 Old Kent Road, London SE1, registered on 29th December 1899. The firm was taken over by Glover & Webb in 1926 to form Glover, Webb & Liversidge Ltd, which was still in business on quite a large scale as goods vehicle bodybuilders, quoting the same address, at least up to the late 1960s. In a picture of No. 9 it is just possible to see the outline of the enclosed chain case of the final drive - Mr Pigg also confirms that they had chain drive. The body design had a roof which was rounded in outline at front, sides and rear, projecting slightly over the windscreen - such use of curves, even if limited in extent, was still quite rare at that date and more akin to a typical mid 1920s style.

### The first AECs

By then further services had been added, a local route serving Shildon, and one to Ferryhill, and further vehicles were ordered. Significant as a pointer to later events were six AEC B-type buses dating from June and July 1913. The Associated Equipment Co Ltd had been formed as a subsidiary of the Underground group, responsible for most of London's tube railways system, on 13th June 1912. Its works at Walthamstow, inherited from the London General Omnibus Co Ltd, by then also part of the Underground group, was already producing the B-type chassis on a large scale, that model having been adopted as the LGOC's standard bus on its introduction in 1910. There had barely been time to develop general sale on the open market before an agreement had been signed with the Daimler Co Ltd in December 1912, under which the latter was appointed sole selling agent for chassis sold outside the Underground group. Clearly United, probably uniquely, had confirmed its order before that date, and thus these chassis, built to a special long version of the B-type design with 14ft instead of 12ft 10 5/8ins wheelbase, are believed to have been the first AECs built for a customer

AEC B-type chassis, bonnet number B2628 (AH 0139), on the occasion described in the text on page 16. *(United)*

outside London, although they were supplied via Daimler in accordance with the agreement by then in force. The B series was used for both the AEC chassis numbers and, for those retained in London, LGOC fleet numbers, the numbers being displayed prominently in raised digits on the bonnet sides as well as the chassis frames. The B-series numbers of the United vehicles and the registration numbers they carried are stated by authors G J Robbins and J B Atkinson in *The London B-Type Motor Omnibus (Third and revised edition, World of Transport, 1991)* to have been as follows:-

| No. | Reg'n No. | Chassis to Daimler |
|-----|-----------|--------------------|
| B2623 | AH 0138 | June 1913 |
| B2628 | AH 0139 | June 1913 |
| B2639 | AH 0140 | June 1913 |
| B2650 | AH 0141 | June 1913 |
| B2664 | AH 0187 | July 1913 |
| B2673 | AH 0189 | August 1913 |

However, this omits the registration number AH 0137, which is discussed below, and whilst AH 0141 is doubtful, AH 0187/9 are seriously suspect, as will become apparent. United fleet numbers, normally also shown on the bonnet side

but in smaller figures, seem not to have been displayed on these vehicles at first, but the photographs confirm that the first two of the above chassis were registered AH 0138 and 0139, both having radiators of a rare style with the full maker's name "Associated Equipment Co Ltd" cast into the top tank instead of the small LGOC lettering hitherto usual; it was already in use on buses supplied to LGOC but allocated for operation in other liveries under various agreements of that era. These two buses at least were supplied with open-top double-deck bodies of typical London style with no weather protection for the driver. The extra chassis length allowed space for a non-standard extra row of seats behind the driver but ahead of the body front bulkhead and hence also exposed to the elements. The standard LGOC B-type body seated 34, with 18 outside on the open top deck and 16 inside on longitudinal benches with seats for eight on each side; the space to the left of the driver not being used for fare-paying passengers. The United arrangement seems to have added a further six, probably with a row of four just in front of the bulkhead - the width of the lower deck of the body was only 5ft, so five would have been impractical - and two alongside the driver - passengers were carried alongside the driver on

*Above:* Two of the 1914 batch of Commers, posed when new in the sunshine. The leading vehicle is AH 0187, but that behind remains tantalisingly unidentifiable. Ernest Hutchinson's new body design is very well illustrated here. *(United)*

*Below:* In a photograph at East Green, Southwold, Daimler No. 25 (AH 0191) had a similar but shorter body to those on the 1914 Commers. This was one of the batch of Daimler B models, a design developed from the AEC B. The vehicle shown was one of the survivors to remain in the fleet into the postwar period. Note that the UNITED fleetname does not yet appear on the buses, although the legal owner lettering is quite prominent. The treatment of the registration number - AHO 191 instead of AH 0191 - was a signwriter's mistake. *(Jack Burton Collection)*

some operators' buses of that era, as indicated by admonishments that no female passengers were to be seated there. This would have given the total capacity of 40 quoted for various buses with LGOC B-type double-deck bodies in the fleet then and after the 1914-18 war.

This was a curious arrangement, making inefficient use of the longer wheelbase, as well as seeming particularly ill-suited to the northerly climate, and raises the question of whether it was intended only as a temporary measure to get the buses into service quickly. The specification of, or conversion to, longer than standard wheelbase was to be a recurring United characteristic throughout the Hutchinson era. In this case, it seems possible that the longer-term objective was to permit fitting

15

*Above left:* Another 1914 Daimler B-type chassis had the fleet number 27 and was registered AH 0193. It had a 28-seat charabanc body which looks similar to that originally carried by 1912 Commer No. 4 (LF 9072) *(see page 9)*. The original caption to this United photograph in the 1921 brochure reads: "Even before the war charabanc business was good. Note the Commissionaire".

*Below:* The line of Daimler B-type chassis, including Nos 24 (AH 0194), 26, 27 (AH 0193) and 30, with bodies removed but still with fleet numbers on the bonnets, ready for departure for war service in October 1914. Number 26 was complete with a small Union Jack in honour of the occasion but the trilby-hatted figure third from the left, which looks very much like E B Hutchinson, appears suitably morose at the loss of the heart of his fledgling fleet. *(Maurice Doggett Collection)*

*Above right:* One of the Daimler chassis which survived the Press Gang. It was fitted with the double-deck body which had been carried by one of the AEC B types, whose registration number, AH 0140, it also acquired. *(Maurice Doggett Collection)*

a single-deck body of adequate seating capacity. A picture of AH 0138 taken at the AEC works *(see page 21)* shows it with a destination board reading "Durham" while one of AH 0139 reproduced on page 14 appears to show it in normal service with "Bishop Auckland" displayed, though the presence of what might be a managerial figure alongside the driver, and the attitudes of various people in the scene, suggest it may have been a posed picture of the vehicle's first journey.

Although the last pair are stated to have been single-deckers, it is not known whether all the others were supplied as double-deckers as delivered, but AH 0138 at least seems not to have lasted long in that form. Another prewar picture taken at Southwold, about ten miles south of Lowestoft, shows the chassis much as built but carrying an enclosed single-deck body, evidently with forward-facing seats, to a style favoured by United in 1914, as described below. The livery is similar to that shown in the picture of Commer No. 9; the picture, reproduced on page 21, is also of interest in showing Mr E B Hutchinson, though

unfortunately he is standing in a position obscuring whatever bonnet number was carried at that stage.

No United fleet numbers are specifically known for the AEC B types. As for registration numbers, it has been said that AH 0137 was an LGOC B type; this description could have meant a B with radiator carrying those initials although it could also be interpreted more strictly as one built when the Walthamstow works was still in LGOC ownership. It seems more likely that in reality this registration was carried by another of the AEC chassis ordered by United, which would give a run of AH 0137-41. On the other hand, it could be a genuine LGOC-built chassis, i.e. dating from before June 1912, perhaps sold from LGOC's fleet, although such an early sale from LGOC's stock would have been unusual. The registration AH 0140 is also quoted as having been at first carried by an LGOC B, rather than an AEC one, but the distinction may have been thought merely academic at that date. Mr Evans, in an article written in 1934, says that in 1912 eight vehicles were owned and that in 1913

16

eight Commers and six AEC B-types were acquired. He had joined United in 1922 and, by comparing with other sources, it appears he included the 1914 Commers in these totals. Given this, the fleet numbers had probably reached 18 by the end of 1912, the AEC B-types probably being allocated the numbers 13 to 18.

Four more Commer single-deck buses were added in 1914, on a longer-wheelbase chassis, very probably the 14ft 3ins version of the WP1 model. These had 36 seats and their registration numbers were AH 0185-8. Mr Pigg quotes Nos 19, 20 and 22 as Bishop Auckland-based "Commers with a longer body, a middle passage, seats for two on each side, and a rear entrance without a door", which seems to fit the above facts well - might the adoption of rear-entrance layout have been a reaction to the accident involving the small boy on the step of one of the previous Commer buses?

These 1914 buses had a new and quite different style of body, which the annual report for that year indicates was designed by E B Hutchinson. It had an almost flat roof, except at the front where it sloped downwards over the cab, barely projecting over the windscreen. There was very slight curvature in the roof in both planes over this front portion but above the cab side windows there was a panel of almost triangular shape lining up with the opening top lights of the main side windows. This rather austere-looking design was to be United's standard 1914 single-deck style for Commer and, in shorter form, for four Daimler buses purchased that year as mentioned below. It was also used for three Daimlers of January 1916, as well as for the rebodied AEC B-type mentioned above.

By 1914, the arrangements between AEC and Daimler were in full effect and what was generally known as the Daimler B was in production at Walthamstow. This was a development of the original B, using the Daimler four-cylinder 5.7-litre sleeve-valve engine, often known at the time as the 40hp unit, in a chassis of slightly heavier build, the prototype of the 3-ton version being B3010. It is known that United took at least five of this model (which had the same 14ft wheelbase as the six special AEC B-types already supplied); two are known to have been purchased in May 1914: B3021, numbered 25 in the fleet and registered AH 0191, which had a rear-entrance single-deck body; and B3025, to which further reference is made under the wartime developments quoted below.

It is stated on page 49 of Robbins and Atkinson (mentioned above), that Daimler supplied ten B-types to United in 1914, with registrations believed to be AH 0190-9, these being described as four with saloon bodies, five charabancs and one with a double-deck body from another chassis. Evidence from motor tax records and from later photographs suggests that these vehicles were more likely to have been AH 0189-94/6-9. All but two of the ten were requisitioned, the survivors being AH 0191 and a charabanc on chassis B3025.

## Wartime

Britain entered what became called the Great War, but now better known as World War One, on 4th August 1914, and large numbers of motor vehicles were soon being requisitioned for military use. It seems that at least four, and probably all six, of United's AEC B-type buses were among them and for a time double-deckers disappeared from Bishop Auckland. Several of the almost-new Daimler B chassis were taken by the War Department in October 1914; a photograph (p.16) shows Nos 24 (AH 0194), 26, 27 (AH 0193), 30 and another with bodies removed but still bearing their fleet numbers on the bonnets, ready for departure. However, No. 32 of the same Daimler B batch, on chassis B3025, somehow escaped this fate, perhaps not being mobile for some reason at the time, and received a double-deck body and registration number, AH 0140, previously carried by one of the AEC B-type buses, B2639, of June 1913. This bus entered service during wartime at Bishop Auckland, regularly being allocated to the local service to West Auckland until after the war ended, although sometimes diverted to the Durham service.

In those days and until 1921, there were no restrictions on the transfer of registration numbers between vehicles, officialdom evidently being satisfied provided a registration number was displayed on any vehicle to be used on the public highway and an appropriate road fund licence corresponding to that number was in force. In United's case, the registration plate was often mounted quite high on the body at both front and rear, simply being moved with it to a new chassis. E B Hutchinson was to write in "Bus & Coach" in June 1940 that all 18 buses in the Yarmouth and Lowestoft area were impressed, with very meagre compensation, and that their removed bodies took up a lot of storage space until the end of the war. This left East Anglia without a single United vehicle and the firm struggled to keep the remaining 17 buses running in the colliery districts of Durham. Writing in retrospect, Mr Hutchinson seems to have included the three later Daimlers 34-6 in his total.

Keeping even the reduced fleet on the road in Bishop Auckland had many difficulties, as recalled by EBH. The staff were all of military age, and eventually every fit man went to the war. When further calls were made their replacements went too, until there were none left capable of military service, though ex-servicemen invalided out of the forces because of wounds were recruited later in the war. "For drivers we got the halt, the lame, the young, the old, and we even tried girls, who through no fault of their own, in the extremely difficult conditions prevailing, were not a success." Early motor buses often had very heavy controls at the best of times and coaxing them along when no longer in the best of condition would have called for skill and experience. Mr Pigg reported frequent boiling and failures to climb hills. He also mentioned the Daimlers becoming "most noisy at even moderate engine speeds through the sleeve

*Above:* On a dull, misty day in Bishop Auckland the driver and lady conductor of wartime Daimler Y type No. 36 (AH 0278) pose for their portraits. Behind the camera was a local photographer from Tow Law, who seems to have made a business of photographing United crews at this spot (at least one other similar view bearing his imprint has survived). The bus was one of the trio which entered the fleet in January 1916, no doubt bringing considerable relief to a fleet much depleted by the depredations of the requisitioners. The characterful, gaiter-clad driver of the rather stern countenance is almost hiding the UNITED fleetname on the side of the vehicle, an innovation which came in with these 1916 Daimlers. *(A O Humphreys)*

*Below:* An unobstructed view of the other side of No. 35 (AH 0277), another of the batch, shows the new fleetname. The chassis were to military specification, drawn from massive numbers built for the Army. In yet another picture obviously taken for the crew rather than the bus, the driver is a handsome young fellow; his lady conductor sports the most peculiar headgear whilst tightly gripping both ticket machine and cashbag. *(John Banks Collection)*

Visual evidence of United buses running on gas in the First World War is not exactly plentiful; had that not been so, the picture above would still have merited inclusion, poor original that it may be. It is of one of the January 1916 Daimlers showing that the wooden box on the roof, designed to carry the gas bag, was enormous: it extended more than halfway to the radiator at the front and there was a considerable overhang at the back, not all of which the photographer managed to fit into his viewfinder. The most important point, however, is the evidence provided by the lettering on the gas bag, above the second half of the word "Brotherton's", indicating that the gas bag was manufactured - or possibly just supplied - by "Barton Bros., Beeston, Notts". The crew is again to the fore: driver with bow-tie and lady conductor again with prominent headgear. Below, in yet another crew portrait, can be seen one of the 1913 Liversidge-bodied Commers, No. 9 (AH 0128). There are a number of detail differences in both holder and gasbag but in either case the extra weight to be hauled around with a less efficient fuel must have affected performance considerably. *(Philip Battersby Collection)*

One of the 1914 long-bodied Commers, in an illustration taken from United's 1921 brochure and unfortunately not identifiable, shows differences again over the previous two pictures. The most obvious is that the gasbag holder had no rear overhang. *(United)*

valves rattling." There is an irony in this experience with the engine design adopted by Daimler because of its quietness - it seems more probable that the noise would have come from wear in the eccentric drive which operated the sleeves, which have given an effect not unlike a big-end failure though producing more of a clatter than the "thump" of the latter, because of the lighter weight of the components involved. However, it seems that women were much more successful as conductors - in EBH's words "they did their job spendidly, and they could control a rough crowd of Durham miners better than the men." Incidentally he refers to them as conductors, although the feminine form "conductress", was to become widely adopted in the north-east by the 1930s. United was then still employing them in quite large numbers, to an extent unusual in peacetime, and one wonders if the good experience in the first war had a bearing on this. However the main factor was almost certainly that they were paid less than the men, as was widespread practice in those days.

Mechanics were a particular problem as munition works paid high wages and offered immunity from military service. Even so, staff were recruited and trained. As already mentioned, one of the Cockton Hill garages was turned into a small factory making aeroplane wings; these would almost certainly have been of wood and canvas construction, allowing some good craftsmen in wood to be retained. A contract was also taken on to supervise ploughing a big acreage using the Fordson tractors by then available, driven by "unfit" soldiers, EBH thereby learning the technology of ploughing.

Obtaining replacement vehicles was almost impossible. However, during the 1914/5 period, the Daimler B, in production at the AEC works at Walthamstow, had been developed into new heavier-duty specifications for manufacture in increasingly large numbers to suit military requirements. They retained the Daimler sleeve-valve engine, successive versions of the chassis

being designated W, X and Y, the last of these having become standard from March 1915. They were numbered in the same series as the B-type chassis though without prefix letter and built in very large batches to meet the War Department's needs. Limited numbers were released to bus operators in 1915/6 and United acquired three of these new Daimler Y chassis in December 1915. Numbered 34-6 and registered AH 0276-8, they entered service in January 1916; they are recorded as having 26-seat rear-entrance bodies, the design being recalled by Mr Pigg as being the same as on the 1914 Commers. These three new buses were noteworthy for the first use of the fleetname "UNITED", at that stage in equal-sized block capital latters, shaded in white. Thereafter, this was quite rapidly applied to other buses in the fleet; the addition of blue lower panels to the grey livery also began with this batch. The Daimler Y-types, which EBH quotes as the only buses obtained during the war, had quite long lives in the fleet by contemporary standards, being recorded as passed to the Sales Department for disposal on 1st October 1925.

EBH reported that supplies of petrol were reduced to 44% of normal requirements and for a time were augmented by a small proportion of paraffin. Then some vehicles were converted to run on paraffin alone using a vaporiser, starting up on petrol as with the farm tractors, but the resulting dilution of lubricating oil caused frequent bearing failures. Then paraffin was included in the rationing allowance, so a fresh alternative was sought. Town gas was also used, being carried in a large balloon-like bag carried in a frame attached to the roof, a method only applicable to single-deckers, most of which were converted. Credit is given by EBH to T H Barton, another lively independent operator, of Beeston, Nottingham, for the idea, and it seems that the bags may have been purchased from that concern, which had patented the construction of the gas-bag. There was a loss of power compared to petrol and the supply had to be replenished every 12 miles or so, but it was regarded as sufficiently important for EBH and "another operator who was similarly placed" - might this also have been Mr Barton? - to rush to London to fight an Order banning the use of gas for operating vehicles, going from office to office until they eventually succeeded. In an account written by A T Evans in "Bus & Coach" in September 1946, it was stated that United was the second largest user of this fuel for vehicle propulsion in the country at that time. It is known that gas was still in use in Spennymoor in October 1918, vehicles so powered being required to have two fire extinguishers.

Fares had to be increased to nearly twice the pre-war levels because of increased costs, but a 1d fare was retained for short distances on all routes, E B Hutchinson claiming that United was the only company in the country to do this. He also reported that the growing Government restrictions of the war led the bus interests of "the Electrical

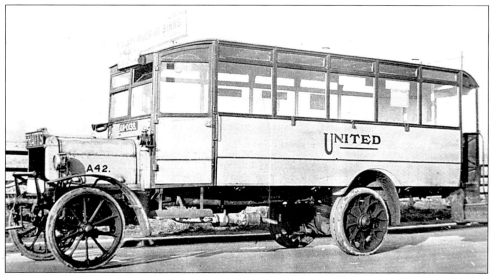

A link between this and the next chapter comes from this trio of pictures of the same registration number applied to three quite different chassis and body combinations.

The upper picture is a fine shot of one of the AEC B types when brand new in 1913 at AEC's Walthamstow premises. B2623 (AH 0138) shows quite clearly the extra space between the front of the body and the driving seat, achieved by mating the standard LGOC B-type 34-seat body to the longer AEC chassis specified by United. This area was used for carrying passengers. Thus United's B types were 40-seaters.

In the centre picture, a year or so later, the same chassis has acquired one of the new standard single-deck bodies designed by E B Hutchinson. EBH is standing in front of the bonnet, consigning generations unborn of United students to wondering what fleet number was on the bonnet side.

The lower picture shows the next stage: in 1919 the single-deck body had been fitted to a new AEC Y-type chassis numbered 42, which had become A42 when seen a year or two later, though retaining the original registration number.

Whilst some of this activity might be explained by a need brought on by a chassis being requisitioned for military use, this sequence of events is an early example of what was to become a United trade mark, for the use and reuse of serviceable bodies on newer chassis was a policy which the Company would pursue well into the post Second World War era. *(Brian Thackray Collection; Maurice Doggett Collection; United)*

21

Federation" - this would be the British Electrical Federation (the organisation set up by the British Electric Traction Co, to act as a central agency for, originally, its tramway company subsidiaries) - to form the Provincial Omnibus Owners Association. Membership was open to independent concerns and this brought him constantly in touch with the leading personalities of the industry; he was later to become a member of Council of the Association. Although still fiercely independent and modest in size, United was beginning to make its mark at a national level.

Another view of AH 0138 in postwar form on the AEC Y-type chassis, one of the best of those taken primarily as portraits of the crew. Here we see a lady conductor with a rather more stylish hat and a driver looking as if all set for a climbing holiday. The advertisement boards doubtless brought in useful revenue but were hardly elegant. The superimposed route number on the destination display was to continue to the end of board displays in the 1930s - in later years at least the number was in red. *(United)*

# 2 Postwar Expansion 1919-1925

The Great War ended with the Armistice of 11th November 1918, and almost immediately a major expansion of the United business was put in hand. The issued capital increased from the £17,242, at which it had remained static from 1915 to April 1919, up to £46,683 in September of that year and then to £180,004 a year later, rising rather more gently to £220,539 by September 1923 and remaining steady for a further two years. The prospectus issued in March 1920 made clear that the capital being sought was required to buy new buses and that an order had been placed with AEC. The extra funds allowed a vast increase in fleet strength and the opening up of many new services. Shareholdings were mainly taken up in small amounts by individuals although the Hutchinson family was well represented.

A 14-acre site was purchased at Laundry Lane, Lowestoft, in 1919 and, in addition to an operating garage and workshop premises, construction of what was described as a coachbuilding factory soon began - it came into operation in late 1920; the first vehicles bodied in it joined the fleet in 1921, as described later. This works became known as "the Coach Factory", remaining so to many of those associated with it through successive changes of title, though officially it became part of the Eastern Counties Omnibus Co Ltd on its formation in 1931 and then Eastern Coach Works Ltd on being split off as a separate business in 1936.

Operational expansion in 1919 included a new group of services in the Northumberland coal-mining area, a further 30 miles north of Durham, previously the most northerly depot. These were centred on Blyth, where a depot was opened in 1919, followed slightly later by one at Ashington. The premises at Cockton Hill, Bishop Auckland, were extended in 1920, as mentioned in the previous chapter, and other depots opened in the surrounding area that year included Crook, Ferryhill Station, Barnard Castle and Darlington. Another leap well outside the existing pattern of routes, this time to the east, was to Redcar on the Yorkshire coast adjoining the mouth of the River Tees. A depot was opened there in 1920, the services from it at first isolated though later gradually spreading westwards to Middlesbrough. A depot was also opened at Stockton at about this time.

In East Anglia, further expansion southwards from the Lowestoft area ran up against a venture by Thomas Tilling Ltd, then mainly a bus operator in south London, who opened a branch in Ipswich in June 1919. This led to the formation in August that year of the Eastern Counties Road Car Co Ltd jointly by the Tilling concern and the British

Automobile Traction Co Ltd, the latter having been set up to run or control motor bus operations by the British Electric Traction Co Ltd, in those days still basically a tramway group. An agreement dated June 1921 with ECRC included a map with boundaries shown as straight lines: Southwold-Thetford; Thetford-King's Lynn; and due west from King's Lynn. It laid down that United would not operate south of this line, the Company giving up two services into Ipswich, while Tilling would not run northwards of the line. It gave United freedom of action in most of Norfolk, turning the main direction of United's expansion in the area towards Norwich. This was significant both as United's first step towards the concept of becoming recognised as a "territorial" operator, and as the first contact with Tilling and BAT, later to play a much bigger role in the United story.

### The Underwood connection

There was a third element to this rapid and exceptionally wide-ranging expansion, although not under United's own name. This was the incorporation, in November 1920, of W T Underwood Ltd, based at Clowne, in Derbyshire, not far from Chesterfield and near the Yorkshire (West Riding) and Nottinghamshire borders. William Thomas Underwood had worked for the Grimsby tramways but had been taken on at United's Bishop Auckland garage in 1914, becoming foreman at Durham garage by 1916 and moving to Great Yarmouth by 1919. Having become a protégé of E B Hutchinson, he was selected to develop the Derbyshire territory, though it may be that its development using his name was also an indication of a degree of doubt as to its success, avoiding the risk of failure damaging the United name.

A controlling shareholding in Underwood was taken by United from December 1920 and most of the vehicles operated under the Underwood name were drawn from the United fleet, some of which, where initially entering service on lease to Underwood, were registered in Derbyshire or the West Riding of Yorkshire accordingly, although livery, and later the fleetname lettering styles, made the link with United obvious. Underwood used its own series of fleet numbers, the first batch, 1-10, receiving registration numbers WR 5132-41, though not in order. These were ex-military AEC Y-series models drawn from United's fleet of the type described below - they had been given United fleet numbers (in this case between 102 and 148, again not in sequence), continuing to be identified as such in United's records. A similar pattern was

*Top:* A102 (WR 5133) was a 1920 AEC Y-type with 32-seat rear-entrance body by Christopher Dodson, of Willesden. It ran from new leased to the Underwood fleet as number 6. *(G Lilleker Collection)*

*Above:* Three Thompson-bodied 30-seat AEC buses came to Underwood from Doncaster Motor Services in January 1922. WY 509/10 and EE 2186 were never owned by United, but fleet numbers were allocated by the Company and by Underwood. These were possibly A165-7 (United) and apparently (UA)44-6 (Underwood) but it is not known which was which. WY 509 is illustrated in this view alongside one of the other two, which a similar photograph shows was fleet number 46. All that can be said for certain about this trio, then, is that WY 509 was *not* Underwood fleet number 46. *(G Lilleker Collection)*

capital needed was largely provided by others. However, a management agreement continued to allow United to keep Underwood in line in regard to vehicle policy and successive livery changes.

United's livery continued to be grey until 1923. A more elaborate form of fleetname, in which the inital letter U of UNITED was extended downwards to align with the additional words "Automobile Services Ltd" in upper- and lower-case lettering, appeared on a timetable in July 1920 and on some vehicles briefly around that time. A scroll ran from the "A", sweeping in curves to link with the final "s", this latter giving a hint of the much later use of a similar idea on the coach version of the fleetname as used from the mid-1930s. Oddly enough, it was applied to the very utilitarian lorry-buses described later, but proved short-lived on vehicles, though it persisted as a letter heading, on timetable covers and in advertisements etc. until the reorganisation of 1929. However, in the 1920/3 period a significant number of vehicles seem to have operated without a fleetname, photographs of new buses over that period showing none, though those already having the plain UNITED form were not altered.

### Post-war fleet expansion

Although the war had virtually cut off deliveries of new vehicles to civilian users, the huge demand for military lorries had expanded production immensely. In particular, from 1917, the AEC factory at Walthamstow, after a brief period of overlap when production of Daimler Y-types continued, had reverted to producing chassis under its own name. The resulting AEC Y-series models, beginning with the YA, were very largely a continuation of the Daimler Y save in regard to the engine, which became the Tylor JB4, a proprietary four-cylinder unit of conventional side-valve type with 7.7-litre capacity, a large engine by the standards of the day, which had been designed to suit the War Department's need for ample pulling capability in difficult conditions rather than speed. AEC output had risen to new heights in 1917/8, sometimes touching 130 per week, and so when the War Department ceased to take delivery of chassis it had ordered as the war ended, large numbers quickly became available for other buyers. E B

followed with later deliveries, which broadly followed the trends in United's own fleet, including numbers of Daimler CB and modified AEC Y-series as described below. Not until January 1922 were any vehicles directly owned by W T Underwood Ltd. In that month three AEC Y-type 30-seat buses were taken over with the business of Doncaster Motor Services. They did not appear in United's financial records but coincide with a gap in the fleet numbers at A165-7. This policy of taking only acquired vehicles into Underwood ownership continued throughout the concern's existence, with a few exceptions. The United financial interest in Underwood only remained at a level giving control until about 1922, after which the increase in

Hutchinson's eye for a business opportunity came into play and substantial numbers were bought not only for the United fleet but for general sale. At that stage, AEC had little in the way of a sales organisation and the Bishop Auckland premises were well sited to supply chassis to customers in the north. This sales role for AEC continued until 1929, the United company at that latter date still being listed as authorised distributors for Norfolk and Suffolk (Lowestoft and 12 miles radius) from its Laundry Lane, Lowestoft, address and for Bishop Auckland, in the latter case quoting the Railway Street address, the sales office having been transferred there from Newgate Street. Dealerships for several other commercial vehicle and car makers were also obtained during the 1920s.

From 1924, when the Coach Factory began to build bodies for outside customers, the AEC connection in particular led to many orders, it then being common practice for the chassis maker to supply complete vehicles, sub-contracting the body construction. This also applied in varying degree to other makes for whom sales agencies were obtained, notably Star and Gilford. Most of these were buses or coaches but goods vehicles were also bodied in the 1925/6 period, including about 50 tankers for petroleum companies.

An initial delivery of 20 AEC YBs - this variant introducing pressed-steel chassis frames instead of the flitched type used hitherto - was taken into United's own fleet, beginning in December 1918, the month after hostilities ceased, and continuing until April 1919, receiving the United fleet numbers 37 to 56, thus continuing the original series begun in 1912. They were followed by sixteen of the YD type, numbered 57-72 in May-July 1919, followed by further YB as well as YC and YD models. The different type letters indicated minor variations, such as the use of David Brown rear-axle gearing on the YC.

By September 1920 the fleet number series had reached 102, some 64 new AEC chassis filling all but two of the postwar numbers. The identities represented by the fleet numbers 79 and 86 remain unknown, but it seems possible that they may have been issued to vehicles first recorded under a new numbering system described later, perhaps as B1 and B2. The drivers at Bishop Auckland welcomed the reliability of the AECs; even though the comparison of the new chassis with the well-worn Commers and Daimlers was hardly a fair one, the ability to climb even steep hills without the need to drop below second gear was a refreshing change, reported Mr Pigg.

Obtaining suitable bodywork for an intake already almost twice the prewar fleet at a time when many other operators were also renewing or expanding their fleets was very difficult and doubtless influenced the decision

to set up the company's own coach factory. Accordingly, these and other early post-war additions to the fleet received an assortment of bodies, drawn from several sources.

United's own records of this period seem not to have been very comprehensive, to judge by what survives - it seems probable that what had sufficed for a small business in the early days proved inadequate amid the problems of a fast-expanding fleet in a time of scarcities - and although a body numbering system was begun in about 1919, establishing the true sequence of events is far from easy, especially as transfers of bodywork were commonplace. Initially, the body numbers were issued in classified series, 1 upwards being charabancs; 100-up double-deckers; 150-up saloons and 251 (or possibly 250) upwards for the lorry-bus bodies described later.

An obvious first step was the use of bodies from earlier chassis, some of which had been stored during the war and others previously on chassis overdue for replacement. New AECs with fleet numbers 37/8, 41/2, 46/7 and 49 received bodies in this category, recorded merely as "old-type saloon"; they were of rear-entrance layout except for No. 38, quoted as "side entrance". Mr Pigg's notes are helpful here, as he records seeing "a body like that of No. 36" (the last of the Daimler Y buses of January 1916, itself with body of 1914 pattern) on a newly-acquired AEC chassis in the workshops, and the emergence of the resulting vehicle as No. 37, the first post-war bus, from the Cockton Hill workshops. It carried the registration AH 0189, which would tie in with the five-bay body coming from the 1914 batch of Daimlers. By contrast, the Pigg account relates that "The next thing we saw in the works was a short Commer body (like No. 10) being put onto an AEC chassis. It eventually came out as No. 38". Here the registration AH 0121 was

A registration number peculiarity is evident in this picture of "AHO 190", which should have been AH 0190. AEC Y-type No. 46 was photographed at Durham depot in 1919, probably. The figure standing proudly beside the vehicle is strongly believed to be the redoubtable W T Underwood himself, at that date manager at Durham. The new chassis carried the body and registration number from a prewar Daimler, and the demonstration route boards were not as used in service. *(John Banks Collection)*

that of No. 6, one of the first Commers with bus bodywork, dating back to 1912, of which the chassis had been taken by the War Department in October 1914; the official record of this body being of "side entrance" layout indicates that it was of appropriate type.

### AEC double-deckers, 1919/20

It seems that only one double-deck body from United's prewar fleet survived into the postwar era,

that being the one, evidently originally from one of the 1913 AEC B-types, still in use on No. 32, a Daimler B (B3025) of 1914. However, steps were taken to acquire a substantial supply of similar double-deck bodies, mostly of London General Omnibus Company origin, in 1919/20. Study of United archives shows that 38 double-deck bodies are recorded as purchased from LGOC; there were also eleven more from other sources or where the vendor is not shown. These were given body numbers 100-28 and 130-49, the number 129 being given to the existing body on the Daimler B, fleet number 32. All the acquired double-deck bodies were mounted on AEC Y-series chassis with a broad spread of fleet numbers, about half going on to vehicles with numbers in the range between 39 and 89 among those acquired new, the rest going on to further chassis of similar type acquired from ex-War Department stock as explained later; those were given double-deck bodies having fleet numbers extending up to 161. An exception was No. 96, which had a Hickman body extending over the cab; it is behind PW 111 in a picture on page 40. The irregular relationship between body and fleet numbers

*Above:* Number 32 (AH 0140), the 1914 Daimler B carrying a body which had started life on one the 1913 AEC B-types, was the only prewar double-decker still in the fleet at the end of the hostilities. In this view in Victoria Road, Lowestoft, the cab had received a fixed roof in place of the canvas top shown on page 16. *(Alan Lewis Collection)*

*Below:* By the start of 1919, United was recovering well from the effects of the war. Fifty AECs were ordered, of which five are illustrated here. The single-decker is No. 38 (AH 0121), which was fitted with the prewar body from 1912 Commer No. 6. The new ensemble retained the Commer's registration number. The double-deckers display another registration numbering peculiarity. Every one of them has a "wrong" registration number in which the numeral 0 has been repeated as a letter after the letters AH, thus: AHO. The buses are AHO 0118 (with an unknown fleet number), 43 (AHO 0199), 44 (AHO 0501) and 45 (AHO 0502). These buses were new in December 1918 and January 1919. AH 0118 and AH 0199 were the second use of these numbers, but in this case attached to "new" bodies on new chassis. AH 0118 is believed to have been a prewar single-deck Commer 3P. For AH 0199 there are no details of chassis make and type, nor of the original body specification. The registration numbers were soon corrected: AHO 0118 became AH 0118 etc. Note how tall the single-deck body is in relation to the double-deckers. *(John Banks Collection)*

*Upper:* This LGOC-style body on a new AEC Y type seen at Walthamstow carried no numbers, but had been rebuilt in United's manner, though painted in more like an LGOC style, perhaps for demonstration use. The combined driving cab and extra row of passenger seating, at that stage open-sided, is well shown. *(Brian Thackray Collection)*

*Centre:* The front portion of the body was later boxed in (no other word could as adequately describe the garden shed-like construction) to protect the driver and passengers using the forward section from the weather. This vehicle was fleet number A141, for which no registration number is known. The picture was taken in Durham. *(John Banks Collection)*

*Lower:* Seen from the nearside, the enclosing of the forward section was a little more elegant. Note that two separate entrances, albeit apparently without doors or canvas screens, were provided for driver and passengers. No. A158 (AH 0584) was a February 1920 delivery. It was photographed on the Norwich to Cromer service at Aylsham. The absence of advertising boards on the upper deck reveals detail of the seating arrangements normally hidden from view, which would not have been allowed in London. *(E G P Masterman)*

may indicate wide variations of time being needed to turn them into serviceable buses or perhaps that numbers were issued retrospectively in some cases.

It seems unlikely that the LGOC would have sold bodywork suitable for B-type buses, at that date still the main type in its fleet, unless regarded as obsolete, damaged or otherwise beyond economic repair, especially as crudely converted lorry-buses were being pressed into service - some of these also found their way to United, as described later. The wide range of LGOC body numbers for the total of 41 ex-LGOC bodies (the lowest 214 and the highest 4103) quoted in the PSV Circle fleet history of United suggests that some of the early ones might pre-date the B-type, perhaps originally built for types such as the X or even chassis of non-LGOC manufacture (De Dion, etc.) The early LGOC body designs mostly seemed to alter only in minor ways, even going back to 1906, and might well have been interchangeable.

Confirmation that some at least of the acquired bodies were not in good order as received comes from an observation recorded by Mr Pigg. A double-decker not seen previously appeared outside the workshop doors at Bishop Auckland, this being before any of the post-war single-deckers entered service and indeed it was the first AEC Y-type with Tylor engine he had seen. The top of the body was "rather bashed in" and there were indications that it had come from London. Surviving United records show that three such bodies were reconditioned by Mann Egerton, of Norwich, and one by Botwoods, and it seems likely that other concerns may also have been involved. In addition to repairs or reconditioning, a number of these bodies - perhaps most - had the area forward of the original front bulkhead enclosed. It will be recalled that the AEC B-types purchased in 1913 had an additional bench seat behind that used by the driver, made possible by the 14ft wheelbase. The surviving body of this type, on Daimler B No. 32, had been fitted with a windscreen and what appeared to be a canvas cover to link it to the original front canopy of the body. Now the idea was taken a step further and what amounted to a front compartment created, improving the comfort of the driver and occupants of the six passenger seats therein, though ill-matched to the rest of the body in appearance - the upper deck was not extended over this new construction. From a study of photographs, it seems that the front bulkhead of the original body was still there. It appears that the front rows of seats were still accessible only from a front nearside doorway, as shown in the accompanying Aylsham photograph *(on page 27)*.

Two of the resulting AEC double-deckers received registration numbers from the prewar series, No. 40 (AH 0133) and No. 43 (AH 0199), but others took new registration numbers, beginning at AH 0501, which was issued to No. 44, followed by 45 (AH 0502), both of the same type. Registrations in the AH 05xx series were used for many of these early postwar AECs with various types of body of 1919/20, though there were some leased to

*Above:* In this bustling view of No. 75 (AH 0552) passengers are boarding and the sunshine seems to have emboldened the ladies to make for the upper deck. A couple have already claimed the back seat, whilst a stout matron in a straw hat waits for them to settle themselves and, no doubt, their bags. Again, there are no advertising boards. *(Philip Battersby Collection)*

*Below:* Remarkably, another picture has survived of a similar bus in the same circumstances. This one illustrates No. 81 (AH 0557) in Lowestoft. The sun is out again, and a policeman watches a lively rush for seats. Once again the upper deck is proving the preferred location for the ladies, some of whom might have been unlucky, judging by the number of people already upstairs. A light, pneumatic-tyred Daimler is in the background. *(United)*

Underwood from new with R (Derbyshire) or WR (West Riding) marks. The fleet numbers were roughly, though not exactly, in the order of the AEC chassis numbers, which ranged from 13106 for No. 37 to 15369 for No. 102 in fairly tidy batches even if not always in order individually, and it seems that some attempt was made to put batches of chassis into a degree of order when purchased, although the bodying and issue of registration numbers was almost inevitably less tidy.

### Single-deck body suppliers

Turning to new bodywork, Liversidge was again a body supplier, with two new examples of 32-seat capacity (with United body numbers 152/3) on buses Nos. 58 and 70 in 1919. Number 58 at least was what seemed a fresh variant of what might be described as United's 1914 style of single-deck body, and quite different from the 1913 version with more rounded roof. Yet it was not identical to the 1914 style. The relatively flat roof still has the downturn at the front, though this is gentler, with a peak over the windscreen having quite a pronounced downward curve each side of the centre-line - the triangular panels over the cab side windows become quadrilateral and appear to be glazed. It rather has the look of a body designed in a response to a "make them like that" instruction, where the coachbuilder's draughtsman thought he could create a more balanced design. The London firm Christopher Dodson, of Willesden, also built a batch of 32-seat rear-entrance bodies. There were at least 27, with United body numbers 178-204, on vehicles with various numbers from 90 to 154, of which a dozen were on this batch of new AEC chassis. The Dodson bodies were fairly square, with the front of the roof having only a very shallow slope. There were also another five Dodson bodies, shown in Underwood's records as being on that fleet's Nos 19-23 (United numbers 151-3/38/45), registered R 6099-101/210/1. These appear to have been the five bodies noted at United's Board meeting on 17th April 1923 as being, unusually, in Underwood's ownership, though on chassis owned by United, which were sold to Underwood following that meeting. It seems likely that the five bodies, which took the Dodson total to 32, were numbered 205-9.

### Ex-WD chassis

Although further new Y-series chassis had been purchased by United, no more from this stock were added to its own fleet after September 1920, the remaining such chassis being sold in an agency capacity. Notable among recipients was Stockton Corporation, whose first six buses were on AEC YD chassis initially ordered in March 1920 as three apiece via two local dealers, certainly one of whom obtained the chassis from United. It is clear from United minutes (for 1st April 1921), that 25 more new chassis would have been bought if a loan could be obtained but if not 20 were to be obtained "from

France". In the event, this latter figure was increased to 27. By that date, disposal of vehicles from the vast fleet of the British Army or other military and associated users, often still in France, was beginning to gain momentum. For its own needs, from fleet number 103 United switched from buying new AEC Y-series chassis to obtaining further examples of the same types from ex-military and related stock, not buying further new AEC buses until 1925. At first, many were almost new and very probably some had not entered service with operational units, so would be in good order, but subsequently vehicles in widely varying condition came into the picture. Gradually both the scale of disposal and the avenues used grew in variety. Some makers adopted a policy of reacquiring their own makes of chassis, reconditioning them before resale where necessary, and some AEC Y-series chassis were handled thus - in 1920, United purchased four examples which became 109-12.

From April 1920, an official organisation, initially called the Disposals Board, based at Slough, came into operation. Vehicles were returned to Slough from military use in very large numbers, eventually including many brought back from the battlefield in poor condition, some of which were rebuilt on a basis of combining good parts from several vehicles, making the original identity uncertain. The Slough Trading Company handled sales and United took six AEC chassis from this source, but about a dozen names appear among the sources for the next 60 or so chassis. In addition to various concerns evidently of British nationality, the name M Marion (Lille) appears for numbers 123-8 and 131 in July 1920 as well as 157-61 in April-May 1921, suggesting that these were purchased from a French dealer. It is known that W T Underwood, then with United's Sales Department, spent about a week in Lille in August 1920 and also had contacts with a firm in Brussels. He visited Slough but was not impressed with the vehicles there, so United probably bought from France until that source dried up, only then switching to Slough. Some chassis were bought at auctions.

Though more of the "used" AEC Y-type vehicles obtained by United dated from 1917 to October 1918 than were of post-war manufacture, the margin was not great, so it seems that the proportion needing major repair or overhaul would not have been too large. They were doubtless bought at much lower prices than equivalent new chassis, and United was among many operators able to build up their fleets with large numbers of sound vehicles at low cost. Among those with fleet numbers from 103 to 123 and evidently entering service between 1919 and early 1921, nine had further Dodson bodies from the above-mentioned order and the four quoted above as acquired via AEC had bodies by Glendower; United records date these as 1919. They were to a conventional rear-entrance style which could be of pre-1914 or circa 1919 origin, with virtually flat roof, and none of the

*Upper:* The 32-seat body of the period in the version by Liversidge, as fitted to No. A58 (AH 0519). This bus was new in May 1919. It was photographed at Cromer Town Hall waiting to leave for Norwich via Aylsham. *(Alan Lewis Collection)*

*Centre:* The Dodson version is seen on No. A105 (AH 0602) of 1921 working in the north-east on the Blyth - Shankhouse - Bebside circular service. *(Philip Battersby Collection)*

*Lower:* This single-decker was No. A109 (AH 0668). Its body was built by a concern named Glendower. Few other details are known but it was probably delivered to United in 1920. The photograph was taken in Cromer. *(E G P Masterman)*

characteristics of the "1914" or post-war Liversidge bodies. The origins of Glendower are somewhat hazy: the firm in question may have been Glendower Aircraft Co Ltd, of 14 Harrington Road, South Kensington, London, which was in business circa 1919 to 1923, though it is not known if its works were at this address. United records quote the body source and description as "Glendower & Morris & Co saloon" for bodies 155/6, on United vehicle numbers 109/10, but "Glendower (AEC), Morris & Co, saloon" for bodies 157/8, on vehicles 111/2; these may have been old bodies, as they were written off in accounting terms by 30th September 1924. These entries seem to mean that the bodies, by Glendower, were refurbished by a firm named Morris & Co, and that bodies 157/8 were obtained through AEC.

### Lorry-buses

The lorry-bus was a phenomenon of the situation in the immediate aftermath of the war, when numerous Army lorries were no longer required and bus operators were in desperate need of serviceable vehicles. The LGOC pressed over 100 into short-term service in June-July 1919 until enough ex-military B-type buses could be made fit for renewed passenger service. They were fitted with seats for 27 passengers within the standard lorry body and what could best be described as a flight of steps at the rear to reach the high floor level. In fine weather some at least ran in open form, operating until March 1920 when they were returned to AEC.

United followed a similar course in 1919 with some of its new AEC chassis; the AEC official photograph on the next page shows No. 80 (AH 0556) freshly painted in United livery and with front and side destination boards

30

*Above:* The lorry-bus in its crudest form, with an open-sided passenger compartment containing wooden seats. Number 80 (AH 0556) was a July 1919 delivery, seen at AEC's Walthamstow works. It was later rebodied as a conventional bus, perhaps before the end of 1919, for it was licensed at Norwich as a 32-seater in December of that year. It was rebodied again, in 1926, with a second-hand body. *(Alan Townsin Collection)*

*Below:* The more sophisticated version, with glazed top cover, is represented by No. 118 (LU 8161), one of those purchased from AEC after they had run as lorry-buses for the LGOC. The photograph is at Bishop Auckland in 1920. Note the short-lived elaborate fleetname style. LU 8161 was rebodied as a proper bus by United in late 1920. *(United)*

but little other departure from the War Department standard lorry body design. Just which United vehicles were involved is not clear, as some official records were literally erased as later bodies were substituted, but 60/1/9, 72/7 and 82/9 are other known examples, and 71, 81/5 are among the possibles, with No. 158 of the acquired chassis also possibly running in this form.

The Regent Carriage Co Ltd, with offices and works at 126 New Kings Road, Fulham, London SW6, was responsible for converting at least four lorry bodies obtained from AEC and fitted to 69, 72, 77 and 82 of the above in October 1919. Other concerns were also involved and, in addition, Nos.116-9 and 122 were purchased complete as

lorry-buses from AEC after they had run in this form for LGOC from June-July 1919 to March 1920, where they had received registration numbers in the LU series; they had begun life as War Department lorries in 1918/9. Number 122 was allocated to Underwood, becoming its number 14, and probably accounting for an apparent United "14" in a list of United lorry buses - another such case was "17", which was probably United 87 under its Underwood number. Bodies

251/2/4/5/62 and three others unidentified are reported as AEC/Regent, an oddly prophetic juxtaposition of names; 259 as Regent; 260/4/5 as Pearson/Regent; 261/3/71 as Pearson/Morris & Co; 270 as Hilton/Morris & Co; and one other unidentified as Express Transport/ Regent. These entries provide confirmation that Morris & Co, previously mentioned, was a separate firm.

The 1920 illustration of No. 118 shows a vehicle with substantial-looking glazed top-cover to the lorry body base, and a windscreen, raising the question of whether the top-cover might have been an addition or whether some at least of these had been ambulances, as has also been suggested. The lorry-buses ran as such until circa 1921 when most, if not all, were rebodied by United to the Norfolk design described below. A United board minute of July 1921 states that there were 25 lorry-bus bodies and as their use was ending at about that time, may indicate the total operated. Relevant to this is a United advertisement, quoting the Newgate Street, Bishop Auckland address, offering 32-seater lorry-buses for sale at £550 each, showing a drawing possibly derived from the above-mentioned photo of 118, and including a note "Many of these vehicles are based on chassis of 1920 manufacture".

### Pneumatic-tyred buses

Until about 1920, pneumatic tyres were available only on car-sized vehicles or very slightly above, the practical limit for a bus being at about the 14-seat class. The pioneering work on what were then called giant pneumatic tyres was done in the United States by the Goodyear concern, soon followed up by its British subsidiary. It is mentioned in an article to mark the 25th anniversary of this development, in "Bus & Coach" of September 1945, that E B Hutchinson, interviewed shortly before the item was written, had visited the US in 1919 to study road vehicle development. "He was greatly impressed by ... the evolution of a light type of bus fitted with pneumatics. He ordered some of these buses complete, and arranged with Goodyear ... to supply giant tyres for fitting to CK-type 26-seated Daimlers which UAS were then introducing." A slightly different account is given in the same article by A S Bishop, of Goodyear in Great Britain, indicating that Daimler had a coach - in reality a charabanc - equipped with Goodyears running experimentally in the latter part of 1919. Mr Bishop's first customer was a Southend coach proprietor, E C Wilkinson, who had a vehicle which ran 8,000 miles in 1919 on a set of pneumatic tyres. An illustration appears in the article showing a charabanc of unknown make, probably seating about 24, with five doors on the offside, including the driver's; the tyres appear to be smaller than used on the early Daimler application.

Notwithstanding the above, United was put forward as the pioneer user on stage carriage buses, and it is clear that it was the first major British operator to adopt pneumatics on a major scale, based on considerable cooperation in the early stages with Goodyear and Daimler. E B Hutchinson was certainly the first major bus

This Daimler CK, registered AH 0742, the first United bus to run on pneumatics, claimed to be the first "heavy motor car" on such tyres in Britain. Briefly it was numbered 124 in the original series before becoming B4 in the new series created for light buses on pneumatics. The 26-seat body, by Regent, was to United's new "Norfolk" style - note the "boot" at the rear. *(United)*

*Above:* Daimler No. A156 (AH 0744) was one of the initial six CK-type chassis, shown here in its original condition with a charabanc body of unknown origin, running on a stage service. It was still on solid tyres, and had therefore been allocated an "A" prefix in the new vehicle identification scheme. United fitted a new "Norfolk" 26-seat bus body in November 1921. At the same time it was converted to pneumatic tyres and renumbered into the B-class as B33. *(United)*

*Below:* Several White chassis came from the American Army, although this 2-ton example, B8 (AH 0746), was one of the initial pair ordered by E B Hutchinson. The 20-seat Regent body, with its characteristic curved top windows, was in similar style to that on Daimler AH 0742 on the previous page, and was a precursor of United's own "Norfolk" body. A number of Whites, including this one, are claimed to have been left-hand drive. The vehicle's classification by the Company was, according to its fleet letter, "light bus on pneumatic tyres." Some smaller Whites went into the D class. *(United)*

*Above:* What a superb social document, redolent of the 1920s, this is. United's Daimler CB of 1922, fleet number C41 (XH 6255), a charabanc with solid tyres, seemed to have been taken over by a party of "flappers" or gay young things (in an era when that word was used with its proper meaning), one of whom, in the apparent absence of the driver (perhaps he was behind the camera) has taken over at the steering wheel. The C-class numbering was for "light buses on solid tyres" and thus is technically correct here, though the body seems to have been manufactured with in-built clearance for the future fitment of pneumatic tyres. The registration number suggests that C41 may have been second-hand to United. It was standing outside "Fermoy House", thought to be in Blyth or Ashington. *(Philip Battersby Collection)*

*Below:* In addition to its business of running bus services over a large part of the country, United engaged in a variety of other motor industry-connected activities, including acting as an agent for AEC chassis. This Y-type 45hp 3-4 ton lorry was used as a demonstrator from the Company's Bishop Auckland premises. *(Alan Townsin Collection)*

operating industry figure in Britain to realise the implications of pneumatic tyres, perhaps of greater importance on rural services than town work at a time when many country roads were not tarred. As it happened, the parish council of Heighington, a village on a route from Bishop Auckland to Darlington, through which United sought permission to operate, agreed provided that a light vehicle with pneumatic tyres was used. This item appears in Mr Pigg's recollections as having been reported in the local paper, but unfortunately no date has been traced; early 1920 seems likely. What the council probably had in mind at that date was one of the smaller models such as the Ford Model T, by then well known. However, it seems logical to deduce that United, and EBH himself, saw this as an opportunity to put the work done on a larger pneumatic-tyre bus to the test.

Among British vehicles, the Daimler CK model was of appropriate size and weight and it proved possible to produce a suitable 26-seat bus with a body of lightweight construction built by the Regent Carriage Co, probably to EBH's design. The resulting vehicle was claimed to be the first officially classified as a "heavy motor car" to run on pneumatic tyres in Britain, and it seems possible that the earlier Wilkinson charabanc on pneumatics may have been light enough for this not to have applied - the limit was 2½ tons, at any rate in later years. Mr Pigg's account mentions its arrival, bearing the number 124, at Bishop Auckland depot from Lowestoft.

Another Daimler CK chassis, with solid tyres and charabanc body, evidently placed in service a little later, was numbered 156. The origin of this charabanc body is not known, but four bodies of this type were bought second-hand from the LGOC in October 1919, at least one later being fitted to a Daimler of similar size. Other charabanc bodies from this source and elsewhere went on to various AEC Y-series chassis; the body-number series began at 1 and reached 13 by the end of 1921.

The Daimler CK belonged to a family of models which began in 1914 with the CB, at first rather conservatively rated as a 2-tonner, built at Coventry as a lighter counterpart to the Walthamstow-built Daimler B and, later, the Y-type. In keeping with Daimler practice, it had a sleeve-valve engine, in this case that known as the 22hp type of just under 4 litres. The appearance was that of a slightly scaled-down version of the Daimler Y. Few examples seem to have reached civilian users before the War Department began taking the entire output. Production continued until 1917. From 1921 this large pool of ex-military CB chassis was to provide a source for many additions to the United fleet in much the same way as with the AEC Y-types. The CK was derived from and very similar to the CB in the latter's longer 13ft 6ins wheelbase form, and United ordered six new CK chassis, including the two already mentioned, which were delivered in 1920. The model had solid tyres as standard, the wheels of spoked type as on the CB; the initial pneumatic version, as used on Daimler's prototype charabanc and United 124, had similarly spoked wheels but with smaller-diameter rims, the rear tyres of larger section than the front; single tyres were used all round. Total laden weight in this form could be up to 5½ tons.

A reflection of the confidence that the future lay with pneumatics was the decision to sub-divide the numbering of the fleet so that vehicles with and without them could be readily identified. This seems to have been taken very soon after No. 124 entered service, although not before the accompanying photograph of it bearing that number whilst working on the Bishop Auckland - Darlington service. This is thought to have been circa July 1920. The new venture was far from trouble-free. In his comments for "Bus & Coach", EBH reported that rapid wear was at first a problem, British roads proving more abrasive than those in America. Goodyear made harder treads and several further modifications.

This renumbering was the beginning of United's letter-prefix system, later developed to convey much more detailed information on vehicle types. A new B-prefix number series, beginning at 1, was used for light vehicles on pneumatic tyres. The series began with two Fords, B1 being listed at first as a van, this word being struck out and "car" substituted, in records for the year ended 30th September 1920. B2 was a Ford touring car recorded as purchased from Timpson, who may

A splendid view of Recorder Road, Norwich, circa 1923. There are about a dozen buses in the line-up, though the first, a Daimler CB numbered B31 (AH 0716), is the only one that can be positively identified. This was one of the ex-military chassis acquired from M Marion, of Lille, and fitted with United's distinctive "Norfolk" style of body. *(Alan Lewis Collection)*

have been a dealer, on 1st August 1920. These were followed by four of the Daimler CKs, B3-6 of which the chassis purchase dates in 1920 are recorded as April (B3), May (B4, which was No. 124, swiftly renumbered), and June (B5 and 6). Body numbers 210-3 were issued for B3-6, of which the registration numbers were AH 0741/2 and 0756/7. The Pigg notes record that B3, 4 and 5 ran from Bishop Auckland.

Another early pneumatic-tyred type was the White, an American make, and it seems that the two first chassis in the fleet were the vehicles recalled as being ordered by EBH during his visit to America in 1919. The chassis of B7/8 (AH 0745/6) were purchased new from the White Motor Company in July-August 1920, being quoted as two-ton models with pneumatic tyres. Their registration numbers and body numbers (314/5) support their purchase being part of the same exercise as the Daimler CKs, although they were appreciably smaller and more lightly built. Their Regent bus bodies seated 20 and they had left-hand drive; later examples of this make in the fleet were right-hand.

*Upper:* **The former lorry-bus chassis, No. A82, fitted with the 52-seat double-deck body described in the text.** *(Alan Lewis Collection)*

*Lower:* **With a seating capacity as low as 14, and much smaller than B7/8, White No. B35 (AH 8099) subsequently went into the D class, which was created for "special" (or "small") pneumatic-tyred buses. The photograph was taken in 1922, when the bus was new, outside the Coach Factory in Laundry Lane, Lowestoft.** *(United)*

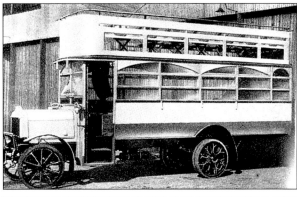

The idea of adding the prefix "A" to the existing numbers of vehicles of heavier types, expected to remain on solid tyres, seems not to have been put into effect until about April 1921. In practice, the changeover from plain numbers to A-prefix numbers did not produce a tidy numerical cut-off point, no doubt because of the varying position of individual chassis in regard to body construction or adaptation, among other factors. Records of dates of purchase of chassis show no prefix up to No. 155, which dated from August 1920. Then A157-60 appear in April-May 1921, yet 161-3 of the same period appear as such. Number A164, of April 1921, marked the beginning of consistent use of the A-prefix. Subsequently, earlier buses were given the prefix letter but this took some time to come into full effect. The remaining two new Daimler CK chassis, registered as AH 0743/4, became B32 and B33 in 1921; these fleet numbers were evidently issued after intervening numbers had been reserved for ex-Army Daimler CB models, as described below. The chassis are recorded as being ex-Sales Dept in April 1921, which raises the question of whether there had been an unsuccessful attempt to sell them after a comparative exercise with the two Whites registered just after them, as detailed below.

The charabanc-bodied former 156, already mentioned, had run briefly as A156 before taking the number B33 on conversion to pneumatics and receiving one of the United Norfolk-type 26-seat bus bodies by then in production, as also fitted new to B32 in place of its original charabanc body. B32 and B33 were allocated to Bishop Auckland. The Daimler CK was judged closer than the White to United's needs as the basis for a pneumatic-tyred bus for general duty, but henceforth ex-military CB models, generally suitably reshod, became the main choice for further additions to this series, the first 20 such chassis, becoming fleet numbers B11-5 and 17-31, being purchased from M Marion, of Lille, in May 1921. Oddly, they had registration numbers slightly lower than the CK models taken into stock earlier, being AH 0695 and 0698-716 in sequence. A further 25 came from Slough Lorries and Components Ltd, an offshoot of the official disposal organisation, in January 1922, followed by 49 more in early 1923.

### United as a coachbuilder

The first design of United-built bus bodies, known as the "Norfolk", was similar to those supplied by Regent on the Daimer CK buses, having unusual arched tops to the side windows, normally covering them in pairs; this arched-top shape also applied to the windscreen. At least one had linkage allowing the driver to operate the door from his seat, evidently an early instance of provision for one-man operation so as to economise on labour costs. A new body-number series beginning at 301 was used for the United-built bodies, the first being on B11 and the initial output provided front-entrance bodies of 26-seat standard capacity for the above-mentioned initial batch of Daimler CB chassis acquired from M Marion of Lille, plus the two CK models, B32 and B33. A total of 38 such bodies was produced for B-class buses between September 1921 and November 1922, plus one of similar design on a Daimler chassis, almost certainly a CK, for display at the Commercial Motor Show held at Olympia, London, in October 1921.

An indication of continuing tyre development was the introduction of larger, fatter tyres on new types of wheel with fewer but heavier spokes and adopting the American style of detachable rim, evident in a photograph of B31, based on one of the ex-Lille chassis, and also a sketch of the 1921 Show exhibit.

Intermingled in the body number list with the B-series Daimlers from November 1921 and into 1922 were 22 of a larger version of the Norfolk style but seating up to 32 for AEC Y-series models, some replacing charabanc bodies, as on A159/60/2/4, or replacing lorry-bus bodies, as in the case of (A)60 and 61. This process was taken a step further when (A)82, another such chassis which had run as a lorry-bus, received body 348, a double-deck version of the Norfolk body, seating 52. After the very limited modifications of old-style double-deck bodies, this was indeed radical in design, retaining the general layout of the Norfolk single-decker, complete with quite narrow front entrance, but with curved staircase immediately behind the driver to the open upper deck. The upper-deck seats and panelling structure were readily removable, with a trap door over the top of the stairs, so as to allow running as a single-decker, and it seems that this may have been more usual. The body was sold in 1924.

At the opposite end of the scale was body 361, a 14-seat version of the Norfolk design built in February 1922 on B35, a White TEBO chassis purchased the previous month from Slough Lorries and Components Ltd and reputedly ex-US Army. It was the prototype for further examples of the TEBO type purchased in 1923/4. Henceforth United became the standard bodybuilder for new additions to the fleet and new bodies for existing chassis, although there were exceptions from time to time for various reasons. The Coach Factory was to

continue in this role as the usual body supplier to the United fleet for some 65 years, unaffected by later changes of ownership. Until 1931, body numbers in the same series continued to be issued to bodies of acquired vehicles and also cases where new vehicles with bodies of non-United make were added to the fleet, as well as for new Coach Factory construction either for use by the company or for sale to others.

By September 1921, the United fleet had become quite substantial, with 124 AEC Y-type, 26 Daimler CB and CK and two Whites plus a few pre-war vehicles still in service; about 30 of the AEC Y-types were on lease to W T Underwood Ltd. The rolling stock continued to expand quite rapidly as the territory covered grew, with methods and policy also evolving as circumstances changed. In 1922 operations in Norfolk expanded and, in the West Riding of Yorkshire, extended into the Ripon area.

Using ex-military chassis meant that vehicles were rarely in tidy batches, even though there was a policy of standardisation, mainly on the Daimler CB in 1921-3 and then returning to the AEC Y-series quite strongly in 1924. It appears to have been the practice to allocate fleet numbers on acquistion of the chassis. This was no doubt necessary to keep track of the work done and the cost involved in bringing them up to standard for operation, but dates of entry into service were often well out of sequence because of the varying amount of work required. To some degree, acquired ex-military chassis may have been regarded as 'stock', to be drawn on as required. Unlike the immediate post-war period, when even ex-WD chassis were often almost new, by about 1923 older chassis, some having seen service in the battlefield, were coming into scope. Although they were doubtless selected as seeming of adequate standard, some of those acquired were not added to the active fleet. This may have been because defects too expensive to be worth rectifying were discovered when dismantling them for overhaul; in some cases, it may have been decided to build say two good chassis from the parts of three as received. Thus there is no record of bodying or registration for nineteen AEC Y-types given various fleet numbers in the range A178 to A255 purchased in 1924, even

From August 1920 United was using three Thornycroft Js, CL3216-8, which had been new in September 1919 to the Great Eastern Railway Co Ltd, London E15, as part of the agreement for United to take over operation of the GER's Norwich to Loddon and Beccles service. The Thornycrofts had 28-seat bus bodies and their GER fleet numbers were 14-6. They are not known to have ever had United fleet numbers and they were soon withdrawn. Number 15 (CL 3217) is clearly in use on United stage-carriage work and has gained characteristic route boards at front and side. It is still in GER livery and was probably never repainted by United. AEC A58 (AH 0519) is also in the picture. *(John Banks Collection)*

though their chassis numbers are recorded against the fleet numbers. Their exit from stock is recorded, three going to the Eastern District for spares and sixteen to "S & S", possibly signifying Sales & Service. The same remarks apply to some similar 'ghost' vehicles distributed among what was basically the B series, mostly in 1924/5. Some of these may also have been chassis not used; if so, no record of even chassis purchase has been found.

From about 1921, registration numbers began to be taken out in larger blocks when this seemed appropriate, an example being the AH 0698 to 0716 run of Daimler CB models already mentioned. Norfolk County Council also moved towards orthodoxy as the heavier types of vehicle ceased being issued with AH 0xxx numbers from 1921, by which time the main AH series had reached about 5000; registration numbers around AH 8xxx began to appear in the United fleet from about mid-1922.

Pursuit of standardisation was doubtless a factor in the early departure of some of the few vehicles brought into the fleet with acquired businesses before 1923. Three Thornycroft J-type 28-seat buses were placed in service in September 1919 by the Great Eastern Railway as its Nos.14-6 (CL 3216-8). They were taken over by United with services from Norwich in August 1920. The J type was designed to meet the same War Department specification as the AEC Y type and the bodywork was much to the specification being adopted by other major users, but these vehicles seem not to have been given United fleet numbers and are quoted as withdrawn by the end of 1920, not appearing in United's records. However, the photograph on page 37 shows No. 15 displaying a United service number, a practice thought not to have commenced before 1922, and these three buses were not sold to a London dealer until April 1922. It is possible that United might never have legally owned them. There are contradictory reports on the make of body carried by these Thornycrofts: both GER (Stratford) and Hora being listed. GER seems more likely. Three others from GER were sold to Thames Valley, where the model was the standard type. Another early take-over was that of Yelland, of Redcar, in November 1921, with a Daimler CK charabanc, AJ 4624, new the previous year. The body was immediately removed and fitted to an AEC Y-type, 159, and a new United-built Norfolk bus body fitted, the vehicle running as B34.

A factor which, for a time, added to the complexity was further elaboration in numbering methods: what had been the B series of fleet numbers now also included vehicles given a new C prefix. This was used for Daimler CB chassis with solid tyres, notably charabancs; there may have been some nervousness about the use of pneumatics on vehicles which might be driven some distance from a United depot, the bulky sizes of pneumatic tyre adopted at first making the carrying of spare wheels impractical. Punctures were apt to be quite common, partly due to poor road surfaces, and the development of pneumatic tyres for use on commercial vehicles being still in

its infancy. There were successive changes in tyres, wheels and hubs which doubtless delayed the process of conversions and may have halted it temporarily from time to time. A further problem reported as applying in the Bishop Auckland area was that the markedly larger diameter of the 'giant pneumatic' rear tyres as adopted for a time from 1921 compared to the solid tyres standard on the Daimler CB or CK caused the buses to perform badly on steep gradients; evidently the rear axle ratio had not been altered to compensate for this. For a time, Daimler CB models with bus bodies were also being placed in service on solid tyres and given C-prefix numbers, although this was regarded as temporary. The charabanc was basically a summer season vehicle, earning little for much of the year, especially in the north-east where the season was short. Some smaller operators removed charabanc bodies in winter to use the vehicles for haulage, and the frequent changes involving such bodies within United's fleet may also have been influenced by seasonal requirements. Hence the idea of bodywork that could readily be converted from covered bus to open charabanc came into quite wide favour around 1922, several bodybuilders evolving differing ways of achieving that end.

### The chara-bus

United's concept, officially known as the "chara-saloon", was basically simple, the closed body structure above the waistline, with three large windows on each side, being made detachable except for the windscreen and front doors on both sides. A folding hood was fitted when operating in charabanc form and the waistline at the rear of the body was swept up slightly to give a higher level where the folded hood was carried. This characteristic also featured on the ordinary bus version of the body and was to persist for a time on later United fixed-roof designs, although sometimes also found on other makers' bodies of the 1920s.

Events of the period around the summer of 1922 added up to the first steps towards a quite different look to the fleet. In addition to the distinctive appearance of the chara-bus body design, there was a new livery, almost always quoted in motor taxation records when vehicles were new as yellow and black, the latter applying to the upperworks, beginning at about July 1922. It was, and indeed still is, common practice to describe colours in the simplest terms for such purposes, and "yellow" could be used for shades ranging from primrose to chrome yellow, or perhaps beige or "biscuit", this last being quoted, unusually and without any other colour being mentioned, for A168 (AH 8451), an AEC YB charabanc first registered in June 1922. As well as the effect of fading with age, there may have been deliberate variations, the effects of successive changes in paint supplier or experimental variations. Some anecdotal evidence perhaps points to the yellow being nearer a primrose shade than in later years, but the strong contrast with black would have heightened such an effect. Some contemporary photos give the impression of quite a dark livery but this is almost certainly due to the ortho film then still common.

At about the same time, the United fleetname began to appear on the side panels in the form, with large 'U' and the remaining letters underlined, that was to remain characteristic until the 1960s, although the style of lettering and size changed somewhat in later years. At first the lettering was in red, shaded in white, standing out well against the yellow panels. Evidently the first United chara-saloon was B58 (AH 8444), on a Daimler CB chassis with body number 362, again with 26-seat capacity, dating from August 1922 and the subject of photographs when seemingly quite new. It had a new type of pneumatic tyre, of smaller section than the earlier type and fitted on disc wheels of the pattern soon to be adopted as standard on most British commercial vehicles. The rear axle used twin tyres of the same size as at the front; the dimensions allowed carriage of a spare under the frame at the rear. The reduced wheel diameter corrected the problem of insufficient gradient capability, although the faster revving of the engine in top gear caused at least one of the Bishop Auckland examples to "knock itself up".

The rear view of B58 in bus form shows 'Waveney Belle' on the rear panels, doubtless to suit its charabanc role; B60-3 (AH 8446-8), were to the same specification as built, and B62 is recorded as being named as 'Beccles Belle' in similar manner, so it seems that this was intended to give a form of local identity to vehicles used on excursion duties.

However, some CB models with the same type of body at first retained the solid tyres on the chassis as purchased after Army service, perhaps while awaiting supplies of the new type of pneumatic tyres, the wheels needed for them and associated chassis parts. A photograph of a chara-bus in this form shows that the mudguard clearances over the wheels were unusually generous, doubtless to allow for subsequent fitment of pneumatics. Its registration number, PW 101, marked United's introduction to Norfolk's newly introduced PW registration series introduced in November 1922. The fleet number is not known, though C71-3 were PW 103-5, and as several nearby fleet numbers in this series also had the C prefix, it seems that a number of vehicles were still on solids when bodied around that time, although evidently soon converted and the prefixes altered to B. Records show C64/7-71 as completed in September 1922 but not taken into stock in the Eastern District until 1923. Further Daimler CB chassis received chara-bus bodies in the period up to June 1924, mostly with 26 seats, the last numerically being B182 (PW 3310). They formed the largest group of the B and C class Daimlers.

It is significant that the total number of Daimler CB and CK buses in stock, as calculated from available information, rose quite sharply from 26 in September 1921 to 116 two years later, while that of AEC Y-types fell slightly from 124 to 120 over the same period, withdrawals outnumbering the small numbers of additional vehicles of the latter type added to the fleet. E B Hutchinson, when interviewed for "Bus & Coach" in 1945, recalled

PW101, the Daimler CB that was United's first in the new Norfolk "PW" registration series. *(Philip Battersby Collection)*

39

*Above left:* A Daimler CB, PW 111, newly in service in 1923, had the fleet number <u>B</u>82 rather than the expected <u>C</u>82 for a solid-tyred vehicle, but generous mudguard clearances had been left in anticipation of the fitment of pneumatics at an early date. The Hickman-bodied double-deck AEC was behind. *(W T Underwood Collection)*

*Above right:* A similar B-series vehicle with pneumatic tyres. By the time of this picture of B72 (PW 104), route numbers were being displayed. The bus is on service 4 from Newcastle to Blyth via Cramlington. *(United)*

*Left:* This trio of photographs of B131 (PW 1067), a 1923 Daimler CB, show how the chara-bus could be used as either an enclosed service bus or a folding-roof private hire vehicle. The body was built by United, and the illustrations are taken from contemporary press cuttings. The roof, side and rear window sections to waist level could be detached as one unit, leaving the windscreen, front door and the driver's side window and framing attached to the lower half of the body. The open version was then fitted with a hood at the rear, making it suitable for private hire and what was described as "char-a-banc" use. The bucket-type seats were a fixture and were not changed. This bus originally had the fleet number C131, indicating that it had then run on solid tyres. Note the smaller-section pneumatics, with twins at the rear. *(John Banks Collection)*

*Below:* The three illustrations on the left are complemented by this nearside-rear view, from which the temporary nature of the fittings holding top and bottom halves together is evident. The vehicle is B58 (AH 8444), a Daimler CB of 1922. It has no fewer than three local authority licence plates, and the additional fleetname "Waveney Belle", which was a local identity applied by United to the vehicle primarily for open-top use. *(Philip Battersby Collection)*

that, once the early problems were overcome, United had found pneumatic tyres advantageous in saving the vehicle from the hard jolts unavoidable with solid tyres on poor roads. Perhaps more important, they allowed increased speeds, hence more journeys in a given time became practicable and the earnings of a 26-seater on pneumatics could prove greater than a 32-seater or double-decker on solids. Hence the ability to fit pneumatics was the factor that tipped the scales in favour of the lighter Daimler models in 1921-3 despite the fact that they carried fewer passengers. There was also some specific choice of small vehicles where use of larger vehicles was impracticable or if livelier and more nimble performance was important when there was direct competition. As in other fleets, such vehicles used to harry competitors were known as "chasers", though often abbreviated to "M.C." within the company, although the meaning of M is not specified.

Two Ford 1-ton models - at that period, this would imply the TT type derived from the lighter Model T - were fitted with new 14-seat United-built chara-bus bodies and joined the passenger-carrying fleet as D65 and D66 (numbered in the B series) in January and February 1923. The Ford chassis of D65 is recorded as coming from W T Underwood Ltd in November 1922, but both may have come from a batch of seven registered AH 4276-82 dating from November 1920, thought to have run as goods vehicles initially. Another Ford, a saloon registered AH 7076, was acquired from Warne & Bicknell, of Letheringsett, in April 1923, becoming D146; it had been new in 1920. However, the main choice for small vehicles in that period fell on further examples of the White TEBO, a total of 35 being added to the fleet. The chassis, acquired between March 1923 and a year later, came from E B Horne, a dealer specialising in American ex-military vehicles, based in Holloway Road, London, where from 1925 new chassis using engines from American makers were built under the Gilford name. These White vehicles were numbered D104/17-20/35-45/9/50/62-78 and also received United chara-bus-type bodies, in this case mostly seating 14, completed between April 1923 and August 1924.

By this stage the categories had become clearly defined, A signifying "heavy cars", B "light buses on pneumatic tyres", C "light buses on solid tyres" and D "special light buses". These descriptions were in use on fuel consumption charts in 1926. The colloquial use of "cars" to mean buses persisted within UAS until at least the 1950s and possibly later.

### Bigger buses back in favour

Meanwhile, interest in larger vehicles had revived after the dormant spell. Development of United's fleet of AEC Y-type buses had largely ceased for a time after 1921, as the lighter Daimler CB on pneumatics found favour. In the year ending September 1922 three further Y-type vehicles,

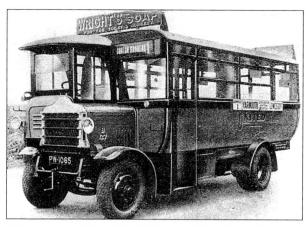

This view of B127 (PW 1065), one of the forward-control conversions of Daimler CB buses made in 1923, gives a foretaste of United styles over the following few years. *(John Banks Collection)*

A168-70, with chassis new in April 1922, are thought to have been the only examples of the type added to the fleet, these receiving existing charabanc bodies previously on 135, 160 and 129. As mentioned earlier, the numbers A165-7 appear to have been given to three AEC Y-types acquired by Underwood at the time of the take-over of Doncaster Motor Services in January 1922, while A171/2 similarly relate to an AEC and a Leyland of East Derbyshire Motor Services when that business also passed to Underwood, in June 1922; none of these appears in United records. Warne & Bicknell were also the previous owners of A175 (AH 0732), an AEC Y-type dating from about 1920.

Forward-control was becoming more widely accepted and in 1923 a number of Daimler CB models were converted to this layout in the course of making the chassis ready for bodying. Some were fitted with United bodywork seating 32 or in some cases 30 - internal records refer to them as "overtype saloons" - built between August and November 1923. There are understood to have been thirteen such bodies, fitted on vehicles numbered B93/9, B109-11/3/23/4/7/9/32-4. The suggestion that the wheelbase was lengthened is not supported by the picture above. Some or all may have been reclassified as SB instead of B, with 109/10/3/23/32 being later classified as XSBs. There are a great many instances of such suggestions or reports which cannot be definitively supported from original source material.

The robust design of the AEC Y-type doubtless influenced the idea of it becoming the basis of more ambitious enlargement exercises than had been applied to the lighter Daimler CB. After annual total purchases reckoned at three AEC Y-types in the year to September 1922 and two in the year to September 1923, the large-scale intake of chassis of this type resumed, and in the year to September 1924, the calculated number rose to 86, although not all were placed in service. The numbers A178-262 were issued to a fairly mixed collection of 85 AEC Y-series chassis built for the War Department

"Big Bertha" must have been more than a handful for United crews, yet the bus pointed the way forward towards high-capacity double-deckers. Its 74 seat capacity would not be bettered in United's fleet for more than a half-century. The centre-entrance and staircase layout was rare in 1923. *(John Banks Collection)*

between 1917 and 1919, all shown in United records as "ex-France" and officially added to stock on 26th February 1924.

United was among a limited number of operating concerns which recovered vehicles direct from France or Belgium. E B Hutchinson appointed two employees, named Eastern and Wylde, to this duty and they spent six months searching the battlefields.

There also exists a reference to "the Belgian Government Commission", which may have been some form of body coordinating aid to that country, to which chassis 13993-4009 and 14361-6 are said to have been supplied in 1919 and all but eleven purchased direct by United, perhaps in unused condition, being collected by United drivers from the Continent. The eleven quoted - 14002/11/7/8/21/6/7/33/4/8/48 - do not all fall within the group, which complicates the issue, but 15 vehicles in the A178-262 range do, so there does seem some link here. Furthermore, 1924 was a very long time after the Armistice of November 1918. Vehicles left lying around the battlefields for five years - by implication, not able to be driven - seem likely to have further deteriorated in that time, even though major units may well have remained sound. Possibly, however, vehicles could have been recovered from the battlefields by local enterprise and stored in rather better conditions. On the other hand, as implied in the Belgian Government Commission case, bureaucracy may have caused some sound vehicles to be left unused. This information is included as being of undoubted interest and relevance; it emanates from an era when written records relating to "scrap" vehicles were doubtless regarded as unimportant. In the aftermath of the First World War, such records were even less likely to have been all that we should today wish.

Calculations indicate that the total of AEC Y-types in stock reached a peak figure of 200 at September 1924, declining to 179 in the following

year as withdrawals of earlier purchases began. With further examples taken over from other fleets, the total of AEC Y-types to have received United fleet numbers reached 221, an indication of the extent to which the company's post-1918 expansion was based on its use.

At that time, local authorities varied widely in their attitude to the regulation of buses and bus services, and there was a lack of national standards, such as on vehicle overall length. As matters stood early in 1923, there was a limit of 27ft 6ins (rarely reached, even for single-deckers) on passenger-carrying vehicles in the area governed by the Metropolitan Police but, remarkable as it may seem, no direct national requirement outside that area, other than one limiting overhang to 7/24ths of overall length. In practice, local authorities in the larger towns imposed their own requirements, refusing to license vehicles of which they did not approve. Two remarkable extended Daimler Y-type single-deckers, nicknamed 'Long Tom', were placed in service by Barton Bros Ltd, of Beeston, Nottingham, whose gas-bag system had been adopted by United in wartime, and these buses also seem likely to have influenced developments of a similar kind that followed in United's fleet.

The first had a 23ft 2ins wheelbase and was bodied to a length of about 34ft with seating for 60 passengers, entering service in late 1922. It was closely followed by another, measuring 36ft 6ins with greater rear overhang, and seating 66, dating from January 1923. Later, when dimensional limits came under uniform national control, such lengths became illegal, remaining so until the 1960s. They both also had centre-entrance bodywork, then a very rare, possibly unique, idea on a British bus, evidently to reduce the distance from the doorway to any seat. Barton did not pursue the idea further after meeting local council opposition and reverted to front or rear entrance for its subsqent buses of more orthodox length. Not to be outdone, in

September 1923 United built an open-topped double-deck body, No. 475, with the then remarkable seating capacity of 74, based on an AEC YC-type chassis dating from 1918, extended and converted to forward-control. The resulting vehicle, numbered A176 (PW 1056), was nicknamed "Big Bertha", after a very large long-range German gun used in the 1914-18 war. The body also followed Barton's practice for its long buses in having a centre entrance, in this case with a single staircase leading from it to the upper deck. It was sent to Northumberland, where Blyth Council refused it a licence in January 1923 - incidentally, quoting it as a 70-seater. In November 1923, it is recorded as going into service on the Lowestoft to Southwold and Oulton Broad routes. It was the subject of bitter argument with Lowestoft Corporation, was banned from Oulton Broad and for a time outstationed at Southwold. It was subsequently cut down to a single-decker, retaining the centre-entrance layout, seating 36 in that form, and evidently was sent north again, working from Ashington depot. We do not have the exact dimensions of this remarkable vehicle. It had the roof extended over the windscreen by some six inches - in itself quite orthodox at that date - and the open top deck commenced some three feet behind the front line of the vehicle - meaning set back from the front of the cab, also then normal on double-deckers.

Apart from its status as an experiment in the operation of very large-capacity buses or perhaps even mainly a publicity stunt, the construction of Big Bertha may have been intended as a test exercise in the lengthening of the Y-type chassis for a more modest venture in carrying more passengers, using a single-deck body, and indeed that its upper deck was simply an addition to the basic design, rather like the double-deck version of the Norfolk body of a year or so earlier.

In 1924, in a significant step towards its recognition as one of the country's leading bus bodybuilders, the Coach Factory began executing orders for bodywork for outside operators, at first largely as a result of being chosen to build bodies, often to AEC specification, for complete vehicles ordered from that firm. The first such case called for sixteen bus bodies for Sunderland District Electric Tramways Ltd; twelve were 26-seaters on AEC 202 chassis, a light, bonneted model on pneumatic tyres, and four were 36-seat AEC 403s, a forward-control solid-tyred chassis of similar design to the LGOC S-type, these latter bodies being full-fronted. They were used in the initial stages of tram replacement for that concern in June 1924; it was then still an independent business, covering areas to the south-west of Sunderland and only a few miles from United's Durham depot - the routes of the two companies met at Easington Lane.

United body orders for outside concerns were by no means confined to AEC chassis. The first municipal order was from Great Yarmouth Corporation, for seven two-door bodies on Guy BB chassis in 1924. Such contracts were intermingled with work for United's own fleet, these first major outside orders being given body number batches among those of bodies for extended AEC Y buses described below. The Sunderland District bodies are believed to have been numbered 578-93 and Great Yarmouth's 599-605.

### The "AA" buses

A large-scale rebuilding programme allowing AEC Y-type chassis to carry longer and more spacious bodywork was put in hand, being applied to 60 of the "ex-France" chassis (all but three of those that entered service in the operational fleet) - A179-83/5-9/91-7/9/200/2/3/7-15/7-21/6-8/30-3/6/7/9-44/6/50-3/6/7/60-2. They mostly received registration numbers in the PW 19xx, PW 30xx and PW 33xx series but a few leased to Underwood had NU registrations. There were also two ex-Underwood buses (A173/4) and two (A58 and A70) that had entered service with Liversidge bodies in 1919, later leased to Underwood but now sold in extended form to that firm. The 64 bodies required were built between July 1924 and September 1925. The chassis reconstruction involved increasing the wheelbase from the original of between 14ft 0ins and 14ft 11ins to 17ft 4ins, probably using new chassis frames.

The chassis were converted to forward-control layout, at first retaining the solid tyres, no pneumatic tyres of suitable weight capacity being available when the scheme began, and with the steering column set at quite an upright angle. The engines (evidently still basically the Tylor originals) were modified using new cylinder heads and smaller cylinder bores, the objective of improved fuel economy being achieved with little loss of performance, it was claimed. A clue to the reduced bore size comes from United statistical returns of June 1926, in which the AA class was subdivided into "5in" and "4½in", the former the original bore size of the Tylor engine; the swept volume would have been reduced by the smaller size, but only to a still quite large 6.26 litres.

At first the rebuilds were not denoted by a different prefix, vehicles running in this form with A-prefix numbers, though later, at latest by the financial year ended September 1927, an AA prefix was adopted, providing a convenient identification for what amounted to a quite distinct vehicle type. A few of the later rebuilds were given AA numbers from the start. The bodies built by the Coach Factory for the extended chassis were to a new design, incorporating several unusual design features and helping to establish the idea of distinctive styles for United's single-deckers. These too were of centre-entrance layout, then rare, and set to remain so for company single-deck buses although taken up in 1925 by several municipal fleets, initially on trolleybuses. The entrance had double folding doors, arranged to open outwards, this latter feature later outlawed for many years on buses operating in Britain. Also very unusual and possibly even unique to United at that date was the

*Above:* This fine sharp photograph shows a lengthened and converted AEC YC-type working for Underwood. The centre-entrance United-built bodywork seated 39 passengers. This is one of the best of the "posed crew" photographs. There is perhaps a resemblance among the three people - perhaps the whole family worked for Underwood. In this photograph the bus, PW 1942, is still fairly "new" (it was delivered after rebuild in July 1924) and still has its solid tyres. It was almost certainly carrying a fleet number in Underwood's own A-class, thought to be A50, but its United identity was A200. The large amount of space left around the wheels pending the availability of suitable pneumatic tyres is again evident. *(EMMS)*

*Below:* Number AA232 (PW 3332) was photographed at the Philadelphia Lane terminus of service 7A at Catton Grove in Norwich. Note how the steering column had had to be moved forward and inclined to give clearance for the pneumatic tyres, and the carriage of two spare wheels. In this circa 1926/7 photograph the crew are driver Billy Hubbard and conductor Stanley Palmer; the latter went on to complete fifty years of service. *(Jack Burton Collection)*

In open-top form, AA197 (PW 3009) is ahead of at least three, maybe more, similar vehicles and a queue of other traffic in a leafy lane. This picture makes a remarkable contrast with the view on page 2 of the same vehicle with the top cover in place. *(Philip Battersby Collection)*

half-canopy front-end, the nearside of the canopy being cut back and allowing quite a deep route board to be displayed above the bulkhead window, the top projecting slightly above the roof-line. At the rear, D-shaped windows gave an appearance in line with contemporary saloon car trends, and as many of the bodies were built on the chara-bus principle with detachable tops, the bold moulded waistline was also a distinctive feature. Unfortunately the impressive overall appearance of these buses, and indeed the fleet as a whole, was apt to be somewhat spoilt during this period by prominent advertising boards mounted across the roof, sometimes at front and rear, as well as in front of the radiator top tank. The seating capacity was quoted as 39 in the official records for almost all the first 43 bodies of this type, built up to September 1924. This would have been tight even at 27ft 6ins overall, with quite a spacious entrance and a not very compact chassis front-end layout, although seat spacing, perhaps influenced by tramway practice, was often closer at that period than would have been accepted later. Thereafter no figure was given, but local taxation records indicate that some ran with seating capacities of 38, 36 and 32, the last-mentioned vehicles were recorded as charabancs, and evidently were built as chara-buses with detachable tops.

About eleven further buses with earlier fleet numbers, mostly former double-deckers - A38, 45/8, 51/2, 62/7, 81, 150/8/61 - also seem to have been rebuilt to AA specification, although there are no recorded new body numbers for seven of them. Of the chassis, only AA52 is positively quoted as such in United records, though the sheets for the above chassis are in a section of the records headed "AA type chassis AEC", strongly suggesting they were also rebuilt to this form. It thus also seems that further such bodies may have been built even though not individually recorded as such, there being gaps in the recorded body numbers which might account for them. A clue might be that records for some of the old double-deck bodies show them as "converted", perhaps an accountancy ploy. The true total of AA bodies thus may have been about 76, including body No. 475, which was regarded as of AA type after conversion to single-deck.

A further stage of modernisation was the conversion of these larger AA-class buses to pneumatic tyres, of a newly-available larger size than used on the Daimler CB buses. These vehicles had disc wheels and twin rear tyres. Photographs show that two spare wheels were carried, in some cases amidships under the high frame and in others at the rear. Some pictures of the extended forward-control AECs show solid tyres with mudguards giving only limited clearance, others with larger-radius mudguards as if subsequent conversion was intended when rebodied. Those on pneumatic tyres had the the steering box moved forward to the extreme front of the chassis, no doubt to provide extra clearance needed for the pneumatic tyres on full lock, resulting in the column and steering wheel being inclined to a greater angle. By that period, pneumatic tyres were no longer regarded as a novelty and in this case no alteration to fleet number prefix on that account seems to have occurred.

Thus, also, the C prefix dropped out of use; this "light buses on solid tyres" category disappeared from the operational fleet by June 1926, the surviving vehicles in that series then all being B or D, the latter prefix still referring at that stage to "special light buses", meaning mainly the Whites and a few Fords. Some indication of the composition of the fleet and the work done by the various classes is given by copies of some monthly mileage, petrol and engine oil returns which have survived. In January 1926, Class B light buses on pneumatics accounted for 57% of the overall bus mileage of 581,521 that month, with Class A, which at that date included what were later classed AA and did not distinguish the type of tyre, accounting for 36%, with Class D accounting for 6.6% and the last few of the Class C running less than 0.5% of the total mileage. The Class A vehicles were consuming petrol at an average of 5.4mpg, compared to 8.7mpg for class B and 8.9mpg for class D. By December 1926, the Engineering Department, by then at York instead of Lowestoft, was sub-dividing its figures to a greater extent. The total monthly bus mileage had risen substantially to 762,397. Of this, the total Class B mileage was just under 45%, the second largest group by then being the new class E buses, described in the next chapter, running nearly 32% of the mileage, but what were then recognised as Class AA accounted for a little under 14%, with "Class A 5in", which translates as unrebuilt AEC Y types with Tylor engines in original state, by then down to a modest 4%. The Class D White buses accounted for 3.6%.

The AA class figures were subdivided to show those on pneumatics, which ran 60% of this class's mileage, and whether they had 5in or 4½in engines, the latter the presumed rebuild size, with other modifications to improve efficiency, these latter covering 57% of the AA mileage. There was also a sub-division of the Daimlers in Class B, one entry being quoted as "22hp", this being the nominal RAC rating of the CB and CK engine as built, derived from the 95mm bore size (the RAC formula was very conservative in relation to actual power, having been calculated from the bore size and number of cylinders back in Edwardian times). However, a second entry headed "Class B, 36hp" accounts for 90% of the recorded mileage for this group. This appears to indicate that these vehicles had received a new type of Daimler engine called the 36hp, still a four-cylinder sleeve-valve unit, as adopted for mildly updated CL and CM bus models introduced in 1925. It was of 104.5mm bore, 150mm stroke and 5.1-litre size. Daimler was tending to depart from using the RAC rating figure, in this case 27hp, for its bus engines. The 36hp may have related to the engine's actual output at a set speed, quite widely used as a nominal figure at that date. There were also small groups headed

"Others" under the Class A, B and D headings, presumably vehicles of other makes by then in the fleet, but together the mileage they covered only amounted to just over 3%.

Four further Daimler CB chassis acquired from various sources and fitted with United 26-seat bus bodies numbered 684-7 were placed in service in 1925, these being on vehicles registered PW 3324/7-9 and numbered B191, 188, 185 and 189, the gaps in fleet numbers possibly indicating chassis drawn from the stock that then existed - these were given BB prefix letters in 1927. This implies they were different from their predecessors with B-prefix numbers to a sufficient extent to be worth distinguishing, though the nature of this variation has not been identified. The fleet number 192 was the number given to an AEC demonstrator registered PW 3322 about which more will be said in the next chapter and D194/5 were two Morris Cowley cars taken into stock through the Sales Department in November-December 1925 - these would have been of the bull-nose type then selling very strongly.

As the fleet grew, so did the territory covered. By 1924, most of Norfolk was served and, in the north, the coverage of County Durham was sufficiently extensive to provide the basis for an agreement with the Northern General Transport Co Ltd under which United were not to operate north of a line from Durham City running eastwards towards the coast at Easington (save for one section of route of about two miles or so to Easington Lane) and similarly so westwards of Durham, while NGT would not penetrate south of that line. In Northumberland, Northern and also Tynemouth & District were similarly prohibited from running north of the line Longbenton-Shiremoor-Earsdon-Whitley Bay. Beyond that line, United was well established in the mining area of Northumberland.

In Yorkshire, it had extended to the Ripon area, although further expansion was blocked by a dispute which led to an agreement with the local Tilling-controlled Harrogate & District Road Car Co Ltd, which in 1928 became the West Yorkshire Road Car Co Ltd.

### The growth of acquisitions

From 1925, the increasing pace of take-overs of existing businesses, usually complete with rolling stock, led to the B/D series in particular gradually becoming the repository for a growing variety of vehicles, although many were soon sold off. Small operators had tended to favour the less expensive smaller models, often on imported chassis, though the A series also gained fresh variety with some acquired Leylands as well as unfamiliar AEC types. Such acquisitions of vehicles were very modest through the early 1920s. After the Great Eastern Railway buses in 1920, only a handful of vehicles are known to have been added to the fleet in the period up to late 1925 including the one from Yelland of Redcar in 1921 and the two from Warne and Bicknell in 1923 already mentioned.

Brunson Bros (Norfolk Motor Transport Co), of Martham, also acquired in 1923, contributed one vehicle, LF 9419, a Tilling-Stevens thought to be an ex-Thomas Tilling bus dating from 1912/3. A body only, taken from a Daimler chassis, came from Saunders and Cribb of Norwich in April 1925. A Lowdon & Sons, of Seaton Burn, taken over in September 1925, contributed a Crossley (doubtless on one of the ex-military chassis and thus probably of about 14-seat size), BB 5185, and, it is believed, a Lancia 20-seater, NL 6437, which became B(?)196 and D197.

The biggest fleet taken over up to the end of 1925 came from W Hemingway, of Skelton-in-Cleveland, in November of that year. Eight vehicles were acquired, of which a 1923 Leyland S4 32-seat bus, WY 8698, became A263, following on from the last of the 'new' rebuilt AEC Y-types, A262. The others included two Lancias (becoming D201/2), a GMC (D198) and a Reo (D203), but the most recent were a pair of AEC 412 models, this being the bonneted version of a new passenger range mentioned in the next chapter, which became B199 and B200. There was also a Maudslay, registered HL 367 and listed in the takeover agreement, but it never appeared in United's records and was probably not acquired.

G A Whitfield, of Darlington, ran a Ford, LD or LP 4954, acquired in December 1925 and A B Barnard, of New Buckenham, was the source of three vehicles in January 1926.

United fleet numbers were allocated to vehicles from two substantial concerns which had been taken over by Underwood in 1925/6. Enterprise & Silver Dawn Motors Ltd, Scunthorpe, with a mixed fleet mainly of Dennis, Karrier and Reo, was the confirmed source of A264-76, D204-6, B207-9. Those numbered A282-91/5-301 and B210-4 had come from Progressive Motor Omnibus Services (Boston) Ltd, largely a Straker-Squire operator, which continued as an Underwood subsidiary, retaining ownership of its vehicles. There were also 20 others from these sources whose United numbers, if any, are unknown.

The stage carriage services of Edgar Helston Robinson, of Scarborough, sometimes using the title "Scarborough and District", were taken over in March 1926, contributing A302-12, all dating from 1922, these being, in order, three AEC K-types, two AEC S-types (numerically the first provincial S-type chassis, 403001 and 403002) and six Leyland S4 models with 42-seat toastrack bodies (see p.59). All were single-deckers at take-over, although the S-types had been London-style open-top double-deckers when new. As such, they had been unpopular with Scarborough residents. All but one had registrations in the North Riding AJ series, the exception being one of the K-types, which had a London number, XB 9084. United sold off the Leylands after just over a year to the United Counties Omnibus and Road Transport Co Ltd of Northampton, whose origins could be traced to the London Central Omnibus Co set up with Leyland-related backing in 1906 and hence a Leyland stronghold.

*Left:* Number B200 (PY 3467), a 1925 AEC 412 with 26-seat front-entrance bodywork, came to United with seven other vehicles (one of them another AEC 412) when the W Hemingway, of Skelton-in-Cleveland, fleet was taken over in November 1925. In this view it is brand new in Hemingway livery. *(Brian Thackray Collection)*

*Below left:* One of a pair of 1924 Hemingway Lancias, which became United's D201/2, seen in High Street, Skelton. Both had been withdrawn and sold by January 1927. *(John Banks Collection)*

Robinson also contributed two Daimler CK buses dating from 1920 and 1922 which became B215/6 and two more, of 1921, B218/9, are recorded as coming from a business in which E H Robinson was a partner with E M Abraham and J Gibbins, also acquired in March 1926. Robinson retained his excursion and private hire business, continuing undisturbed at that stage although later also acquired by United, as recorded in a subsequent chapter. Even the bus business continued to use the fleetname "Robinsons Motor Services" under United ownership for a year or so; a new AEC bus, E3 (see the next chapter) being operated under that name and in Robinson blue and white livery when delivered in June 1926.

The final A-series fleet number, A313, was given to a vehicle acquired slightly earlier, from Adamson & Thurlow, trading as "Gypsy Queen", of Croft Spa, North Yorkshire, in February 1926. It was an AEC Y registered in 1923 as HN 2828, and had a 30-seat bus body by Edmond, of Middlesbrough. There was also a Daimler CB, U 3742, which became B217. These various acquisitions brought the total number of Daimler CB and CK models in United's fleet to a peak figure of 138 as recorded in United records in September 1926.

Thus the era in which United's business had grown immensely on the basis of the use of AEC and Daimler vehicles of types originally intended for military use drew to a close. The company's character was beginning to alter, partly as a direct consequence of its growth but also in a way indirectly connected to this expansion, as senior staff were selected to join the company and brought their own experience and personalities to bear on its management. An example of this was Albert Thomas Evans, appointed accountant in March 1922 at the age of 31. He had come from the Bristol Tramways & Carriage Co Ltd, in those days still primarily a concern with the interests conveyed by its name, though also running motor buses made in its own workshops. That firm had no connection with United at that date, even though the history of the two concerns was to become interwoven in later years as fellow members of the complex network of associated companies that dominated much of the British bus industry.

The archive papers show what may well be Evans's influence in a distinct improvement in the standards of United's record-keeping from about 1923. With effect from 1st January 1926 he was appointed Secretary to the Company and his subsequent promotion - adding the role of Traffic Manager from 1st May 1930 and then becoming General Manager in July 1934, remaining in that post until 1959 - gives an indication of his range of capabilities.

Another key appointment was that of Bernard Venn Smith as Engineer, with effect from 1st October 1924. Previously he had been Assistant Engineer to the Birmingham & Midland Motor Omnibus Co Ltd, better known as Midland Red and already one of the most important bus companies in the country, though his earlier career had also been with the Bristol Tramways concern. Here, too, a man of considerable potential had been appointed, his title becoming Engineer and Operating Manager in September 1928; he remained with the company until resigning as Chief Engineer in December 1935 to become General Manager of the Western National and closely-related Southern National companies. He was to do much to develop United's capabilities in regard to maintenance and overhaul of its vehicles.

# 3 New Buses by the Hundred

## The E class

There was a distinct change of direction for United's fleet policy with the 1926 intake of 100 vehicles, all based on one batch of new chassis to a standardised design, the AEC model 415. An order of such size for one operating concern was, as it still would be, a major event in the bus industry, even meriting brief mention in the 'Daily Mail', underlining the position that United had achieved as one of the largest company undertakings outside London. Even so, competition was increasing and the measures adopted in the first few years after the end of the war in 1918 had left a legacy of buses with outdated bodywork and inadequate performance to cope with the nimbler buses, often on imported makes of chassis, chosen by the numerous small independent operators. This big intake of new buses was set to become an annual event through the rest of the 1920s.

The origins of the AEC 415 could be traced to a Ministry of Transport proposal that buses on pneumatic tyres might be permitted to travel at up to 20mph, instead of the 12mph maximum then officially applying, if their unladen weight with body was under 3¾ tons. It seems probable that this line of thought had been set in motion by existing bus designs in the mid-sized range, such as United's B-class Daimlers. Before joining United as Engineer, B V Smith had experience of the development of Midland Red's first own-design SOS model, a bonneted 32-seat bus with 25ft overall length designed to run on pneumatic tyres and weighing just under 3¾ tons complete, of which prototypes were built in mid-1923 and of which 84 production vehicles were built in 1923/4, including examples for two of United's neighbours, the Northern General Transport Company and the Peterborough Electric Traction Company.

AEC's reaction to the proposal was to introduce two new light passenger models intended to meet the anticipated 3¾-ton limit, the forward-control Renown, model 411, and the equivalent bonneted Blenheim, model 412, announced in March 1925. They were relatively short, the Renown having a 14ft 6ins wheelbase and being designed for 30-seat bodywork, a complete bus measuring about 24ft overall. It had a 5.1-litre four-cylinder side-valve engine, basically as used in the London S and NS double-decker, large enough to give quite a lively performance by the standards of the time in a vehicle with weight thus restricted; maximum power was quoted as 45bhp at 1500rpm. The 411 had the footbrake arranged to operate a transmission brake, the rear wheel brakes being worked only by the handbrake, but a revised design

had both foot and handbrake acting directly on the rear wheels, this being given the model number 413, and the bonneted model became 414, though this had the handbrake acting on the transmission.

Examples of the 411 and 412 began reaching operators in the summer of 1925. They were often fitted with bodies of uniform style based on AEC drawings, of which Short Bros, Strachan & Brown and United were the main bodybuilders. At least one of the two 412 models for the Hemingway fleet of Skelton-in-Cleveland dating from June of that year, PY 3467, which became United B200 in November as illustrated on the opposite page, was a case in point. A Renown 411 chassis, retained by AEC for use as a demonstrator, received a United body, number 677, built to AEC specification; this body is recorded as purchased by United for its own stock on 1st August 1925, i.e. from new, even though the chassis to which it was fitted was not. Chassis makers' demonstrators sometimes took registrations from their first place of use, and this one was registered PW 3322 in a batch mainly used for United vehicles. Hence the vehicle may well

have been intended initially as an AEC demonstrator to United although also sent to at least one other operator. The above photograph shows it bearing the fleetname of White's Motors, Cardiff, a concern which was a regular AEC user though seemingly not retaining this vehicle. No entries for this chassis appear in surviving United documents. The bus was allocated the number 192 in the B/C/D series. However, the document recording body 677 and hence evidently dating from August 1925 shows it as E192, the E prefix confirming the link to the subsequent vehicles bearing this prefix. The vehicle, under its registration number, appears in Norwich hackney carriage records as a 26-seater in July 1926 and April 1927 so was presumably in United service at those dates. No withdrawal date is known, but the

*Above:* The majority of United's E-class buses were to a standard front-entrance design intended for service-bus work. E93 (PW 8632) was photographed when new. *(United)*

*Left:* Number E16 (PW 8205) is seen waiting in the rain in Morpeth Market Place to depart on the Morpeth to Newbiggin service. The United staff make a charming group. They are identified on the back of the original of this photograph as follows: "Left - Driver T Towers (deceased), Centre - Driver J Glancy, Right - Con. Miss I Morton, now in Morpeth ticket office." Driver Towers is noted as "carrying his toolkit, every driver had one" and the livery of the bus is described as "yellow and black". *(Fred Kennington Collection)*

body, still seating 26, was transferred to B5, one of the Daimler CK buses dating from 1920. This implies either that the body was converted to suit the bonneted chassis or the chassis rebuilt to forward-control to suit the body. As other basically similar Daimler chassis had been altered in the latter way, that seems the more likely option.

The AEC 411 chassis, still with registration PW 3322, was running as a goods vehicle for a Leatherhead operator by September 1934. It seems clear that PW 3322 played a part in securing the order for 100 chassis mentioned above, agreed by the United board on 15th December 1925. The announcements made in the trade press in January 1926 stated that the type was to be the model 413, the version of the Renown with modified brake system, and that the buses were to have 36-seat front-entrance bodies. Such a seating capacity was well beyond the standard 30-seat size for the model but was in line with United's interest in buses capable of carrying more passengers, already indicated by the AA conversions. The promise of the relaxation of the speed limit to 20mph faded, not to be fulfilled until about 3 years later, and hence the pressure to keep within 3¾ tons unladen eased.

What was not mentioned publicly was that the initial order on AEC called for 100 chassis and 50 bodies, rephrased as for 50 complete vehicles and 50 chassis at the meeting of 5th January 1926.

This approach was adopted as part of a complex hire purchase agreement to defer the cost of 50 of the bodies. To meet United's specification, the chassis were of 16ft wheelbase, and a further increase of passenger space came from the removal of the petrol tank from its position behind the bonnet on the 411 and 413 - this being a legacy of Metropolitan Police preferences found on LGOC and other AEC models of the day. Instead, the tank was fitted under the driver's seat, an idea also being adopted by Midland Red for its first forward-control SOS buses. Although these did not appear until 1926, one wonders whether B V Smith might have kept in touch with developments in that company; the idea was not adopted for other AEC or ADC types. Despite these changes, it proved possible to retain the 36ins x 6ins tyre size of the original 411 and 413. The engine was basically the same 5.1-litre four-cylinder unit as used on these models, now designated A119 by virtue of minor improvements.

AEC decided to give the model number 415 to the chassis with these features supplied to United, the initial batch being numbered 415001-100. United broke new ground with its fleet numbering system at this point by numbering these vehicles in a separate class as E1-100, although by then the existing fleet had developed in such a way that the A-class was almost all composed of AEC Y-type vehicles in various forms, while the B class was mainly Daimler CB or CK, even though there were still the D-prefix lighter White or Ford vehicles intermingled among them. At that date, the idea of using a class letter numbering system in bus fleets was extremely rare outside London, and it seems probable that United may have been influenced by the LGOC in that, as well as in other matters involving the fleet and its maintenance, such as removal of bodies at overhaul and, later, maintaining a float of spare bodies for each of the main types. It may have been the result of opportunities to observe LGOC methods in the course of senior management contact with AEC in arriving at the specification of the new fleet, bearing in mind the close links between LGOC and AEC.

In November 1923, Arthur Henry Hawkins, a personality with strong London ties, had joined the United board. He had founded the East Surrey Traction Co Ltd in 1911, this concern operating services on behalf of the LGOC in its area from 1921, using LGOC-style vehicles, although not becoming a subsidiary of that concern until 1929. He would have brought some knowledge of LGOC methods to United board discussions but seems unlikely to have supported the adoption of LGOC-like fleet numbering as East Surrey did not follow LGOC practice in this respect. This divergence in regard to numbering continued when it was enlarged and renamed London General Country Services Ltd in 1932. Even when London Transport took over, the country area, of which Hawkins became General Manager, still did not use fleet numbers until its engineering organisation came under direct Chiswick control in 1935. Remarkably, Hawkins continued as a United director until November 1952, this being unaffected by the various successive changes of ownership and control of both his employers and United itself.

Another prominent industry figure who had become a United director, in this case in December 1925, was William Johnston Thomson, also founder of a famous fleet, that of the Scottish Motor Traction Co Ltd. Knighted by 1936, he remained a United director until his death in 1949. This was no doubt to prove helpful in regard to Anglo-Scottish services and may have had some bearing on the one order for United bodywork placed by SMT, when 20 bus bodies were built on Maudslay ML3B chassis in 1928. In this case, influence in regard to fleet numbering methods may have come from United when SMT and two of its major operating subsidiaries, Alexander and Central SMT, followed suit by adopting a letter-prefix system from 1932.

Build dates of the 100 415-type chassis for the E-class vehicles at AEC's Walthamstow works began with 415001 in April 1926, though United records show the first chassis delivery, of 415018, which became E6, in June. During the production run of this batch, AEC and Daimler once again became linked by the formation of the Associated Daimler Co Ltd on 26th June 1926. It was agreed to market vehicles under the Associated Daimler name, often abbreviated to ADC, but in United

records all but E83-100 of the E-class vehicles are shown as purchased from AEC and it is thought that all carried the AEC style of radiator. It seems that, for sales purposes in regard to existing contracts, the changeover date was September 1926 and was related to invoicing dates, so was artificial in relation to the vehicles themselves.

AEC's original intention, as recorded in United Board minutes of 26th January 1926, had been to give the order for the construction of the 50 bodies it was to supply to Short Bros, and these would have gone on 415051-100 which would have been E51-100. Later it was agreed that United would build bodywork for the whole batch, perhaps because of a shortage of other work. It may well be relevant that this was the year of the General Strike, and although that was brief, it reflected the economy of the country being in a depressed state. Of the bodies built by the Coach Factory for the E-class chassis, 90 were 35-seat buses, built in two batches, numbered 812-41 and 933-92 (this latter beginning with the 50 ordered via AEC), and ten, 842-51, officially described as charabancs with 26-seat capacity, retaining the folding hood of that type but of the transitional type with centre gangway and glass side windows by then in favour. These charabanc bodies were fitted at first to E26-9 and E34-9, not in order, but the 40 directly-supplied bus bodies originally intended for the remainder of E1-50 became mixed with the 50 ordered through AEC. However, E1-50 still had the first 50 chassis and E51-100 the second 50, even though not individually in sequence.

It is noteworthy that the first body of the series, 812, fitted to E3, was initially painted in Robinson's style for use on the services taken over from that Scarborough operator. It seems that the majority, possibly all, of the E-class buses had front-entrance layout, but pictures of the coach version all show rear-entrance bodies.

The bus body design had the half-canopy cab as a common factor continued from the forward-control rebuilds of the AEC Y-type buses but the overall design had a tidier appearance as well as being on a more neatly-designed chassis, though the square-cut upper corners to the rear windows gave a slightly more angular look. Interest was beginning to grow in what was apt to be called all-metal body construction, meaning the use of metal rather than wood framing, and one such front-entrance bus body was built, given the body number 1000, and mounted on E68. It was constructed in September 1926 and delivered to the operational fleet in November. Although of the same basic outline, with front-entrance layout, it differed in having a deeper roof curvature and omitted the hinged top-lights above the side windows, giving a rather more modern appearance. At that stage the idea seems not to have been taken further and metal framing was not adopted generally at the Coach Factory until well into the ECW era, in 1948. It released one standard body as a spare although an additional body, 1276, was also constructed as a spare for this batch in January 1928. Body

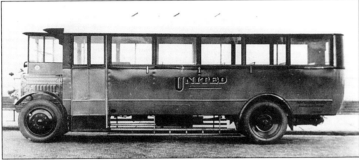

*Upper:* The vehicles of the E class may well have been regarded as a standard type, but from the outset there was some variety. Fleet number E36 (PW 8225) was one of the ten convertible canvas-roofed coaches. *(R Harrison)*

*Centre:* The non-standard body of all-metal construction was fitted to No. E68 (PW 8612). *(United)*

*Lower:* E64 (PW 8608) worked on hire for W T Underwood for a time in 1926/7. It was in Pond Street, Sheffield on service 3 from Sheffield to Mansfield. The Underwood fleetname is on a detachable board hung over the United transfer, a ploy which did little to deceive United's opponents. At an enquiry in Sheffield in 1923, the General Manager of Sheffield Corporation had made a statement to the effect: "Let no-one think that Underwood is a small operator; this is an offshoot of United Automobile Services Limited." *(G H F Atkins)*

the relationship with dates and chassis numbers was haphazard. There were still the last eleven of the batch of PW 33xx registration numbers unused so E1-11 became PW 3340-50 in sequence, after which E12-56 were PW 8201-45. E57-68 then started a new series with PW 8601-12 before E69-73 completed the previous one with PW 8246-50, and then E74-100 were PW 8613-39. If not perfect, this was much tidier than the existing fleet. Delivery of standard E-class vehicles was completed in the period from June to October 1926.

By December, the summary of fuel returns showed a creditable average petrol consumption of 9mpg, better than any of the A or AA variants, some of which were barely achieving 6mpg; such figures have to be viewed in the light of the 12mph overall speed limit in force for such vehicles in those days. In fact, United timetables were based on a speed of approximately 13mph, which itself implied breaking the law: a law discredited and regarded with some contempt by most transport operators, as was to happen in the postwar period with the 30mph limit. The timetables were worked out based on road speed and distance, without regard to the time needed for acceleration and braking, climbing hills and allowing passengers to board and alight.

The matter of scheduled speeds was discussed at a high-level meeting held at York in November 1926 to discuss how to combat increasing competition. It was attended by E B Hutchinson, W J Thomson and W T Underwood as well as the Traffic Manager and District officials from Yorkshire, Durham and Northumberland. It was felt that speeds should be increased where this could be done conveniently. With regard to vehicles, it was considered that if modern and comfortable vehicles were provided in sufficient quantities to carry all the passengers, the incentive for competitors to come on the road would be reduced, thus providing a rationale for the continuing large orders for new buses over the following few years.

Acquisitions of other fleets were at a modest level at that time and apart from those already mentioned, the only other to occur in 1926 was that of Norfolk Road Services Ltd, of King's Lynn. From them a fleet comprising six Dennises with 32- or 33-seat bodies, four on 4-ton and two 2½-ton chassis, which became B221-6, plus a Lancia 20-seater and a Napier 14-seater, numbered D227/8, with D229 reported as a further Dennis, was acquired in April of that year.

reconditioning tended to be a slower process than for chassis and as in the LGOC fleet, body transfers within batches of United vehicles at overhaul became standard practice.

Some attempt was made to put the E-class fleet and registration numbers into blocks, even though

These two pictures of E3 (PW 3342) make an interesting comparison. The bus is seen *(above)* in Robinson's livery. It was purchased by United on 30th June 1926, some four months after the take-over of Robinson's bus routes in Scarborough. It is obviously new: apart from being in shiny condition, it has the destination box in the original position, set right back under the canopy; the box is not in use, perhaps pending the arrival of suitable blinds, and an ill-fitting route board has been fixed to the front of the box. The photograph was taken at Holbeck Hill, Scarborough, perhaps on 1st July 1926, which would have been the vehicle's first day in service. Another interesting feature is that the legal owner lettering gives United's address as 29 St Nicholas Street, Scarborough, rather than the usual Laundry Lane, Lowestoft. E3's livery was royal blue and white. In the view below, also in Scarborough, E3 has the United fleetname and the revised style of destination box, brought forward to the front of the canopy, which contains a purpose-made blind. The livery is still royal blue and white, and the side route-board appears to be the same as in the earlier picture. Roof-mounted advertising boards are another addition, but it is not thought that this picture is later than 1927, and it could even be 1926. *(Philip Battersby Collection)*

*Above left:* Second-hand acquisitions at around the time of the introduction of the E-class were few, and surviving photographs of them are even fewer. They included this little 1922 Strachan & Brown-bodied Daimler CK 28-seater, which came from Edgar H Robinson, of Scarborough. AJ 7894 became United's fleet number B216. *(Alan Pickup Collection)*

*Above right:* In the top levels of rarity are pictures of Dennis buses in United livery. This one, B221 (AH 8736), was one of the fleet of eight acquired from Norfolk Road Services Limited in 1926. It was a 1922 4-ton 32-seater, and was the oldest of the eight. It was withdrawn by United in 1929. *(Jack Burton Collection)*

*Below:* The smiling driver has managed not to obstruct either fleet or registration number in these views of ex-Norfolk Road Services Dennises B225 (PW 5495) and B221 again. *(Jack Burton Collection)*

Since February 1920, United's registered office had been in London EC1, but, from November 1926, it was moved to Kilburn House, Fulford Road, York; the above-mentioned meeting was one of the first held there. In one sense, the new location was quite a logical choice, bearing in mind the spread of areas by then covered by the company's services and York's position, readily accessible by rail. On the other hand, the city was not in United's operating territory, having already been reached by the Harrogate and District Road Car Co Ltd as well as having a municipal tram and bus undertaking providing local services.

### The F class

An even larger intake of new vehicles occurred in 1927, this time financed largely by capital subscribed by the LGOC, a new development consistent with the policy explored at the November 1926 meeting. Some 90,000 shares of £1 were taken in late 1926 in the name of C W Reeve, then the LGOC's - and the Underground Group's - General Stores Superintendent, evidently known personally to E B Hutchinson. At 30th September 1926, United's issued capital was £228,939 but, with other new investment, this rose to around

A United F-class bus in the days when the company still operated under its own name in East Anglia. F101 (PW9901) was in the Market Place at Bungay and was about to depart for Lowestoft via Broome, Beccles and North Cove on service 2. The view was taken for a commercial picture postcard but the driver and conductor have made sure of being immortalised on the photographer's glass plate. Although for our purposes the bus, in an excellent view replete with all the day-to-day details - route boards, advertising, crew and their uniforms and accoutrements and, of course, passengers - is of prime interest, the photograph was certainly taken for the other aspects of the scene, including the bandstand, church and the region's typical architecture. There is a remarkable lack of other traffic: animal, pedestrian or vehicular. Perhaps it was a quiet Sunday morning and some of the passengers had been to morning service. *(Jack Burton Collection)*

£400,000 by 1927. The LGOC/Underground, via a nominee, thus covertly owned about a quarter of United, far in excess of any other holding. There is no evidence of LGOC involvement in the operational policy decisions of UAS, though another member of the Underground Group benefited, this being AEC, whose works were to build most of the chassis, as explained below, even though at that stage they were sold under the Associated Daimler name. C W Reeve became Managing Director of AEC in October 1929, though the holding in United had passed on by then.

By 1927 the Associated Daimler name was being applied to production models, and thus the further 415-type chassis - initially 150 were ordered, later reduced to 140 - which were to form United's F class had a new type of radiator with top tank designed to display that name across its width. However, there were more than cosmetic differences. At the United Board meeting of 12th August 1926, it was stated that the frames for the F-class buses were to be stronger and longer than on the previous 100, with larger tyres. The intention was doubtless to produce a larger and

slightly heavier-duty bus to take up the type of work then being handled by the extended-wheelbase AA rebuilds of the AEC Y-types. For the F-type, the wheelbase remained at 16ft but the rear overhang was increased and the tyre size was increased to 38ins x 7ins, using ten-stud instead of eight-stud wheels.

The main idea behind the formation of ADC was renewed cooperation between AEC and Daimler; this time the basic idea at the outset was that manufacture of the chassis would be at AEC's new works already under construction at Southall in the western outskirts of London, with engine supply switching largely to Daimler. The latter had introduced a new range of six-cylinder sleeve-valve engines for its cars, from which certain types were to be the basis of versions for use by ADC. Many bus operators, including United, had experience of the earlier generation of Daimler four-cylinder sleeve-valve engines and although lubricating oil consumption, even when new, was heavier than on most engines with conventional poppet valves, they had proved generally reliable so, although some operators expressed doubts, the scheme was at

Two F-class buses negotiating the roundabout outside Scarborough railway station in the early 1930s. F86 (PW 9886) and F21 (PW 9821) illustrate the red and white (or cream) livery introduced in 1930. F86 has advertising boards at both sides and none at the front; F21 has a front board and one on the nearside. Although longer than the E-class buses, most Fs retained the same AEC four-cylinder engine; only F115-40 had the Daimler six-cylinder unit. *(Philip Battersby Collection)*

first widely accepted as a promising one. However, such sweeping changes were bound to take time and be liable to encounter difficulties.

Most of the F-class chassis retained the 4-type A119 four-cylinder 5.1-litre side-valve engine of AEC design, basically as used on United's E-class buses. They went into production at Walthamstow, beginning at 415101, some 72 being shown in AEC records as built in January 1927, delivery to United starting at the end of that month and proceeding at around five per week. A further eight Walthamstow-built chassis, 415160-3 and 415177-80, were also intended for United as its first examples of the new Daimler-engined version but, instead, A119 engines were fitted, evidently before the chassis left the premises. They were renumbered 415251-8, and diverted to other customers, four going to Agar, Cross, the ADC agents for South America, and four to Rhondda Tramways; these chassis also had build dates in January-February and were delivered to the bodybuilders concerned in March. It is interesting to note how, for a time, the UAS and AEC stories became so interwoven.

There was then a pause in chassis production while the transfer of the various manufacturing departments and their machinery from Walthamstow to Southall took place, output of 415 models resuming at the end of April, chassis numbers 415181 to 235, all having A119 engines, being completed during the following month. Of these, 43 were for United but four (415181/6/9/91) were supplied to Ralph Bros, Abertillery; three (415193/6/200) to Gough, Mountain Ash; two (415213/8) to Gordon, Cavan; two (415220/2) to Pelican, ADC's Yorkshire distributors, and one (415232) to the ADC Leeds depot. Although ADC did not promote the 415 as a model for general sale, the emphasis being on the new 416 and 417 by then in production and described later, it was no longer exclusively a United model as had been so in 1926. A factor in this may have been United's decision, agreed at a Board meeting on 31st May 1927, to cancel five or ten of the ADC buses on order so as to purchase light vehicles with which to fight competition from Brook, this referring to Eastern Express, with Chevrolet buses in the West Hartlepool area. In fact the ADC 415 order was reduced by ten to 140.

There had been delays in putting the six-cylinder Daimler engine intended as the future standard for ADC single-deckers into production in this form, supplies not reaching Southall until April 1927. It was derived from that used in the Daimler 25/85hp car model of the day, generally chauffeur-driven. In commercial-vehicle form, it was known internally as the CV25, though confusingly described as the 40/70hp in ADC publicity, apparently because it was felt that a '25hp' engine did not sound large enough for a full-sized bus. It was of 3.568-litre capacity and, although capable of producing

56

greater power than the 4-type engine of 5.1 litres, had to run at higher speed to do so. In theory, suitably low gearing should have enabled this to be accommodated but in practice use of this engine in much heavier and less sedately-driven buses was to reveal severe inadequacies in the lubrication system.

Output of 415D chassis with the CV25 engine for United took place in May 1927, when chassis 415236-50/9/60 are recorded as being passed out, together with what seem to have been replacement chassis numbered 415160-3 and 415177-80 for those diverted earlier. Some records show such vehicles as having a suffix D added to the chassis number, others are given as 415D160, etc., while some, including those of the makers, do not show any addition to the plain number. Thus the F-class comprised 115 vehicles with the AEC four-cylinder engine, numbered F1-115, and 25 with the Daimler CV25 six-cylinder unit, the latter receiving the fleet numbers F116-40, according to contemporary archive records, and not at this stage the FD-prefix numbers as sometimes thought. It is noteworthy that the latter chassis were not recorded as taken into stock by United until various dates between July and October. This time the registration number series, PW 9801-940, not only ran in one sequence but the last two digits matched those of the fleet numbers. This degree of tidiness was very rare among bus fleets at that date and was to remain characteristic of most later United batches over the years, so far as practicable.

The bodies built in the Coach Factory for the F-class buses were broadly similar to the E-class design in general appearance, with half-canopy front-end, although there were several detail changes. The overall length was slightly extended by increasing the rear overhang, which had been quite short on the E-class, and this enabled the maximum seating capacity to revert to the 39-seat figure as on the AA class buses. The entrance was set back slightly from the front bulkhead and one seat, intended for the conductor, was in this corner - some local authorities did not count this when recording the seating capacity and this accounts for some such buses being recorded as 38-seaters. The first F-class buses joined the fleet in February 1927, and a report in "Motor Transport" of 4th April 1927 indicated that all 150 then on order were to be of 39-seat capacity.

This also described how the timber framing was machined to allow rapid assembly, using a line system. Each body was assembled, panelled, wired and mounted on its chassis during a working day, ready to go to the paint shop. The original intentions on seating capacity were modified to some degree, although surviving records conflict on the details, evidently because changes began to be introduced before the batch was completed or at any rate before some vehicles entered service. The main run of body numbers, 1008-143, completed by September 1927, was for the most part in sequence for vehicles numbered F1-136, save for a few brief runs where individual buses were out of

order slightly. It seems clear that these were at first all to be 39-seat saloons, but then it was decided that some were to be 30-seat, F54-9 and F82-136 being altered to this form, possibly before entering service. The vehicles with the final four numbers F137-40, completed in October-November 1927, were described as De Luxe saloons and are recorded as having body numbers 1225-7 and 1145. Again, records differ as to their seating capacity, one version showing F137-9 as 25-seat and another 20-seat, with F140 as 30-seat, with yet another quoting body 1225 on F137 as seating 21.

In addition, there were at least two spare bodies, 1144 and 1146, and others, 1147-52 and 1223/4, recorded as not built, although there is an alternative version that three of these were further spare bodies passed to Eastern Counties in 1931. It may be significant that the complete runs of all the foregoing body numbers 1008-152 and 1223-7 add up to 150, the size of the original F-class order as first planned, so it is possible that sets of parts were already in existence, used for extra spare bodies. This class of vehicles was subject to various further modifications - the 1931 and 1933/4 rebuilds are recorded in a later chapter.

No firm information has come to light on the duties for which the F-class vehicles finished to De Luxe standard were intended, but one possibility may have been the Yarmouth-London express service for which some of the K-class vehicles were similarly equipped the following year. The Anglo-Scottish services from Newcastle are thought not to have started until 1928 but the De Luxe vehicles may have then been used on them.

### Sleeve-valve difficulties

The Daimler CV25 engines were soon in trouble; 23 of the 25 in the United 415D vehicles suffered major failures, with broken sleeves, damaged pistons and bearings over the next few months. Other operators using this type of engine were having similar experiences. United's Chief Engineer visited the Wrexham & District concern (which had suffered failures of all fifteen of its engines of this type within three months) to compare notes on how to deal with them. By the end of the year it was reported within ADC that almost every engine of this type had given trouble, with about half replaced, some more than once, the engines returned having to be rebuilt with many new parts. United cancelled an order for 20 further Daimler CV25 engines which were to be fitted to earlier vehicles.

As early as January 1928, a number of users of these engines had become so exasperated with repeated failures that they were driven to the length of replacing the Daimler power units in some of their ADC buses with four-cylinder AEC examples. No evidence has so far come to light from the archives to suggest that United adopted this policy; it may be that the Engineer's Department succeeded in making them run satisfactorily.

### More small buses

Added to the fleet in July-September 1927 were fifteen Chevrolet LM models purchased as "chasers", funded by the cancellation of ten of the original F-class order. They received 14-seat bus bodies built by Waveney, a small bodybuilding concern based at Oulton Broad, Lowestoft, presumably because United's own coach factory was too busy. Numbered H1-15, the first ten were registered PW 9941-50, the balance of the booking of 150 made for the F class. The remainder were registered as VF 1381-5, Norfolk having moved on to these letters from March 1927. A further fifteen generally similar buses were to follow in 1928, as detailed later. The Chevrolet, at that stage with four-cylinder 2.8-litre engine, was becoming the most popular of the lightweight goods and passenger models of American origin being sold in Britain; the Ford model T and TT were by then regarded as outdated. From 1923 Chevrolet vehicles had been assembled in Hendon, on the north-western outskirts of London.

A development among medium-sized vehicles was the rebodying of six of the B-class Daimlers as seaside runabouts for the Scarborough Promenade

The rebodied Daimlers for Scarborough's sea front service are known to the compilers in very few photographs. In a pre-1930 view *(upper)*, B11 (AH 0695) was in the yellow and black livery at the Corner Café terminus. The canvas roof was closed. In almost the same spot on a sunnier day *(lower)*, D17 (AH 8445) had its roof fully open and was in the 1930 red and white livery. In the foreground is an ex-Pioneer Dennis, B2 (or possibly B3) (PY 7368), and between the two Uniteds is a 14-seat charabanc, DL 2633, of local operator F D Bulmer. *(United; Roy Marshall Collection)*

One each of the 1927 and 1928 batches of Chevrolets. H7 (PW 9947) was an East Anglian allocation and one of the batch H16-30 was working in Scarborough. The Chevrolets had a short life with United. Three of them, H21-3, went to East Midland in 1928, and most of the remainder were withdrawn in 1929. *(A Norris Collection; United)*

service. The new United bodies, which had roll-back canvas roofs, were fitted in July 1927 to one of the CK-type chassis dating from 1920 (B6) and five CB-type chassis first placed in service by United in 1921/2 (B14/9/25/8/43). The innovation was well enough received for a further thirteen Daimler CB chassis to be similarly treated in April-May 1928; these new bodies, again built by United, seated 25 passengers. Those chosen for this second batch (B11/2/29/30/4/8/49/51/3/6/9/68 and 107) dated from 1921-3. All were allocated to Scarborough and became a distinct class as D1-19 under the partial renumbering of 1929.

### Formation of East Midland

Following the departure of W T Underwood from its board, W T Underwood Ltd was renamed East Midland Motor Services Ltd on 1st July 1927, E B Hutchinson continuing as Managing Director. As had been so since 1924, United did not have direct financial control, holding only 6,131 shares out of the total number issued, which in 1926 reached its maximum of 57,517, though a management agreement continued to keep policy and methods in such matters as livery under United control. W T Underwood remained on the United board, which he had joined in 1925, for three months, until 30th September. The Underwood head office at Central Avenue, Worksop, continued to be used by East Midland though Kilburn House, Fulford Road,

*Above:* The rebodied Daimlers replaced some ex-Robinson Leyland S4 toastracks dating from 1922, acquired by United in 1926 to become fleet numbers A307-12 (AJ 8528/31/2, 8630-2). Two are seen here in Pickering: a rather precarious mode of travel for a nonetheless relaxed-looking party of be-hatted and be-fox-furred ladies. *(Alan Pickup Collection)*

*Below:* The 1927 G-class consisted of 50 Short Bros-bodied ADC 416A front-entrance 32-seaters. United ordered these buses and allocated its own body numbers 1300-49, but they never ran in United service or carried the United fleetname. G1-50 (RR 7401-50) did, however, have United's yellow and brown livery when put into service with the East Midland concern. By the time of this photograph of G8 (RR 7408), the cream band had been added, and the destination blind moved from its original position under the canopy. *(G H F Atkins)*

York, at first quoted as "the managing director's office", was the address given for EMMS on the agreement with the makers dated May 1929 concerning the AEC Reliance buses then added to the fleet.

East Midland's activities were now concentrated on the area, mainly in Derbyshire and Nottinghamshire, implied by the name, and it did not continue those in Lincolnshire for more than a few days; some of these became a direct United responsibility for the first time.

In a reversal of the usual pattern of empire-building, the operations in the Scunthorpe area were sold to a newly reconstituted Enterprise and Silver Dawn Motors Ltd, registered on 8th July 1927 by Arthur Drury, one of the directors of the former company of the same name which ceased trading in late 1925, after the purchase of its business by Underwood. Four of United's E-class AEC 415 buses, E59, E60 and E77/8, were sold in August 1927 to the new E&SD company, which was to prove a long-lived concern, with a fleet largely composed of AEC buses and coaches. It survived until 1950, when it sold out to the Lincolnshire Road Car Co Ltd, a concern which was also to figure more directly in the United story.

The class letter G was omitted from United's own sequence, being allocated to a type of vehicle selected for the East Midland fleet. This was the ADC 416, the forward-control version of a new standard single-deck model introduced for the 1927 season - the bonneted equivalent was type 417. Both adopted the 16ft wheelbase of the 415 but introduced a new frame, slightly cranked over the front and rear axles to permit a lower floor level, in response to contemporary trends. They were available with the same choice of engine as the 415; the East Midland batch, consisting of 50 vehicles, were 416A, with the AEC four-cylinder A119 engine. The 32-seat bodywork was built by Short Bros to that firm's usual style for the model, based on an ADC specification, and quite unlike the F-class buses. As built, they had shallow roller-blind destination boxes hung under the full-width front canopy. However G1-50 followed the latest United practice in having suitably matching registrations RR 7401-50, this being a Nottinghamshire series in consequence of the move of the administrative headquarters to Worksop in that county from Clowne in Derbyshire. They were supplied between July and September 1927 as complete vehicles on hire purchase from ADC and hence the bodies were sub-contracted from ADC, thus discharging an obligation that had been left by the cancellation of the 50 bodies ordered on a similar basis for United's E class buses.

Photographs of these buses when new show that initially they had no cream band, but otherwise they bore the livery to remain associated with the East Midland fleet until 1955, despite successive changes of ownership of that company. In the simple terms quoted in motor tax records, they could be described as yellow and brown, though some memories are of the yellow as nearer a beige shade, sometimes called "biscuit", and the brown as quite a rich chocolate, at any rate by the mid-1940s. It thus seems that the intention at that stage was to draw attention to the renaming with a new and distinctive livery, as United's fleet continued with the "yellow and black" until the final deliveries of F-class vehicles in the autumn of 1927.

Though doubtless influenced by that carry-over from a previous episode, the arrival of 50 new buses represented a huge inflow in relation to the size of the operational fleet. Because almost the whole Underwood fleet had been leased from United, individual buses coming and going and being replaced by others, it is difficult to be precise on the number in service at the point of the name change. However, a good indication is given by United's pressure on W T Underwood Ltd for the 75 vehicles on lease at the end of March 1927 to be returned because of its own needs. Indeed, it seems that, despite EBH still being in charge, there was a marked change in the relationship between the two concerns leading to East Midland generally relying on its own rolling stock, the new ADC 416 buses being able to cater for a high proportion of the operational needs.

Although no 416 or 417 models were purchased new by United, examples of both types were later to come into the fleet with acquired businesses. Despite the above episode and the close relationship to the 415 model, they were treated as non-standard, early ones at first being given numbers in the B series, but later added to the E series but with EB or other prefix letters, often in an apparently illogical way. Similar remarks applied to other AEC or ADC models of this era.

A further boost to East Midland's fleet which took place in October 1927 was the purchase from United of 30 Daimler CB models with fleet numbers in the range from B60 to B180, many of which had been operating for Underwood on a leasing basis. In view of the request for the return of leased vehicles made earlier that year, this may seem a surprising development, but United's fleet had meanwhile received the 140 F-class vehicles and what by then were probably regarded as fairly elderly 26-seat buses may no longer have fitted United's needs. Among further consequences of the ending of the Underwood era, United acquired garages and six buses, all of Straker-Squire make, that had come from the fleet of Progressive Motor Omnibus Services (Boston) Ltd, which had been an Underwood subsidiary from February 1926. They had been used on services in the Boston and Holbeach areas which came into direct United operation in July 1927. They had already been allocated United numbers A283/6/8/90, all of which were 32-seat single-deckers of 1921/2, and A300/1, which were 60-seat open-top double-deckers of 1922/3. Little if any use was made of them before they were sold.

In addition, two previously mentioned vehicles of United origin, though hitherto run by Underwood, were re-acquired from East Midland in October 1927. They were both extended forward-control rebuilds of AEC YD models, by then having new bodies and AA-prefix designations, AA58 and 70; they had originally entered service with United with Liversidge bodies in 1919, and had been sold to Underwood in February 1925, after having been leased from 1921.

## The 1928 fleet programme

United started its ordering process for the new vehicles needed for 1928 in July 1927, the Board minutes for the 29th of that month stating that an order was to be placed with ADC for 75 complete vehicles, the bodies sub-contracted to United as part of a hire-purchase deal in the manner that had applied with part of the E-class in 1926. Then on 25th October it was agreed to purchase a further 75, with no details specified. The vehicle type is not recorded and may not have been settled at that point but United would have been aware of developments at ADC, for whom Laurence Pomeroy was supervising the design of new chassis following his appointment as its Chief Engineer, the work being done at Daimler in Coventry. The ADC management continued to express confidence that the future lay with its sleeve-valve six-cylinder models, claiming that a revised version of the CV25 engine would eliminate the problems experienced with the earlier units.

Examples of the new models so powered, type 423 (forward control) and 424 (bonneted), were exhibited at the November 1927 Commercial Motor Show. These had revised frontal appearance, with a radiator similar in style to that on Daimler cars of the day except that the top was not fluted in the way by then characteristic of that marque. The chassis design made extensive use of aluminium alloy to reduce weight. A bus body was ordered by ADC from United for the second 423 chassis, number 423002, and delivered in November in time for demonstration use at the Show, giving an early opportunity for United to assess the model in relation to its own requirements and develop the new style of 35-seat two-door body (No.1267) it carried, which was to be adopted as the 1928 standard for the company's own fleet. This vehicle was purchased by the Crosville Motor Co Ltd, numbered 276, registered FM 4751, and delivered in February 1928, but was to remain unique in that fleet, already firmly standardised on Leyland vehicles, though there were many parallels in the stories of the United and Crosville concerns.

United, keen to buy six-cylinder buses, wanted all 150 of its order on ADC for delivery in 1928 to be of the 423 model - it was probably around this time that a run of 150 registration numbers VF 2701-850 was booked, in what was becoming standard practice. Yet, behind the scenes, there was considerable unease within ADC as more reports of trouble with existing CV25 engines flooded in, resulting in delay in putting the new models into production. It was decided by ADC that only limited quantities of the 423 and 424 would be built, at Daimler, until it had been shown that the

problems with the CV25 engine had been overcome. Instructions were given in January 1928 that even the handful of chassis already built were not to be released to customers until modified and tested. A further sign of retreat from ADC's confident line of the previous autumn was the decision that the 416A type, originally scheduled to be dropped, was to continue in production at Southall for 1928. It retained the AEC 4-type four-cylinder side-valve engine already familiar in the United fleet in the E- and F-class buses, though now mildly updated and designated A127 in its latest form, with detachable cylinder head and other changes. Reluctantly, United agreed in January 1928 to revise its order to call for 50 of the 423 type and 100 four-cylinder buses, at that stage quoted as 416A models. However, it was recorded that ADC was willing to replace the latter by further 423 models, subject to financial adjustment, if found unsatisfactory, up to Christmas 1928. There were thus two influences at work - getting the 423 up to a satisfactory level of reliability, and arriving at an acceptable specification for the four-cylinder buses United had reluctantly agreed to take.

It was doubtless to enlist United's help in pursuing the former, and perhaps also to bolster its faith in ADC's own preferred choice, that one of the very early 423 buses built for the 1927 Show was lent to United from February 1928. This was a demonstrator on chassis 423004, dating from November 1927, and having a Short Bros body initially - it seems to have been the exhibit with rear-entrance bus body of that make on the ADC stand at the Show held that month, as mentioned above. The ADC record card for this chassis confirms that the body was by Short Bros; that firm had also built other bodies for ADC vehicles at the Show. It seems likely that it remained unregistered before delivery to United, where it was registered VF 2871 on 3rd March.

United's Coach Factory would have wanted to start work on the 150 bodies and the prospect of production of two dimensionally different designs, with continuing doubts on quantities, would have created fresh problems, especially as body production had become quite highly mechanised, with machine-cut timber and jig-built assembly. It is likely that initial work might have begun on the original basis that the 423 chassis was to be used, and indeed United's big order was probably particularly in mind at ADC when the model was offered in long- as well as short-wheelbase form. The concept of producing a four-cylinder chassis that would accept basically the same body design as already built for the 1927 Show vehicle sold to Crosville provided a solution to that problem, and ADC was in no position to resist such a request. Thus ADC built another "United special", the 425 model.

The 425 was closely related to the long-wheelbase version of the 423, but the engine was the latest A127 version of the four-cylinder unit. The front axle was moved back slightly, evidently for some installational reason related to the change

<< *Opposite page:* These three views sum up the story of the 1928 fleet and the link between the ADC 423 and 425. The ADC 423 demonstrator *(upper)*, numbered F151 and registered VF 2871, is seen soon after receiving the United-built bus body in place of its Short Bros original. This represents what United originally had in mind as its standard bus for 1928, including the new yellow and brown livery. In practice, the 125 standard buses that year proved to be on the four-cylinder ADC 425 chassis, creating the J-class, though the body specification was as planned. In a view *(centre)* of J8 (VF 2708) outside Jesmond depot, Newcastle, in post-1933 red and cream livery, the 425 model's slightly set-back front axle can just be detected. Only 25 of the six-cylinder ADC 423 model were supplied, becoming the first, short-lived, K class. Most were elaborately equipped coaches; K14 (VF 2839) is seen *(lower)*, probably in 1929, at a rest break on the London-Yarmouth express service with a new-looking Bristol B behind. The legend "Buffet Car" echoed railway practice but provision of toilet and buffet facilities in a coach was about 35 years ahead of general matter-of-course provision of such things and an immense advance in the 16 years since United's first buses; an interior view appears on page 66. Note that the rear door, left open here, was not intended for passenger entry. *(United [2]; Roy Marshall Collection)*

of engine, and thus the 425 wheelbase was 17ft and 5/8ins, which was 3¼ins shorter than that of the long-wheelbase 423 - in similar manner the 16ft wheelbase of the 416 had become 16ft 3¼ins on the 423 in short-wheelbase form. Even so, the main structure of the body design as already produced also suited the 425, the slight change in axle position only affecting the cab, which was of the 'floating' type supported separately from the front end of the chassis. The front end was of similar appearance to the 423, using the same style of radiator, and shortly afterwards this styling change was also adopted by ADC for new four-cylinder chassis for general sale, types 426 and 427, both retaining the 16ft wheelbase and otherwise identical to the later 416A and 417A with the A127 engine - examples of these were also later to find their way into the United fleet with acquired businesses. This gave United the ability to go ahead with body production while allowing freedom of action on the vexed question of the engines and hence the chassis.

This was just as well, for the chassis order was altered again in March 1928 to call for 125 of the newly-created 425 model and only 25 of the 423, this figure being set by ADC's declared inability to deliver any more chassis of this type. Delivery of the 425-type chassis began in March 1928 almost immediately after this further revision was confirmed, and completed vehicles began to reach the fleet the following month. It had been decided that these vehicles would form United's J class, being numbered J1-125 and registered VF 2701-825 in sequence, the chassis being numbered 425001-125, though, as it turned out, not in order. The body design for these vehicles was almost identical to that on the ADC 423 sold to Crosville, apart from minor details. By comparison with previous generations of United bus, it took advantage of the lower-built chassis in having reduced floor height and lower overall height, in line with the trends of the time, this latter also applying to the raked windscreen. The roof, with full-width canopy at the front, had a mildly arched profile and with the radiused top window corners created a distinctive look that was to continue on United's 1929 single-deck bus deliveries. Provision of doors at front and rear was fairly common at that time, though new to United, partly accounting for the reduction of seating capacity to 35 from the 39 of the F-class buses, though the seats themselves seem to have been slightly more comfortably raked.

Unlike the Crosville bus, no front destination box was provided, United's standard practice in the late 1920s, first established as standard on these 150 vehicles, being the provision of a deep but narrow board mounted on the front bulkhead alongside the bonnet.

The financing arrangements applying to the total of 150 bodies for both types of chassis were as had been laid out in July 1927. Half had bodies built by United at its own direct expense, these going on to the vehicles numbered J1-75. The remaining 50 of the J-class buses, J76-125, had bodies built to ADC order but the body numbers of the two groups were intermingled to some degree, delivery of completed buses beginning in April and continuing until August. The 25 bodies needed for the ADC 423 chassis, to be designated the K class, were also built to ADC order, and the first five of these which were also 35-seat buses were also intermingled with those of the J-type buses; the 130 bus bodies for J and K chassis received the body numbers 1350-479, followed by 1480-99 for coach bodies on the remaining K-types, to be described later.

Along with their new styling the new J and K class vehicles introduced the livery listed in motor tax records as "yellow and brown" to the United fleet, where it made its appearance in March 1928, the last to be finished in the yellow and black style being the final F-class ADC 415 deliveries of the previous autumn. It was only to remain current for United for 18 months or so, but what seem to have been identical colours had, as described above, already been adopted by East Midland, where the livery had a much longer life. Again, the shade of yellow is a matter for debate, though half-tone photographs strongly suggest that the East Midland and United colours were the same in the 1928/9 period. "Biscuit and brown" was a phrase sometimes used, and both fleets added a cream waistband for the single-deck deliveries of 1929.

None of the 423-type vehicles entered service until June 1928 but meanwhile the demonstrator, 423004, was taking a more clearly defined if still mysterious part in the story. It was fitted with a United two-door bus body, numbered 1552, outwardly identical to those of the J-types. The Norfolk motor taxation records give the colour when first registered in March as yellow and brown, which, unless the Short Bros body was itself yellow and brown, suggests that the new body had already been fitted. It may well have received the fleet number F151 at the same time. Official United

photographs show the vehicle with this new body in United livery, and bearing these fleet and registration numbers. On the reverse, one bears the pencilled inscription, seemingly contemporary, "181-'J' Type. May 1928. 423 chassis". The figure 181 may simply have been a photographer's reference, but the date implies that the vehicle existed in this form at that date, possibly that it was then newly fitted with that body. The chassis does not figure in the surviving United records, evidently remaining in ADC ownership and retaining demonstrator status throughout its stay with the company. However, the body, numbered 1552, is shown as supplied to "Management", i.e. built for the operating fleet.

Several questions arise. Why was the vehicle given the number F151? This suggests that it was allocated before the J and K series of numbers were confirmed, and perhaps around the time of registration in March as already suggested, being tacked on to the previous series for full-sized buses, of which the most recent examples had basically the same Daimler CV25 engine. The register presumably used for allocations might still have included numbers up to F150 although the last ten had been cancelled. Although the registration number VF 2871 was higher than the pre-booked batch used for the J and K vehicles, it was lower than those of a further batch of Chevrolets which had begun entering service in April, which is also consistent with the March registration, an action which may have been encouraged by ADC for their own test programme. The body number 1552 comes immediately before those issued to this Chevrolet batch, so again does not rule out relatively early construction.

The production ADC 423 chassis were delivered

**Three, and possibly all four, of the Leylands that had been on order by independent operators when United took over their businesses in 1928 are shown here. All were delivered directly to United in the yellow and brown livery.**

*Upper:* **B269 (VF 4178), which was one of two PLSC3 Lions ordered by the Pioneer Bus Service Company Limited, Whitby, was photographed on 5th September 1928 when brand new.** *(Senior Transport Archive courtesy BCVM)*

*Centre upper:* **One of the pair, VF 4178 or VF 4179, at the old Silver Street, Berwick (in use until 1938 when the new bus station and depot opened) rented depot on Good Friday 1935, was in the by then well-established red and cream livery and had been renumbered into the Leyland series as either AL28 or AL29.** *(Fred Kennington Collection)*

*Centre lower:* **Pioneer had also ordered a TS2 Tiger with 32-seat Leyland bus bodywork. This emerged as United's B271 (VF 4180). It was photographed when new in November, on delivery to United, at the Quayside, Berwick, and was not on the Glasgow service.** *(Robert Grieves Collection)*

*Lower:* **This splendid Hoyal-bodied PLSC3 Lion, B290 (VF 4669), had been ordered by Amos, Proud, of Choppington. The location looks like Edinburgh and the bus is on the service to Newcastle. The trees, sun and shadows indicate a summer photograph, probably 1929. The bus was in the yellow and brown livery but had been repainted red by August 1930.** *(Philip Battersby Collection)*

in May-June and bodied in June-August 1928, numbered K1-25 and receiving the registration numbers VF 2826-50. They were in two distinct batches, of which the first, K1-5, on chassis 423023-6/2 respectively, received 35-seat bus bodies, with two-door layout, at any rate as built. The random distribution of the body numbers, 1354/9/84/52/74 respectively, among the first of the J-type bodies, strongly suggests a virtually identical design.

The remaining twenty, K6-25, on similar chassis 423038-57 (not in order), were completed as coaches, with front-entrance layout - though there was an emergency door at the nearside rear - and different pillar spacing. On K6 at least, and probably all, there was a recessed spare wheel housing accessible from the offside just aft of the driver's door. K6-11 were to quite an elaborate design with very comfortable seats for 20 passengers, toilet compartment and servery at the rear, the rest having 25-seat capacity. They had body numbers 1480-99 in order. A photograph of K8 when new shows it carrying a Yarmouth-Lowestoft-Southwold-London route board.

By June 1928, the Associated Daimler era was at an end, the troubles with the CV25 engine, still not fully resolved, being largely responsible. AEC and Daimler agreed to go their separate ways, though remaining on friendly terms with continuing co-operation in some respects, one being that existing contracts would be executed by AEC or Daimler under the control of ADC, which continued to exist as a company, after which the two makers would act independently. AEC continued to offer some of the four-cylinder models developed in the ADC era, including the 426 and 427, now simply retitled as AEC products - the lack of badge on the radiator proving helpful.

In August of that year, after being used in various parts of the Company's territory, the demonstrator F151 (VF 2871) was returned to Daimler. There it received an example of the larger CV35 engine, similar in general design to the CV25 but of 5.76-litre capacity, which was to become Daimler's standard bus power unit for the next few years; this was used in the new CF6 model announced later in 1928 and was very similar in general appearance to the 423 from which it was derived, save for having a fluted finish to the radiator top. It is reported that VF 2871 then went to East Surrey in December 1928, as a demonstrator, and to AEC in January 1929, which seems slightly odd, since it was more of a 'Daimler', though no doubt some ADC 'winding down' was still to be done. It lost its United body in favour of a Short Bros replacement, which seems almost certain to be the original, reinstated. A photograph shows VF 2871 with Short Bros body and livery as at the 1927 Show, but clearly with CF6-type fluted-top Daimler radiator instead of the previous plain one. The appearance is otherwise virtually identical to that of the vehicle displayed in 1927.

A United record in a 1930s file of vehicle valuations reports a spare J-class body being purchased in January 1929, without number or explanation and this ties in well with the report that the ex-F151 body went to a United J-class bus that same month. This again seems to confirm the dimensional compatibility of the 423 long-wheelbase and 425 models, but the purchase of body 1552 by United at this time appears to show that it had been the property of ADC. Although, as already noted, the Coach Factory records show the body as supplied to "Management", it does not appear in the Company's capital records for the time. VF 2871 then passed to H Phillips of Long Buckby, taken over by United Counties in July 1932, the vehicle running until 1938.

Two early casualties among United's J-class buses were J51 and J113, burnt out, together with three of the AEC 415 charabancs, E27, 28 and 37, in a fire at the ex-Dunham depot (see p.67) in Norwich on 15th October 1928. Somewhat surprisingly, the United Board decided on 30th November 1928 to exercise the option made in January to exchange what were described as the ADC 416 chassis for 423 chassis, although no quantity was mentioned and clearly no action was taken. By then, a new supplier had been chosen for the 1929 fleet requirements as recorded in the next chapter. Just how an exchange would have been handled remains a matter for conjecture - manufacture of complete new chassis and accepting the return of what were clearly the 425-type chassis after around six months' use seems unrealistic especially in view of the break-up of ADC, though conversion from 425 to 423 specification seems more feasible even if of doubtful benefit, given hindsight.

As already mentioned, there were also a further fifteen Chevrolet 14-seat buses taken into stock between April and June 1928, numbered H16-30 (VF 3001-15), again reputedly primarily for use as 'chasers', though one is shown in a contemporary photograph (page 58) being used on a Scarborough local service. This time the chassis model had moved on to LO, though the design was not changed fundamentally, retaining the four-cylinder engine as on the previous batch. Waveney again fulfilled the body order, these being numbered 1553-67 by United. They, and H1-15 dating from the previous year, had short lives with United, though the departure of H21-3 to East Midland in May 1928 doubtless reflected response to a need from the associated company. Most of the remainder were withdrawn in 1929, although two evidently remained in United ownership long enough to be sold to Lincolnshire Road Car in July 1930. Thereafter, no new buses or coaches in the classes below 26-seat capacity were added to the United fleet for over half a century, despite the many rural services operated, until the special circumstances of the advent of deregulation and the minibus era of the mid-1980s. However, United acquired many small vehicles with taken-over businesses, some of which were kept in service for quite lengthy periods.

*Above:* The troubles with the Daimler CV25 engines in the ADC 423 models caused Daimler to agree to rebuild the chassis with the larger, and livelier, CV35 engine, effectively converting them to CF6 models. The former K14 (VF 2839) is seen here having received the fluted-top Daimler radiator as standard on the CF6 and forming part of the conversion. It had been repainted in red livery and doubtless bore its new fleet number NA28. *(Jack Burton Collection)*

*Below:* The interior view, looking forward, of these vehicles reveals a luxurious ambience. This is K8 (VF 2833). *(United)*

# 4 The Fleet Under Changing Regimes 1928-1933

Major changes affecting the United company and its fleet were afoot during the latter part of 1928 but there was no outward sign of this at the time. Meanwhile, the pace of take-overs of independent operators began to speed up. Unlike the situation in 1926, when larger vehicles from such acquisitions were put into the A class, by 1928 vehicles of the quite wide variety of makes involved were all being added to the B series, taking its numbers up quite briskly and gradually altering its character to become more of a miscellaneous class, even though the Daimler CB was still the most numerous group within it and much of the acquired stock was sold off quite quickly.

J W Rines & Co, of Scarborough, taken over in April, contributed three Vulcan buses, two 20-seaters and a VWBL 30-seater, which became B245-7 until sold off in 1929. They were followed by B248-53, from another Scarborough operator, Allan's Motor Service, taken over in May, these comprising two Chevrolets, a Beardmore, a Karrier and a Morris, all 14-seaters, plus a Vulcan 20-seater; most had turned up with other users by 1931, at least two as lorries. R C & R E Dunham (Central Bus Services), Norwich, acquired in about June 1928, was another such case but the mixed bag of eight vehicles was sold off very quickly and evidently not numbered into the fleet. Pioneer Bus Service Co Ltd, of Whitby, taken over in July, was rather more substantial, with thirteen vehicles, which became B255-67. Here again there was quite a mixed fleet, including a Willys-Overland 14-seater, a Graham-Dodge 20-seater, and three Guy 20-seaters, the larger types included two Albion PFB26s and two Dennis Fs dating from 1927 and a 1925 Dennis 2½-ton model. However, there had been a growing preference for Leyland, two PLSC1 Lions having been added in 1927 to join a 1923 32-seat charabanc of that make. The Dennis buses and the PLSC1s had bodies by W G Edmond, of Middlesbrough. In addition, two Leyland Lions of the longer PLSC3 type and one of the six-cylinder Leyland Tigers introduced at the 1927 Show, a TS2, all with Leyland 32-seat bus bodywork, had been ordered. These were delivered directly to United, being given the fleet numbers B269-71 respectively and registered VF 4178-80, the Lions in October and the Tiger in December 1928. Most of the ex-Pioneer vehicles were sold off by 1931; the two PLSC1s found a new home with Thomas Allen and Sons of Blyth when sold in January 1934, only to be reacquired by United on the take-over of that business later in 1934. The two new PLSC3 buses lasted until 1936/7 and the Tiger until 1939, this vehicle being converted to a fire engine by the Scarborough Auxiliary Fire Service in 1940.

Morris Cowley cars, acquired or new, were given numbers D244, D254, D268, D272 and D273. An indication of United's expansion northwards was the take-over of W W Pile, Wooler, Northumberland, only about a dozen miles from the Scottish border yet running a service to Newcastle, in November, with a Studebaker 20-seater and two W&G buses, which became B274-6.

Larger than any previous acquisition by United was Amos, Proud & Co (1928) Ltd, based at Guide Post, near Choppington, Northumberland, taken over with 33 vehicles in November 1928, the fleet numbers issued running from B277 to B310, including one vehicle then on order. The business had been begun by J W Proud, later joined by J H Amos, further reconstructions leading to the final title, as quoted above, in February of 1928. As well as local routes, there was a Newcastle-Edinburgh service and it was doubtless for this that four new Leyland Tigers, very early examples of the type, TY 3677/8 and 4493/4, had been added to the fleet in January and April 1928, becoming B285/8/7/6. They, like the example ordered by Pioneer, had the rather square-cut Leyland body as then offered for this model, at least one having the layout with internal luggage space alongside the rear entrance as supplied to some other early customers for long-distance use.

Also added to the Amos, Proud fleet in the spring of 1928 were four ADC 416s with LGOC 32-seat bus bodies, TY 4343-6, becoming B292-5 despite their affinity to United's main types of that time, though later renumbered EB102-5. However, the largest group of full-sized buses from the Amos, Proud fleet were nine Leyland Lion PLSC1 and PLSC3 models with Leyland bodies dating from 1927 (B277-84 and 289) but there was also a Guy BB 32-seater of that year (B310). Earlier stock was in the 20- to 26-seat category, including eleven Lancias dating from 1922-6 (B299-309), three Dennis 2½-ton models of 1926 (B296-8) and a 1927 Reo Gold Crown (B291). The number B290 was allocated to the vehicle on order, an additional PLSC3 32-seat bus, delivered directly to United in December 1928 and registered VF 4669 - it was unusual in having bodywork by Hoyal. The Lancias were not used and were sold to dealers in January 1929. United and SMT had established a competing joint service when Amos, Proud & Co began its Newcastle-Edinburgh route so United's takeover upset the balance.

In April 1929 it was decided that the Scottish Motor Traction Co Ltd should receive four of the ex-Amos, Proud vehicles as part of their share of the business relating to the service to Edinburgh, two of the Tigers (B285/8) and two Lions (B277/89, which were TY 2423 and 3066) being transferred. It seems that during the period when owned by United these four had already been running in SMT livery because, it is said, Edinburgh City Council had refused to issue licences for them, although this may have reflected a transitional stage pending transfer of the licences to SMT.

Further independent businesses based in Northumberland whose purchase took place during December 1928 were those of C F Wright, of Rothbury (B311-3: a Thornycroft A6 and two Laffley 20-seaters); W & C E Curtis, Monkseaton (B314-7: a Leyland Lioness, a Beardmore 14-seater and two Dennis 20-seaters); J W B Thursfield, of Whitley Bay (B318/9: two Dennises): T M Walton, Whitley Bay (B320, a Beardmore) and J Lee, Rothbury (B321-9: a Renault, a Chevrolet and seven Lancias). Many of these vehicles were sold off within a couple of years and most of the rest by about 1932, though the ex-Curtis Lioness survived, as AM41, until 1934. The following month, Blyth Motor Services Ltd followed, two Albions, a Reo and two AECs becoming United's B331-5.

### The choice swings to Bristol

The decision taken in the autumn of 1928 to place a large order for Bristol B-type buses was a turning point, in several respects, which ultimately had repercussions extending well beyond United. The inter-related problems of supply and reliability, detailed in an earlier chapter, seem to have tried United's confidence in the Associated Daimler Company to the limit, notwithstanding the special financing arrangements covering nearly 400 new buses in 1926-8 which had contributed crucially to United's expansion over that period. Even the end of the ADC regime, in June 1928, was itself doubtless unsettling until AEC and Daimler could re-establish their own identities and reputation as bus makers.

When the orders for the J- and K-class vehicles were amended for the second time, in March 1928, the United board had resolved that a Leyland six-cylinder chassis was to be purchased for experimental purposes: at that date, this could only have been the new Tiger model introduced the previous autumn and mentioned above. Offers of Maudslay and Albion chassis were also to be reconsidered when six-cylinder models were available. In the event, none of these was purchased, though it is interesting to speculate as to what might have happened if this had been pursued, particularly in regard to Leyland, in the spring of 1928. Even so, it is clear that the climate for United to switch to a new supplier was promising. But why Bristol?

By 1928, the Bristol Tramways & Carriage Co Ltd had built up a modest business as a builder of bus and lorry chassis, producing two or three of these per week as an adjunct to its core activity of running the electric tramway system in the City of Bristol and providing motor bus services in surrounding districts, the latter using own-make vehicles. At that date the only alliance to which BTCC belonged to was the dwindling Imperial Tramways group - a very few Bristol motor vehicles had gone to the Imperial branch on Tees-side and to the Corris Railway in Wales. At that stage, Bristol buses were being bought mainly by municipalities or companies which quite often had a tramway background - an example in the north-east, not then associated with any other operator in the area, was the Sunderland District concern - or by small independent operators. Conspicuous by their absence at that stage among the users were members of the big Tilling or British Electric Traction groups of operating companies or that of the jointly-owned Tilling & British Automobile Traction Ltd, the new name given to the former British Automobile Traction Co Ltd in May 1928 to mark the rationalisation of the many instances where both groups had direct or indirect interests in operating companies.

Although United's decision to buy Bristol chassis went to the company board, with E B Hutchinson then still in place as Chairman and Managing Director, various factors may have helped to influence it. For example, A T Evans, by then Secretary who would from May 1930 take on the duties of Traffic Manager as the next step in his rise towards becoming General Manager, had as already mentioned joined United as accountant from Bristol Tramways in 1922. A more traditional source of influence on vehicle matters was the Chief Engineer, and B V Smith, appointed Engineer at United as from 1st October 1924 as previously stated, had been trained at Bristol Tramways, although his appointment with United was from a post with Midland Red. He had just been appointed Engineer and Operating Manager to UAS in September 1928, his employment being put under a three-year contract. A contemporary, D H J Flooks, who had been in the experimental department at BTCC in 1928-34, specifically gave Smith the credit for United's order for B-types going through, in reminiscences which appeared in the house magazine "Bristol" of February 1967 when he was about to retire as Chief Engineer of Red & White Services Ltd. He indicated that BTCC's continuance as a vehicle maker was in doubt at the time because of lack of sufficient orders and that the United order may well have saved the day, adding another dimension to its importance.

By the late 1920s, the Bristol B-type chassis which had been announced in 1926 was selling quite widely, though in modest numbers. It had a simple four-cylinder side-valve engine of 6-litre capacity, about a litre larger than most competing models and obviously acceptable to United, despite the latter's preference at that time for six-cylinder buses, because of the lively performance it could give. Shortly before the United batch was built, the engine design was modified, a new cylinder head and pistons being developed for it by Harry Ricardo, then best known as a wizard in getting side-valve petrol engines to perform well. The B-type prototype, with chassis number B101, built in 1926

*Above:* The Bristol B enters service: the second and third of the L class appear in this interesting view of Loftus depot in 1929. The Bristols were still very new and were being serviced before going out of the depot. L2 (VF 5102) was being oiled and watered (note the driver's toolkit on the ground) and L3 (VF 5103) was being fuelled. The bus on the right was F21 (PW 9821). Several drivers and conductors were present and the photographer's activities had drawn an interested crowd of depot staff and the odd passer-by. *(John Banks Collection)*

*Below:* When still new and very shiny, at least four (maybe six and possibly more) B-type Bristols were allocated to a private hire assignment in Scarborough. The route number boxes appear to be in use to identify the buses for the members of the party. L77 (VF5177) and the unidentified bus behind it are Nos. 3 and 4. It would be logical to suggest that the other two visible buses were Nos 5 and 6 and that Nos 1 and 2 were out of the picture ahead of L77. If so, and if all seats were taken, the private hire party must have numbered some 190 or so. *(United)*

*Above:* A dramatic accident to a Bristol B occurred in treacherous conditions on Lythe bank, just north of Whitby, on 17th August 1931. Loftus depot's L11 (VF 5111) skidded and span through 180 degrees near the top of the 1 in 4½ gradient. By the time the photographer appeared, help from the depot had arrived using sister vehicle L29 (VF 5129). At this date both vehicles were in the new red and cream livery. *(John Banks Collection)*

*Below:* Summer sunshine in Scarbrough Avenue, Skegness, near the Pier Head, in July 1930, and East Midland's United-bodied AEC Reliance M3 (VO 738) was waiting to leave on service 25 to Chesterfield via Worksop. This is a rare picture, for it shows both of the classes unique to East Midland in United's numbering scheme: standing behind the Reliance was G3 (RR 7403) and another member of the G class of Short Bros-bodied ADC 416As, neither of which had yet had the cream band added to the livery. G3's destination blind was set to show "Special". *(G H F Atkins)*

70

but retained as a demonstrator, received the modifications and was sent out to potential users in October 1928, perhaps just in time to have helped to influence United's decision.

Characteristically, United specified a longer wheelbase. The B-type as built in 1926-8 had a 15ft 7ins wheelbase, intended for an overall length of just under 26ft, but the United vehicles were the first with a wheelbase of 16ft, thereafter adopted as standard for B-types for other users. On 30th October 1928 it was reported to the Board that it was planned to buy 150 Bristol chassis, but the order as signed and sealed at the Board meeting on 14th December was for 130; even so, this was easily the biggest single order for chassis Bristol had received. In March 1929, it was proposed that the balance of 20 be made up of Star, AJS, Gilford and "other similar faster vehicles"; United then held sales agencies for all these makes as well as bodying them for independent operators. Although this was not pursued, it indicates that possession of some lively vehicles was regarded as important despite the tight official speed limits of the time.

The bodies for the Bristol B chassis were, as usual, built in United's own Coach Factory at Lowestoft, to a style similar to that on the J-class ADC 425 buses, though with single entrance doorway, at the front, and seats for 32 passengers. They were intended as buses though, as with the J class, were rather more comfortable than the maximum-capacity types of the mid-1920s. This layout and capacity could be accommodated on the 16ft wheelbase and in the 1929-31 period United

adopted a length of about 26ft for most of its new single-deckers, perhaps with the idea of building up a new medium-sized fleet to take over the role of the somewhat smaller B-class Daimler CB buses.

Though the deep destination board on the bulkhead was perpetuated on the Bristols, a two-track route number box was added at roof level. The B-type buses were given the next vacant class letter, L, becoming L1-130 and were tidily registered VF 5101-230 in the usual manner. The invoice for the first chassis, L1, was dated the day before the United Board confirmed the order, and chassis delivery began on 19th December 1928, indicating that the deal had already been agreed at director level and the work put in hand. Further chassis followed from late January and the final chassis of the batch left Bristol in May 1929. Entry into service of bodied vehicles began in March and extended to August. They are said to have been quite fast in their heyday and gave the company very good service; most were still in use with United until 1948/9, although by then they were rather less appealing to passengers, being prone to quite severe propellor-shaft vibration as speed built up.

Although United's own intake of new buses in 1929 did not include any AEC buses there was an East Midland order reflecting what proved the last instance of United influence on that company. It was for ten of the then new Reliance, type 660, introduced by AEC as an interim model, which featured a newly-designed six-cylinder engine in a modified 426-style chassis, following the break-up of ADC. These were given the class letter M, which

After the M class, which, as we have seen, was allocated in its entirety to East Midland Motor Services, the next class letter in United's orderly alphabetical progression was N. The N class of 1929 consisted of 14 Daimler CFs, N1 - N14 (VF 6301-14), which were renumbered in 1935 as D4 - 17. N12 (VF 6312) was brand new in this 1929 photograph, and survived until 1946/7. *(Senior Transport Archive)*

was the next available in United's system. They were delivered in May and had United 32-seat bodies of similar general style to those on the L-class Bristol Bs, with United's contemporary type of destination display. As described later, unforeseen events were quite soon to cause United to build up a substantial fleet of AEC Reliance buses, even though none had been ordered by the firm.

A batch of fourteen Daimler CF6s dating from July 1929 and numbered N1-14 (VF 6301-14) might be counted as an epilogue to United's ADC era, perhaps also as a fulfilment of the search for vehicles with more lively performance, possibly replacing the earlier plan to buy 20 "faster" vehicles of other makes. This model was outwardly almost identical to the ADC 423, though its larger CV35 5.76-litre six-cylinder sleeve-valve engine soon made it widely recognised as a refined model well suited to express service use. The CV35 proved much more reliable than the CV25 as used in the 423, even though still notorious for heavy lubricating oil consumption, an inherent problem of sleeve-valve engines. In this case the United-built bodies were of more rounded outline than those on the L-class buses and had 26 coach seats.

At this point, it is appropriate to mention that the 25 K-class ADC 423 vehicles were renumbered NA15-39 before the end of 1929. This was part of a wider renumbering scheme covering several classes, as described later, in this case related to a plan to fit these vehicles with the larger CV35 engines. An offer by Daimler to "recondition 23 ADC 423 chassis to specification at £160 each" was accepted by the United Board on 18th October 1929. In this context "recondition" was evidently a euphemism for conversion almost to CF6 standard, which made NA an appropriate classification. The modest price suggests an attempt at restoring better relations after the troubled spell centred on CV25-engined vehicles from 1927. The 23 new engines are reported as being fitted to NA15/6/8-36 and 38/9 in March-May 1930; presumably NA17 and 37 were altered independently.

The pace of acquisitions of smaller operators slowed during the earlier months of 1929 although, on 28th March, People's Balmoral Bus Service Ltd, of Scarborough, was taken over, with six small buses which became B336-41: three Leylands, an Albion, a Dennis and a Karrier. Aside from the transfers related to the railway connection described below, there was also the purchase in October of the business of Albert Brand, of Richmond, with five Maudslays, three Thornycrofts and an Albion, which took the numbers B343-51. As it turned out, that was to prove the highpoint of what could be described as the "old" B series so far as buses or coaches were concerned.

### The LNER involvement

There had been growing interest in bus operation by the four main-line railway companies although there had been some ambiguity as to their powers in regard to this until the passing of their Railway (Road Transport) Acts in August 1928. The previous month, United, conscious of the implications, suggested to the London & North Eastern Railway that it should consider a policy of cooperation. Also taking note of the changing situation was Tilling and British Automobile Traction Ltd, concerned at the implications for its group of operating companies and, at a meeting with the railways in November, the principle of the railways and TBAT taking equal shareholdings in operating companies was established, although in the meantime this did not prevent a continuation of competitive bidding; it is unlikely that United knew of this meeting. There was interest on the part of both LNER and TBAT in the major independent operators within the former's area, which covered much of eastern and north-eastern England, and of which there were quite a number at that date. In December 1928 TBAT made an approach to United offering financial assistance should the company desire to raise capital, but no immediate specific action followed. In January 1929, the LNER suggested an amalgamation with them on the basis of the formation of a new company and active negotiations were put in hand.

By June agreement was all but reached when, on the 14th, a direct approach was made by John F Heaton on behalf of TBAT to E B Hutchinson. That same month Heaton was appointed Vice-Chairman of Thomas Tilling Ltd in the aftermath of the death of Richard Tilling and was making his mark as an increasingly dominant figure in the industry. Despite TBAT's earlier contact with the railway companies, he was uneasy about the threat of railway control of United to the bus groups. The purchase of the Crosville concern, not unlike United in its character and status, by the London Midland & Scottish Railway, completed on 1st May, may have heightened these fears. Events moved rapidly from that point, though by no means without trouble: the BET directors of TBAT were at first not in favour, but were persuaded to allow Heaton to pursue the matter, and negotiations with the LNER were far from smooth. Even so, by 3rd July, a joint LNER/TBAT offer based on the equal shareholding principle had been agreed for sending out to United shareholders. It won the day and the official take-over date was 1st August 1929, E B Hutchinson, his brother P K Hutchinson and L L Livermore having resigned on 24th July to make way for the new Board appointed that day.

Arthur Hawkins and William Thomson remained and, although clearly not regarded as part of the old regime because of their "outside" status, they provided a degree of continuity because of their appointments dating back to 1923 and 1925 respectively. The roles of A T Evans and B V Smith as Secretary and Engineer respectively, first appointed in 1922 and 1924, also seem bound to have expanded well beyond day-to-day matters in the new circumstances. An indication of LNER's strong position at this point was the appointment of Thomas Hornsby, who was North-Eastern Divisional Manager of the LNER, as United's new

Chairman, J F Heaton being Deputy Chairman, with Reginald Tilling and W S Wreathall also on the Board. The latter two were present as TBAT directors but Wreathall is noteworthy as the only one of the three TBAT representatives who was a BET rather than a Tilling man - United's long era under Tilling influence had begun. The appointment of a railwayman as chairman was a pattern not repeated in subsequent instances of joint railway and bus group control of bus operating companies. Although a general settlement between the railways and TBAT reached on 30th October 1929 was based on the United model, in practice the principle subsequently adopted generally throughout Britain was that the railways would leave the management of bus companies in which they held shareholdings, and in particular, the provision of chairmen on their boards, to the bus company groups.

A General Manager for United was now required. The post was advertised, and an appointment made on 18th October. The successful applicant was H P Stokes, who had been General Manager of the Plymouth Corporation undertaking since 1919. Transfers of ex-municipal men to senior positions with major operating companies belonging to the big groups were rare events, such vacancies normally being filled from within the group. It is interesting that the latter path was not followed in this case, perhaps suggesting that the TBAT members on United's new Board might have deferred to the Chairman's view on the matter. General Managers, particularly in municipal undertakings, could exert considerable influence on fleet policy, but although Leyland and AEC buses were about to enter service in the Plymouth undertaking, Mr Stokes seems not to have had an opportunity to influence United policy in this respect during his short period in office. Perhaps his main claim to fame is that of being the father of Donald, later Lord, Stokes, who became Chairman and Managing Director of the British Leyland Motor Corporation on its formation in 1968 after a career in which successes in sales of Leyland buses overseas played a key part.

The first new buses to be added to the fleet after the takeover had been completed were 25 Leyland Titan TD1 double-deckers, the order being authorised on 18th October 1929; it was evidently a decision made by the Board as it then stood, with no General Manager in office, although doubtless other officers of the Company may have been consulted. Nineteen of the buses arrived in November, suggesting that Leyland had made a special effort to give quick delivery and in all probability this had been agreed informally in advance of confirmation. They had the Leyland closed-top 48-seat bodywork standard for the type; the makers had coined the name "Lowbridge" for this patented body design, later to become part of the industry's vernacular, and they were to the latest enclosed-staircase specification. At that date, United's Coach Factory had no experience in building double-deck bodies, save for the two one-

off exercises, the open-top version of the Norfolk design on (A)82 in 1922 and then 'Big Bertha' on A176 in 1923. The Leyland body was widely accepted across the industry as offering good value, even the standard destination display often being adopted, as in the case of United's examples. The Titan, with smooth-running six-cylinder 6.8-litre overhead-camshaft petrol engine, had been introduced two years earlier and in that time had become firmly established as the leading double-decker on the British market, and the first to be widely used on inter-urban routes. Its choice for this large-scale venture into double-deck operation was thus in line with many companies in most of the main groups as well as independent concerns and municipalities.

The question of livery had been discussed in October and it was agreed to change to red - recorded as the preferred choice - or green, but that the matter would be left to the Chairman. Thus it came about that, when new, these first TD1 buses in the fleet were painted in LNER green - believed to be the apple green shade used on LNER express passenger locomotives - with what is quoted in Norfolk Tax office records as white relief but seems likely to have been what was then sometimes called "broken white", i.e. cream. It is worthy of note, however, that the old United board had been considering a change of livery in the autumn of 1928. The fleet numbers 1-19 of the first Titans initially had no prefix, but it seems likely that this was simply because fleet numbering practice was under review, not least because of the introduction of these vehicles and their close relationship to the Tiger single-deckers already in service, of which more were soon to be added.

### Partial renumbering and revision of classes from November 1929

There were other cases where inter-related models were joining the fleet and means of identifying them as such would be of practical value. The result was a partial renumbering affecting roundly 150 out of the 750 or so vehicles operated, and creating several new classes, although most vehicles in the big E, F, J and L series continued undisturbed. The scheme appears to have been implemented from November 1929, in some cases not becoming evident until relevant vehicles came into scope over the succeeding few weeks. The alphabetical principle remained, but was used more effectively to identify specific types, in some cases with suffix letters to make sub-divisions clearer, as explained later. It was decided that a new A series was to be used for Leylands and the first batch of Titans became A1-25 - their registration numbers showed continuity with previous practice in again being a Norfolk issue, VF 7617-41. The remainder of the initial Titan batch were delivered by February 1930 with the new A-class numbers, and the earlier ones were brought into line. The first fifteen went to the Northumberland area and the other four were used mainly on service 21(Darlington to Redcar).

The third of the TD1 Titans, No. 3 (VF 7619), photographed in November 1929. The panelling, rear dome and upper window surrounds were green; the middle and front of the roof were possibly silver but more likely white, the lower window surrounds and the three bands were white. *(Senior Transport Archive courtesy BCVM)*

At that time there were still a number of buses in service from the earlier A series of "heavy cars", but most were AEC Y-type buses rebuilt to forward-control and by then reclassified AA, so there were only a few true A-prefix AEC Y buses. They mostly had much higher fleet numbers than the new Leylands and in any case were almost all withdrawn within the following year. The original B series, at first "light buses on pneumatic tyres", had developed something of a split nature. There were about 48 Daimler CBs still in the operational fleet, though with various types of body and function; by that time the D-prefix within this same series was being used only for service vehicles or cars. Since 1926, from fleet number B196, the B series had been used for acquired vehicles, causing the numbers to rise quite quickly and become a very mixed collection of makes, the series reaching B351 by October 1929, even though many of these vehicles had been sold off quite quickly. Numbers D352-60 had been allocated to cars - eight Morris Cowleys and one Austin Six - then on order, though they entered service as IC5-13.

A new D series, starting at D1 and forming part of the late 1929 renumbering, was used, initially for the Daimlers that had been rebodied as seaside runabouts in 1927/8, all by then licensed as 23-seaters and allocated to Scarborough. They were given numbers in the order of their original fleet numbers, D1 thus being the solitary Daimler CK so rebodied, formerly B6. The remainder of this first group from D2 were the CBs, often erroneously called "toastracks", with former fleet numbers taken in sequence from B11 and ending with D19, the former B107. Then, possibly at a slightly later stage, other surviving B-class vehicles were also renumbered into this new D series, beginning at D20, which was also a CK type, the former B5, the series running to D48. Again, it seems that they were given new numbers in the order of their previous B numbers. Fleet number D20, the former B5, survived until 1931 and, as indicated previously, had been recorded as receiving the body from the AEC Renown, PW 3322, so some rebuilding to reconcile a hitherto bonneted chassis and a forward-control body is implied.

A fresh, purely miscellaneous, B series, intended for types thought unlikely to figure in the fleet in quantity, was begun in the course of the reorganisation of classes. Its use was more restricted, more types hitherto numbered in the later part of the old B series now having their own individual series. Where this was not so, vehicles which the Company intended keeping more than very briefly were moved from the old to the new B series, taking much lower numbers.

United's connection with East Midland Motor Services Limited came to an end as from 1st October 1929 upon acquisition of that company's shares by the LMS and LNER. East Midland thus drops out of the United story, although it should be recorded that the United fleet numbering system was retained for many years, as well as the livery. The transfer freed the letter G, used for East Midland's ADC 416 fleet, which was now used for Guy vehicles acquired by United, often from LNER-associated fleets. The association of initial letters in this case, as with D for the renumbered smaller Daimlers, may have been fortuitous; there would be other occasional instances, hinting at the more radical renumbering that was to follow in 1935.

The letter K had become vacant with the movement of the ADC 423 vehicles into the N series as NA, so a new K series was used to identify the new or nearly new AEC Reliance buses, also mainly from LNER-related sources, as described below. As already mentioned, East Midland had adopted M for a batch of AEC Reliance buses with United bodies in May 1929, but this had now also become a vacant letter so in early 1930 United adopted M for Thornycroft, a type which came into the fleet in fair numbers for a time. The letter H, already in use for Chevrolet, was also applied to GMC, another product of the General Motors combine.

The use of second letters to signify sub-variants had begun in 1926 with AA, and BB in 1927, but now began to be used more specifically, sometimes conveying the precise model, although using a common numerical series for each group. Thus A was Leyland Titan, but AL signified Leyland Lion and AT Leyland Tiger, while AM was at first used for other Leyland types such as the A9 and Lioness. Sometimes the second letter had a specific meaning common to more than one type - it appears that M used in this way sometimes signified a bonneted vehicle, as may have applied here. Thus, though EB was used for the ADC 416 and EC for the AEC 426, both being forward-control, EM was used for the AEC 414, ADC 417 and AEC 427 models, which were all bonneted, though the logic became a bit confused by the inclusion of AEC 411 and 413 forward-control types. The complexities of model identification and variety of types coming into the fleet seem at times to have defeated the staff involved. In a fleet so widely spread, staff may well not have seen the vehicles in question and not have been familiar with maker's type codes, which were much less widely publicised than in later years. Hence it seems possible that CM, which became applied to Albions in general, might have begun in a similar way, as many of the Albion buses acquired at about that time were of bonneted types such as the PJ26 or PK26 of the 30/60hp Model 26 series. Many of these came from railway-associated fleets, even though these also included equivalent forward-control models such as the PM28, PMA28 etc, which, together with various other Albion types, were also given fleet numbers in the CM series. At that stage, there is no record of C being used as such, though one vehicle acquired in 1930 is recorded as CA29, this being HH 4363, ex-Emmerson and previously Wallis of Carlisle, quoted as a PM28 - reports that this was "articulated" run up against the fact that any form of articulated passenger-carrying trailer was then illegal and suggest some misunderstanding. No mention in United records of the code CH, as has been quoted for some Albions, has been traced.

Another noteworthy acknowledgement of a variation was the introduction of the prefix FD for the ADC 415D models with Daimler sleeve-valve engines, which are shown in United records as F116-40 up to late 1929 but as FD, using the same numbers, by March 1930; those remaining in the fleet being noted as reverting to F from dates between 1932 and 1934, suggesting that the Daimler engines had been removed although it may also have indicated the loss of their original coach status.

Existing classes E, F, H, J, L and N continued, although some had sub-variants added or denoted by new two-letter codes. The new classes introduced in November 1929 were:-

*New A class* - for Leyland Titans; other Leyland variants denoted by AL, AM, AT and, later, AN and AH, included in same series.
*New B class* - for miscellaneous vehicles, this being a new series for those not transferred to new classes.
*New CM class* - for various Albion types.
*New D class* - for Daimler CK and CB types, initially the seaside runabouts and, later, other remaining examples.
*New G class* - for various Guy types.
*New K class* - for AEC Reliances (K had

Examples of vehicles in the new numbering series were Leyland Titan A72 (VF8515), a new, 1930, purchase in a new class; and Lioness AM130 (TY 5609), which came from William Wharton, of Fourstones, near Hexham on 1st April 1930. It took its place in the A series, but with an "M" suffix, which may, initially, have been used to denote bonneted vehicles. *(Jack Burton Collection; Mrs B Norris)*

become available as a result of the renumbering of ADC 423 vehicles as NA).
*New IC and IL classes* - for inspection cars and lorries in a single series of numbers. The vehicles had previously been classified respectively as D, and A and B. The term "lorries" was defined fairly broadly and included parcels vans.

*Notes:*
All except the new K class drew some existing vehicles from the old B class.
G, hitherto used by East Midland, became available as a result of the ending of the direct link with that company.
M, another former East Midland class, was introduced in about March 1930 for various Thornycroft types. The first 13 of these, at least, had briefly been in the new B class.
P was added for Tilling-Stevens later in 1930 and R for AEC Regal in 1932 when the numbers coming into the fleet were considered to justify the creation of fresh series, as described later in the text.
Subsequently, C was used for some Crossley buses acquired in 1934.

### LNER-controlled operators

The LNER considerably influenced the content of the United fleet in that period, the repercussions extending well into the 1930s. Soon after the main-line railways obtained bus-operating powers in August 1928, the LNER began acquiring interests, usually giving full control, in various existing concerns. It acted through its subsidiary Thompson, McKay & Co, which had been the cartage agent of the Great Central Railway before the 1923 amalgamation brought it under the LNER umbrella. In regard to their effects on United's fleet over the following few years, the more important of the LNER-controlled businesses acquired were Robert Emmerson and Co Ltd, based at Throckley and operating services running west from Newcastle to Hexham and Carlisle; Eastern Express Motors Ltd, of West Hartlepool; Redwing Safety Services Ltd, of Redcar; and Scarborough District Motor Services Ltd. Another significant case was that of Blumer's Motors Ltd of Greatham, near West Hartlepool, though in that instance absorption into United's fleet did not occur until 1934 and is covered later. Several other firms were also involved, an example being Billingham and Haverton Hill Motors Ltd, an offshoot of Eastern Express, and the history of the whole episode is very complex.

New vehicles had been ordered by LNER for these and other operators, most notably a total of 74 of the then new AEC Reliance single-decker model, type 660 - this was the largest fleet of the type ordered by any one concern. The Reliance was the first application for a new AEC six-cylinder overhead-camshaft 6.1-litre petrol engine. The rest of the chassis was based on the previous 426 model, the combination being an interim step towards AEC's new Regent and Regal models. There had also been some earlier ADC or AEC models in the LNER-controlled fleets; other makes favoured were Albion, Guy and Thornycroft, though some went to other areas. The first batch of 24 Reliances, for which 32-seat bodies with full-fronted cabs had been ordered from Strachan & Brown, were delivered in February-April 1929. Ten (registered EF 4118-27) entered service with Eastern Express and the remainder, having GU (London) registrations, were intended for Emmerson's, though three were diverted for direct LNER operation on routes in the Durham area. The full-width cabs on these buses were later altered to half-cab form, probably at quite an early stage in their lives.

The construction and ultimate distribution of the balance of 50 LNER-ordered Reliances was more complex, being affected not only by the railway involvement with United but also by further developments involving other operators. Official records are complicated by the fact that Thompson, McKay remained official owners of buses while they were being acquired by operating companies under hire-purchase agreements. Delivery of these later Reliances from the bodybuilders began in July 1929, 32 having bus bodies to a new 32-seat design with conventional half-cab layout from new but with a more rounded outline at the rear than the previous batch. At least 28 were built by Dodson, but there is evidence indicating that Strachans (by then that firm's title had changed from Strachan & Brown) built two, possibly sub-contracted from Dodson, with some uncertainty on the remaining two. Early deliveries were registered EF 4239-46, 4261-8, 4280 and 4283, all for operation by Eastern Express, the pair thought to have Strachans bodywork being EF 4266 and 4280 - they were shown as such on AEC record cards, the others of these EF registration batches being shown as Dodson except for EF 4261, for which there no bodybuilder was quoted - the remaining similar case is mentioned later.

In March 1929 the LNER also took a shareholding in Wakefield's Motors, of North Shields, at that stage associated with Eastern Express and having the same principal directors, and EF 4239-44 of the above AEC Reliance buses, although licensed to Eastern Express in July 1929, are thought not to have entered service before being hired to Wakefield's that same month. The Northern General Transport Co Ltd, the BET group's principal bus operator in the area, covering most of the north-eastern part of County Durham, took a holding in Wakefield's in November 1929 as a preliminary to the LNER taking a shareholding equal to that of BET in NGT itself in December 1929.

United took over Emmerson's in January 1930, acquiring 54 vehicles. In addition to the eleven Reliances as detailed below, there were 23 Albions, mostly bonneted PK26s (which became CM7-29); four ADC 416s (EB111-4), four AEC 426s (EB115

Vehicles of direct or indirect LNER origin which fitted into the new class lettering system included M7 (XV 1194), a Thornycroft BC with Hall Lewis body, which had briefly been numbered B33, seen here at Durham railway station; and K31 (EF 4121), an AEC Reliance, one of eleven taken over from Eastern Express, and by then half-cab, photographed at Ryhope circa 1934. A Sunderland District Leyland Lion follows. *(John D Watson Collection courtesy Miss B Allan; R L Kell Collection)*

and EC116-8 - suggesting a change of mind in classification); a mixed bag of five AEC/ADC vehicles, AEC 411, 413, 414, ADC 417 and AEC 427 (all lumped together as EM119-23); four Gilfords (B27-30); two Daimler CF6s (NA42/3 - logically, they should have been plain N) and a Lion PLSC3 (AL45). Although legally absorbed into United, the company being placed in liquidation straightaway, this concern's services continued to be run as an identifiable block for about two years, the vehicles used on them, not all ex-Emmerson's, having the words "Emmerson Services" below the United fleetname. At least one of the Reliances delivered direct to United as described below, K23, registered VF 7611, nonetheless began life on 27th February 1930 in Emmerson livery complete with fleetname "Robt. Emmerson & Co." on the waistband (but without "Ltd.") - it seems likely that there may have been others. There would have been plenty of time for the painting instructions to have been changed to United livery had this been desired, so the retention of the Emmerson identity was clearly deliberate.

The Billingham and Haverton Hill Motors business had been absorbed on 1st December 1929, with five ADC 416s which became United EB106-10 and three Chevrolets (H35-7). There was also a Leyland single-decker of which the chassis

dated from 1913, having begun life as a double-decker with the Wellingborough Motor Omnibus Company and now briefly numbered in the United fleet, apparently as AM44, though one source quotes AN44. Eastern Express also became wholly owned in January 1930, but this led to an assertion from Northern that the territorial agreement between that firm and United was thereby being broken. It took some months to resolve this but 23 of Eastern Express's vehicles passed to Northern in April and 32 to United in May, after which Eastern Express was wound up. The United share comprised eleven Reliances, eight ADC 416s (EB131-8) and seven AEC 426s - this time these latter became JA129-34, it being decided that their appearance as well as the 4-type engines made them more at home with the J class. The similar ex-Emmerson buses EC116-8 were renumbered JA126-8 at the same time. Also from the Eastern Express fleet were two Thornycroft BC Forwards (M34/5), a Dennis 26-seater (B69), and three Chevrolet LM 14-seaters (H39-41).

The LNER had acquired a 50% interest in Redwing Safety Services Ltd, based at Redcar, in March 1929 and this firm had also received an allocation of the AEC Reliance buses, as explained below, by the time the LNER holding was transferred to United in January 1930. Redwing became a wholly owned United subsidiary in November 1931, continuing until absorbed in November 1932. Further details of the vehicles transferred are given later. The United K class of AEC Reliance buses began to take shape from the beginning of 1930, the GU-registered Reliances from the Emmerson fleet, plus the three from the Durham LNER branch, becoming K1-14. The last fifteen new Reliances, all but one confirmed as bodied by Dodson, were delivered directly to United and became K15-29, receiving registration numbers VF 7603-16 and 7643 - the body of unconfirmed make being on VF 7607. Then followed K30-4, five of the Reliances dating from April 1929 from the Eastern Express fleet, EF 4120-2/4/5, and K35-40, drawn from the later

Eastern Express buses, registered EF 4245, 4262/3/6 and 4280/3. Four Reliances dating from July-August 1929 were registered VN 616-9 for Redwing but then put into Eastern Express livery and stored for a time by United - the records of the storage charges show understandable confusion about ownership. These had bus bodies by Edmond, of Middlesbrough, and became United's K41-4 in about March 1930. Another stored Edmond-bodied Reliance in Eastern Express livery was still unregistered and became United K45 as VF 7602 in April 1930 - this registration number from the VF 7601-700 series booked by United had not previously been issued. VF 7601 was used in November 1929 for the Austin Six saloon IC13 already mentioned, purchased for use at the Head Office, which was then in York.

There had been five additions to the K series resulting from other acquisitions before the main part of the Redwing fleet was given fleet numbers in the United series in November 1931, so the eleven further Reliances from that source, the final part of the LNER legacy of AEC Reliance buses, became RK51-61, all with VN registration numbers. The R prefix stood for "Redwing" - this being the usual method of signifying vehicles in the fleets of various subsidiaries wholly owned and managed by United. Some - notably those of London-service coach operators to be mentioned later - were applied quite rigorously but others, possibly including the Redwing case, may have been more of a paper exercise. Later they were dropped when the businesses were absorbed. These Redwing AEC Reliances included five having Clark coach bodies, but the remaining six received United bus bodies and were very similar to the ten Reliances bodied by United for East Midland Motor Services in May 1929, that fleet's last batch of vehicles showing United influence. Thus although United had ordered no Reliance models for its own fleet, it found itself with some 56 new or recent vehicles of the type by the time the dust had settled on the consequences of the LNER deal. Northern got seventeen (including the six that had been with

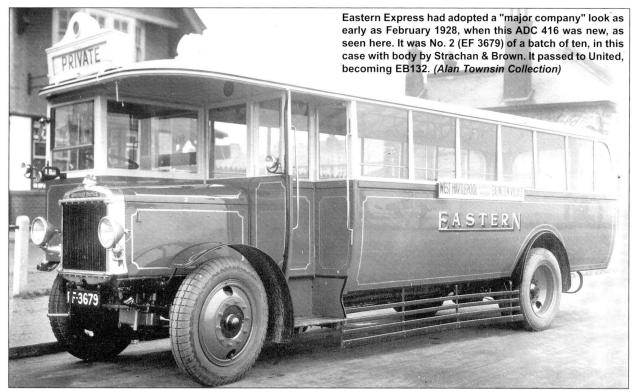

Eastern Express had adopted a "major company" look as early as February 1928, when this ADC 416 was new, as seen here. It was No. 2 (EF 3679) of a batch of ten, in this case with body by Strachan & Brown. It passed to United, becoming EB132. *(Alan Townsin Collection)*

*Above:* With its original United fleet number on the waistrail just behind the entrance, K24 (VF 7612) was caught laying-over whilst working service 34 Newcastle to Carlisle. It had a cream roof, pre-1933 fleetname style and a destination board. *(United)*

*Left:* AK34, formerly K16, (VF 7604), seen on the Newcastle to Hexham service in a 1946 view, taken at Marlborough Crescent bus station, Newcastle. The bus was in postwar livery with red roof, had been fitted with wartime replacement small headlamps and had lost its destination board in favour of an enlarged destination blind box. An Albion of Venture Transport stands behind. *(R C Davis)*

Wakefield's) and one, with horsebox body, was retained by the LNER. The Reliance was to remain a familiar sight in both the United and Northern fleets until 1948; they were smooth-running, as with all types having that engine, although the appearance, gearbox note, and the rather ponderous right-hand gear-change combined to identify the Reliance as a child of the late 1920s.

## A time of expansion

United's fleet was expanding strongly in this period, and not only because of the large input resulting from the link with the LNER. A total of 273 vehicles was acquired from other operators in 1930, of which 129 were from the railway offshoots, as compared to 120 new buses, which latter figure includes the above-mentioned sixteen Reliances forming part of the railway order but registered by United. Even after withdrawals, the fleet strength rose to about 1,000 at the end of that year and comfortably over that figure if associated former railway and other subsidiary fleets later absorbed are included. Midland Red is thought to have been the only larger provincial fleet, being second in size only to the LGOC's bus fleet in Britain at that time; by then, the National Omnibus & Transport fleet had been broken into its Eastern, Southern and Western parts. In Scotland, the Alexander fleet had then reached about 700, rising to about 1,000 in 1931.

The acquired vehicles included an assortment of makes and models, and the variety makes it easier to review the fleet as it stood in this period in terms of the various classes, makes and types. This is doubtless partly why the classified numbering system was strengthened just after the link with LNER, which made so mixed an intake inevitable. At one end of the scale, the AEC and ADC buses of types such as the dozen 416s, eleven 426s of 1928/9 and various other types, largely from the Emmerson and Eastern Express fleets, were close enough to standard United classes to be given numbers tacked on to the E and J classes as explained above; most of them ran until the mid-1930s. The ex-Amos, Proud ADC 416 buses had already been similarly renumbered from B292-5 to EB102-5. Also worthy of mention here were a pair of 1928 ADC 423s acquired from Archer Robinson, trading as Bridlington Green Bus Service, in November 1929, recorded as Daimlers and numbered NB40/1, following on from United's own 423s NA15-39, as then renumbered from their

original K class. NB40/1 had bus bodywork by T G Bell & Co Ltd, of Doncaster, and passed to the Eastern Counties Omnibus Co Ltd on its formation in 1931.

Leyland had become the new standard make at the beginning of the 1930s and thus acquired modern examples became generally also regarded as permanent additions to United's fleet; some were so permanent as to remain for over 20 years. Vehicles such as the ex-Amos, Proud & Co Tigers and Lions acquired in 1928, at first regarded as miscellaneous and given B-series numbers, were renumbered into the A series with AT or AL prefix letters according to type. A further designation, AN, was added, at first for an example of the small Leveret but later applied to Cubs, though these were rare in the United fleet. Further modern Leyland buses came from several acquired businesses, including Redwing, in the early 1930s and are described later.

In addition to the ex-Emmerson Albions already mentioned, Scarborough District Motor Services Ltd, another railway-associated fleet, contributed 20 buses of this make, which became CM38-57; most were PJ26 or PK26 bonneted buses but six were forward-control PMA28s. The largest number of Albions to come from an independent operator were the 21 from Blue Band Bus Services Ltd, of Normanby, near Middlesbrough, taken over after the firm ceased trading in March 1930, which became CM58-78. The earlier ones included six PK26s and three other Model 26 bonneted vehicles, mostly buses and four PM28 buses, but the last eight, dating from 1929, were six-cylinder Viking Six PR28 or PMB28 coaches. From the mid-1930s these coaches ran on excursion duty from Scarborough for several years, rebuilt and repainted in Robinson's white livery of the local coach operator by then absorbed, as explained later. With other Albions from acquired businesses, this series of fleet numbers reached CM101, though many were sold off, 23 passing via dealers to W Alexander & Sons Ltd in 1932: ten in 1933 and four more in 1936 joining that concern's C and D classes. Other bonneted Albions became United parcel vans, remaining a familiar sight after Albion buses had disappeared from the fleet.

Another make briefly quite prominent was Thornycroft, from M being adopted as a class letter in 1930. M5-13 and M34/5 were ex-LNER and associates, comprising ten BC Forward 32-seat buses and an A2 20-seater, but M17-33 came from W H Johnson & Sons Ltd of King's Lynn. These

---

>> *Opposite page upper:* **Blue Band Motor Services Limited, of Normanby, Middlesbrough, provided a sizeable fleet of Albion single-deckers when taken over by United in 1930. One of the coaches, CM75 (DC 9498), a Viking Six, type PMB28, was working the long-distance London to Middlesbrough service in August 1930. It was photographed during a refreshment stop in Grantham. This was one of the six-cylinder Albions later painted in Robinson's white livery for excursion work from Scarborough.** *(G H F Atkins)*

>> *Opposite page lower:* **The business of Farrer & Faulder, of Carlisle, was acquired on 17th February 1930. Three 1929 Maudslays with 30-seat front-entrance bodywork were added to the fleet. B40 (HH 4609) was one of them, and it was photographed on the turntable inside Scarborough garage. Upon B40's withdrawal in 1935, its body was fitted to K47 (VY 1288), a second-hand AEC Reliance ex-Ovington Motors, York.** *(United)*

vehicles, taken over in March 1930 and originally intended to carry the numbers B51-67, ranged from a J-type of 1920 to five BC Forwards and two LC Forwards of 1929/30. With vehicles from other independent fleets, the series reached M42 by 1934, but only a few were to survive beyond the 1935 renumbering.

Guy was another somewhat similar case after receiving G as its class letter in 1930. The numbers G2-9 were issued to Guy FBB and other models of 1926-8 acquired from Reliance Express Motors Ltd of Darlington, with which the LNER had reached agreement for a purchase in January 1929, but this did not take place and the business was taken over by United in October. Six Guy OND buses with Guy 20-seat bodies had formed part of an LNER order for eight, Eastern Express receiving four in May 1929, becoming United G10-3 later that year, ahead of the main transfer of that fleet; all four passed to Lincolnshire Road Car in January 1931, but G12 and G13 returned to United and then passed to the new Eastern Counties fleet in July 1931. The other four had been supplied to Scarborough District of which two came to United as G14 and G15 via LNER's Durham branch. All of these had vanished from the fleet by 1935. A borderline case in terms of United stock was that of four Guy 32-seat buses in the Redwing fleet dating from 1929 and registered PY 9868-71 - the last two are recorded as of type FC, this being Guy's full-sized six-cylinder model of that time. Two had been sold by 1931 but the other two, PY 9869/70,

received fleet numbers RG17/8 (it is not certain in which order) in the United system in November 1931, though disappearing when the fleet was absorbed at the end of November 1932.

Among the more notable acquisitions of independent operators in this period were two which could be counted as related to the Emmerson take-over. In February 1930, three Maudslay buses which became B40-2 were acquired from Farrer and Faulder of Carlisle, showing how United's activities now extended to that city. Blaydon 'A' Omnibuses Ltd had been a major competitor to Emmerson on certain routes running west from Newcastle, but sold out to United and Newcastle Corporation jointly in March 1930. United took all 25 vehicles, most if not all bonneted types, including eight Albions of the Model 26 series (CM30-7); four Leylands (AM46-9: two Lioness PLC1s and two Leveret PLA2s); three Thornycrofts (M14-6); two ADCs (EM124/5); and eight miscellaneous vehicles (B43-50: three Minerva, three W & G du Cros, one Star and one Crossley Hawk). All but two were sold off almost immediately.

Inevitably, large-scale acquisitions of businesses brought in a wide variety of vehicles, quite often of non-standard and sometimes quite obscure makes and models. An example was the group B71-8 from the Scarborough District and associated Blue Bus Service (Bridlington) fleets in 1930, which comprised a 1924 Berliet, a 1927 Vulcan VWBL, a 1926 Reo W, three 1927 Karrier 26-seaters, a 1923

United's extensive split-level garage in Vernon Road, Scarborough, with its distinctive fascia, soon after its opening in Autumn 1929 - note the tram tracks. The Scarborough District Albion PMA28 is VN 227, new in May 1929, which went to West Yorkshire in May 1930. When this picture was taken, Scarborough District was in United's ownership pending the three-way split of the fleet among United, East Yorkshire and West Yorkshire. Of 13 PMA28s, United received six. *(United)*

Atlas and a 1923 All-American, while H42-9 from the same fleets were six Chevrolets and two GMCs dating from 1924 to 1927. Most survived in the fleet until December 1931.

Problems related to area agreements also sometimes complicated matters: Scarborough District, indeed, under United management from October 1929, was involved in a complex three-way split when absorbed in April-May 1930. East Yorkshire took its share on 1st April, United on 1st May and West Yorkshire on 4th May, some vehicles passing to each. Even quite modern acquired buses of makes regarded as standard were sometimes sold off quite rapidly. Condition, varying widely, would be a factor and, overall, rationalisation of services when competing businesses were acquired tended to produce a surplus of vehicles. Some vehicles sold via dealers were to find homes with independent operators within United's area and there were occasions where sold-off buses reappeared in the fleet.

### Reorganisation under Tilling influence

Evidence of TBAT and, in particular, Tilling influence on United began to strengthen during 1930. This might have been a consequence of the policy agreed in the general settlement reached between the main-line railway companies and TBAT on 30th October 1929 feeding through and superseding that which had been worked out earlier for United in isolation. J F Heaton had managed to convert what was about to be a pure railway takeover of United to the joint one and he may have felt constrained to accept the LNER chairmanship and a degree of influence despite his own instinct for taking control - he was what might nowadays be called a "control freak". A further relevant matter to United's policy decisions is the way in which, although TBAT was presented as a monolithic structure, in reality it was always an uneasy alliance between BET and Tilling which eventually blew apart in 1942. It was usually very obvious where either Tilling or BET influence was, or had been, dominant and it may be that personal shareholdings in operating companies were used to influence the balance of control. Certainly, from July 1929 onwards, United seemed always to belong firmly in the Tilling camp in the balance of its directorships and in most of its vehicle policy, even though the company's size and the often strong personalities of its management quite often allowed individuality to shine through.

As matters stood in mid-1930, there was a well-established in-house Tilling bus chassis make, going back to the association with W A Stevens Ltd, of Maidstone, in the development of petrol-electric buses which led to the first Tilling-Stevens production models of 1911. From 1926, the Express B9 and then B10 models, the first of that make to have conventional gearboxes, became the standard single-decker for a number of Tilling and TBAT companies. The West Yorkshire Road Car Co Ltd was a large-scale user, being the first of the group to turn to United for the bodying of new vehicles with a batch of 20 B10A2 models in spring 1930 - a little earlier there had been a shortage of work.

To prove more directly involved in the story of United as an operating company in 1930/1 was the Eastern Counties Road Car Co Ltd, based at Ipswich, where Thomas Tilling Ltd had begun operating Tilling-Stevens petrol-electric double-deckers in June 1919. ECRC was formed to take over and expand the business in August 1919 - it was created as part of BET's British Automobile Traction group despite predominant Tilling interest. The LMS and LNE railways, acting together, became equal partners in its control with TBAT from December 1929 and the ECRC fleet continued to be standardised on Tilling-Stevens buses, mainly Express B9 and B10 models, although modern double-deckers were Leyland Titan TD1s.

The management of the Tilling/TBAT/BET group favoured a regional structure and the concept of United as an operator with services stretching from Lowestoft to the Scottish border no longer found favour. It had never been completed as a continuous area, with several existing combine companies well entrenched at various points. A process of breaking up the original "grand concept" began to take effect and it was remarked at a Board meeting in November 1929 that it would probably be to the advantage of the company if its activities were confined to north of the Humber. An amalgamation of United territory in East Anglia with that of other companies was suggested, with the possibility of the East Yorkshire undertaking being transferred to United in compensation. The first part proved prophetic but the latter did not materialise - BET may well have been unwilling to give up a promising concern in which it was the dominant partner. East Midland Motor Services Ltd, with services partly in the territory of the LMS Railway, had already ceased to have any direct relationship with United. This was an obvious consequence of United coming partly under LNER control, and East Midland subsequently came under direct joint LMS and LNER ownership; it became a TBAT/railway company from February 1931, though in that case under BET management for most of the 1930s, switching to Tilling briefly before becoming a full BET subsidiary from 1942.

The possibility of a merger of the TBAT's associated operating companies in East Anglia was now given serious study, involving not only that part of United's operations and Eastern Counties Road Car but also two further TBAT companies in which BET was the dominant influence - the Ortona Motor Company Ltd, based in Cambridge, and the Peterborough Electric Traction Company Ltd. These two were noteworthy in running fleets comprising both Leyland and SOS buses, the latter initials being the marque-name then adopted by Midland Red for its own-make vehicles. By May 1930, the merger was agreed in principle and from 1st June that year United's traffic and commercial management in East Anglia was put under the

*Upper:* The Tilling-Stevens B10A demonstrator, KR 1658, acquired by United in 1930. Its body was by John C Beadle, of Dartford. In this, the only photograph known to the authors, the vehicle is seen in 1948. *(Philip Battersby Collection)*

*Lower:* Short Brothers, of Rochester, gained the contract to body the production batch of B10A2 chassis; there was little or no conformity to United's contemporary standard. This one is P3 (VF 8524) when brand new. *(John Banks Collection)*

control of Joseph Worssam, ECRC's General Manager. He was thus given considerable authority in the area and there was evidence of this in regard to United's rolling stock. However, it was over a year before the merger took place, partly because it was decided that a new headquarters should be built in Norwich.

The arrival of a Tilling-Stevens Express B10A demonstrator with Beadle body, KR 1658, and its acquisition by United in March 1930, may have set some contemporary observers wondering whether this was a clue to future policy; it was at first numbered B70 among other miscellaneous types. Then it was renumbered P1 and sixteen more, P2-17 of type B10A2, were added to the fleet in July-August, registered VF 8523-38, though not before a larger fleet of new Leylands had arrived as described below. Later events strongly suggest that P2-17 had been purchased in accordance with Eastern Counties Road Car policy with the planned merger of operations in East Anglia in mind. They had Short Bros 31-seat front-entrance bus bodywork, of up-to-date though rather plain design, with no indication of having been built to conform to United's style of the period. The choice of constructor may well have been due to pressure of work in United's own body shops.

As it turned out, while these vehicles were being delivered there was a reconstruction of Tilling-

Stevens Motors Ltd in August 1930, the title of the company becoming T.S.Motors Ltd and marking the withdrawal of the Tilling financial connection. In practice, some Tilling or TBAT companies did continue taking Tilling-Stevens buses for a couple of years or more, perhaps because of long-term contracts, but United took no more and the new Eastern Counties company placed only one order for the make, for ten B39A7 models in 1933.

The adoption of red as United's main livery colour which began by January 1930 seems likely to have been another sign of growing Tilling influence: it is known that nine vehicles from the F class switched to it between then and April. The shade is thought to have been that which remained standard for United and several other companies under Tilling management and then adopted as one of the two alternative main colours for Tilling group buses from circa 1944. The relief colour has sometimes been quoted as white, perhaps on the basis of Norfolk taxation records which give the new livery as "red and white", continuing thus up to the last new United vehicle registration entry there in 1932; but in this context "white" probably included what was then often called "broken white", meaning cream. The livery was certainly red and cream by the time the writer first took fairly serious notice of United buses in about 1935. Indeed both colours then continued unaltered right up to the introduction of the National Bus Company corporate livery and the consequent switch to poppy-red and white from 1972. Official pictures of United single-deckers when new in the period from May 1930 and more generally in the next year or so show red lower panels and light upperworks, a style also applied around that time to existing buses in the fleet, though later to be confined to coaches.

The main supplier to United in 1930 was Leyland. There were a further 30 Titan TD1s delivered in May-July, to add to the existing 25, numbered A50-79 (VF 7694-700 and 8500-22). Of these, A50-64, allocated to the north-east, were in a style with red upper- and lower-deck sides with cream window surrounds and roof. However A65-79, allocated to United's Eastern District, were in a half-and-half style identical to that of Eastern Counties Road Car Titans supplied the previous winter, further evidence that Mr Worssam had been given a free hand on such matters.

In addition, there were 50 Leyland Tigers, entering the fleet from May to August. These were numbered AT80-129 (registered VF 7644-93) and had bodies by United, perhaps best described as saloons, with comfortable seats for 29 passengers; as built, they had roofs with panels over most of the length which opened sideways - the design, known as Lif-Top, is believed to have been designed and patented by United. They were on the recently introduced TS3 chassis, this having a 16ft 6ins wheelbase and intended for 26ft overall length - hitherto the main Tiger model had been the TS2 with the same length but 17ft 6ins wheelbase; the original TS1, nominally of 27ft 6ins length, was rare at first but was revived in 1931; all three were

Whilst VF 7694 was the first TD1 to be *delivered* in the new "sandwich" livery, here is 1929's A19 (VF 7635), originally in the LNER green and white scheme, which had been *repainted* in the new colours. It was at Exchange bus station, Middlesbrough. *(Philip Battersby Collection)*

mechanically similar. Some 19 of the VF 76xx Tigers were to pass to the new Eastern Counties company in 1931, those remaining in United's fleet being downgraded as 30-seat buses, with roofs fixed, by the later 1930s. Some were sold off or taken for civil defence or military use in wartime

but even in post-war years the survivors were pleasant vehicles in which to ride.

The large-scale take-overs of 1930 produced a surplus of rolling stock; in addition the depression was beginning to affect the demand for travel, especially in industrial areas. United's new vehicle intake for 1931 was very small, though of interest in switching to the NG registration mark then recently introduced by Norfolk County Council. There were four more Tiger TS3s with United bodies, AT133-6 (NG 986-9), dating from June. These 26-seat coaches were to a rather more elaborate style which set a precedent for later vehicles, most obviously in the twin destination indicators. As built, they had a hinged entrance door near the front but in 1937 they were rebuilt to rear-entrance layout, reseated to carry 32 passengers and fitted with standard indicator boxes; they were used as buses until scrapped in 1950. There were a further three standard Leyland-bodied Titan TD1 double-deckers, placed in service in November to augment services in Scarborough, where United had just taken over operation in the town from the local tramway company. They were

The new "half-and-half" red and white (or cream) livery carried by the 1930 TD1 Titans that stayed in East Anglia is illustrated on A65 (VF 8508), photographed on 17th April 1930 *(below)*. The similarity with the colour scheme applied to contemporary vehicles in the Eastern Counties Road Car Company fleet is evidenced in the views *(<< opposite page)* of ECRCC No. 141 (DX 8356). The Leyland lowbridge body remained virtually unchanged. *(Senior Transport Archive courtesy BCVM)*

*Above:* **AT85 (VF 7649), from the batch of 50 TS3 Tigers delivered in 1930, was one of those that was transferred to Eastern Counties in 1931.** *(Alan Lewis Collection)*

*Below:* **AT111 (VF7675), on the other hand, became a north-eastern vehicle. It is seen here circa 1934, outside Jesmond depot, in the livery that superseded the "half-and-half" version seen on VF 7649 above.** *(United)*

*Bottom:* **A not-very-good copy of a contemporary press cutting - but it is all we have - of one of the elusive 1931 Harrington-bodied AEC Regal 32-seat coaches. Originally numbered KA49, this is R1 (NG 1442) at Middlesbrough's Exchange bus station. They remained in service until 1950.** *(AEC Gazette)*

numbered A159-61 (NG 1800-2) and were noteworthy because of a change to what was to be United's standard bus livery until the postwar years. Most of the bodywork was now red, with three cream bands and cream roof, though the rear dome was red - single-deck buses were treated similarly, though with one cream band at waist level. However, there is photographic evidence of an earlier application of this mainly-red style, possibly experimental. A picture dating from May 1931 taken at the Coach Factory shows Leyland Tiger AT81, new just over a year previously, in this livery but with Eastern Counties fleetname despite having legal lettering reading "Albert Thomas Evans, Secretary and Traffic Manager, United Automobile Services Ltd, Kilburn House, York". This may have been a trial to help decide on the style to be adopted for the new merged fleet in East Anglia, made just before the changeover described below came into legal effect; AT81 was one of those transferred.

Two further new coaches, dating from July 1931, were AEC Regals with Harrington 32-seat rear-entrance bodies, orginally numbered KA49/50 (NG 1442/3), having been ordered by a concern taken over in October 1930. This was Harrison and Ives Ltd, of Norwich, with 27 vehicles of varied make, trading as Eastern Motorways, and it seems that another vehicle it ordered, a Tilling-Stevens B10A2, had already joined the United fleet in December 1930, after bodying by United as a 25-seat coach, being registered VF 9980 and numbered P18. Eastern Motorways, though independent, had already been a customer of United for coach bodywork, notably on two Bristol B-type coaches of 1929, VG 1550/1 (which became L132/4) and an earlier Regal supplied in 1930, VG 2284 (KA48). There were also two slightly earlier Bristol Bs, VG 1150/1; five Daimler CF6s, VG2555-9; and an AEC Reliance, VG 2773, with coach bodywork by Eaton, the trading name of a Norwich coachbuilder, H E Taylor,

dating from 1929 and earlier in 1930: these became L133/1, N44-8 and K46, the Reliance being a stock chassis supplied to Taylor in May 1929.

More complex in their history were four ADC 416Ds and four 417Ds originally supplied to Wrexham and District Transport Co Ltd in 1927. As mentioned earlier, that firm, a BET subsidiary, had, as had United, experienced trouble with the Daimler CV25 engine fitted to these models, and in that case the eventual outcome had been replacement with new Daimler CF6 chassis in 1929, the bodies and, most unusually by that date, the registration numbers being transferred. Harrison and Ives received the 1927 chassis and, with bus bodies, the 416D models were reregistered VG 2282/3/5 and 2774 while the 417Ds became

*Above:* Jesmond depot, Newcastle, was the location for this official photograph of 1931's Leyland Tiger AT134 (NG 987). The illustration became familiar when a tinted version of it was used for some time on prewar timetable covers. The United-built body style pointed the way to later United coach and bus standards. *(United)*

*Below:* One of the United-bodied Bristol B-type coaches acquired from Harrison & Ives Limited, of Norwich (Eastern Motorways), in October 1930. The four ex-Eastern Motorways Bristol Bs were left in East Anglia when the new Eastern Counties Omnibus Company was formed, whereas the 130 similar chassis of United's L class were regrouped in the north-east. The body was visually quite different from those built for United's own fleet. *(Alan Townsin Collection)*

VG 2775 and 2925-7. They were numbered FD142-5 and FD146/1/7/8 by United, thus following on from the mechanically similar ADC 415D models already in the fleet. Although the two new Regals were to remain in service with United until 1950, the ex-Eastern Motorways fleet itself, plus the

Tilling-Stevens, was to remain part of the United story for only a few months before they passed to Eastern Counties, with whom all the vehicles mentioned ran until 1938 or later; several were rebodied and received Gardner 4LW engines. Another ex-Wrexham ADC 416D, reregistered as

VG 2474, in this case with an Eaton coach body, went to J L Brighton, of Long Stratton, and had also come into United ownership when that concern was taken in June 1930, initially as EB139, but then joining the others as FD149. There was also a Graham-Dodge which became B87, both also going to ECOC in 1931.

Ovington Motors Ltd, of York, was the subject of a partial joint takeover with the West Yorkshire Road Car Co Ltd in October 1930, United receiving three Reo buses, sold off after a year or so, and a 1929 AEC Reliance, VY 1288, with Cravens bus body, which became K47 and remained in the fleet until 1947. Further take-overs, mostly of operators with one or two vehicles apiece, continued in 1930/1, and included other firms in the Blaydon area - the vehicles were usually sold off quite quickly. From time to time there were exceptions to this pattern, such as a Leyland Lion LT1 with Leyland body registered in Bradford as KW 6786 by Tillotson, the dealer, for Robert Dunning, of Great Ayton, whose business was taken over with two vehicles in August 1931, the Lion becoming AL151 and remaining in service until 1950, latterly as LT4-3.

The Lincolnshire Road Car Co Ltd had been formed in 1928 to take over an existing business under the TBAT umbrella and, as a further step in rationalising the group's structure, United's operations in the county were transferred to it on 1st January 1931 with 38 vehicles: 20 AECs and ADCs from the E and F classes; seven Leyland Lion PLSCs (from the ex-Amos, Proud fleet); seven Chevrolets; three Guys and a Vulcan; plus a motor-cycle. Agreement for a take-over of L H Smith and J Tait (Smiths Safety Services), of Boston, Lincolnshire, had been reached with United on 1st December 1930 but the business, with two Leyland Lioness PLC1s, two Lion PLSC1s and two ADC 423 buses, passed directly to LRCC, also on 1st January 1931. The BET influence was to be dominant in the Lincolnshire fleet until 1942, the company then being transferred to Tilling when TBAT was split between the two major groups.

A further signal of the strength of the Tilling/TBAT position in regard to United occurred on 28th April 1931, when Thomas Hornsby stepped down from being Chairman to be succeeded by John F Heaton, who was to retain that role until 1949. The chairmanship was thus held by a bus group representative rather than a railway one, as had become usual elsewhere in similar circumstances by that date. Hornsby was also on the board of several other bus companies in the north-east in which the LNER held an interest but even the role of Vice-Chairman he then held with United until 1936 was the only such instance - he continued to be actively involved. Heaton's star was to continue rising at a national level through the 1930s with the chairmanships of both Thomas Tilling Ltd and, from 1936, TBAT, the latter on an alternating year basis with Sidney Garcke, who represented the BET. George Cardwell became a Director on 31st March 1931, replacing Reginald

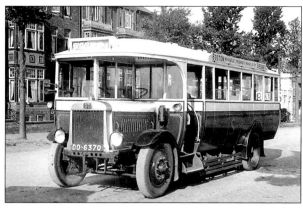

*Upper:* DO 6370 was a Leyland Lion PLSC1 of Smith's Safety Services, Boston, Lincolnshire. The business and vehicles were to have been taken over by United at the end of 1930 but passed to the Lincolnshire Road Car Company on 1st January 1931. The photograph was taken in Scarbrough Avenue, Skegness, in July 1930. *(G H F Atkins)*

*Lower:* United's ancillary services included the carriage of parcels and by 1931 a useful fleet of vans existed for this work. Sometimes converted buses were used, but two new vans in that year were Morris-Commercials, NG 1882/3, which United numbered IL42/3. Both are shown in this view of United's parcels receiving depot in Princess Street, Newcastle. *(United)*

Tilling as a representative of TBAT, though recorded in the minutes simply as a Director of the West Yorkshire Road Car Co Ltd. He was another major figure in the industry, having been General Manager of the North Western Road Car Co Ltd from 1923 to 1930, and at an earlier stage in his career he had been manager of the BET's Hartlepool Electric Tramways Company from 1907 to 1912. It is noteworthy that he was appointed Managing Director of United from 28th April 1931, the day Heaton became Chairman.

The United minutes of 30th September 1930 had recorded that the appointment of Mr H P Stokes as General Manager was terminated with effect from that day, with payment in lieu of notice, which suggests there may have been a fairly major disagreement of some kind. Until July 1934, United did not have any holder of this post, though A T Evans is understood to have acted as such in most day-to-day respects.

The planned rationalisation in East Anglia took effect with the registration of the Eastern Counties

Omnibus Co Ltd on 14th July 1931, Mr Worssam duly being appointed its General Manager. An amalgamation of the ECRC, Ortona and Peterborough Electric Traction businesses (contributing 133, 98 and 77 vehicles respectively) with the East Anglian section of United Automobile Services Ltd (with 226 vehicles) was put into the charge of the new company, giving an initial fleet strength of 534. The new Eastern Counties company also took over what was usually known as the Coach Factory in Lowestoft, of growing importance as supplier of bodywork to associated companies though no longer building for the wide variety of other operators, including independents and municipalities, as had been the case previously. United had a 43.2% shareholding in ECOC, so in that sense it could be said to have remained an offshoot of United, though TBAT had a direct holding of 27.6%, the LNER 24.3% and the LMS 3.3%, these latter adding up to the same as TBAT, as was the usual pattern.

The buses transferred to Eastern Counties were largely those already in the area, although there were some movements. There were contributions from most of United's main standard types of the time: 40 E-class AECs; 33 F-class, 28 J-class and 22 NA-class ADCs; 19 AT-class Leyland Tigers and 15 A-class Titans; plus the 17 P-class Tilling-Stevens (although the ex-demonstrator, P1, stayed with United). To these were added others that had been acquired by United mainly from local ex-independent fleets, notably twelve of the ex-Johnson Thornycrofts and the former Eastern Motorways fleet, plus a few others that had been transferred south. However, a number of L-class Bristol B buses that had been allocated to East Anglia were moved north, all of the 130 thus remaining with United, although Eastern Counties received the four B-type coaches that had come from Eastern Motorways.

The dominance in numbers of the ex-United contribution to the new company's fleet led to some aspects of the latter's methods being a continuation of United practices. The United fleet number prefix letters were adopted for the whole ECOC fleet and L still signified Bristol with Eastern Counties on new vehicles until 1966, remaining in use until they were withdrawn circa 1982; United in its new north-east stronghold moved on to another system in 1935. The 77-strong P class of Tilling-Stevens B10 vehicles, mainly from ECRC, was ECOC's largest single class at its formation, though run fairly close by its initial fleet of 65 Leyland Titan TD1 A-class buses, from all four constituent fleets.

ECOC official instructions of the time quote the livery as Eastern Counties 'Foochow' red and broken white, with black mudguards, chassis items and mouldings. Despite the reference to Eastern Counties, the Foochow red is thought to be what became recognised as Tilling red and this livery seems to have been adopted for both UAS and ECOC at that point. As to broken white, the Oxford English Dictionary includes the following meaning, dating from 1882, for "broken": "Of colours: reduced in tone by the addition of other colours." Hence it seems that broken white in this context meant what is nowadays usually called cream. It is noteworthy that a management instruction called for "Built by Eastern Counties" transfers to be applied to "all recent types built by the Coach Factory, excluding J type and previous". The "United built" transfers were to be taken off in all cases: a good example of officialdom seeking to rewrite history and incidentally create pitfalls for future historians of the companies.

### Concentration on the North

All this left United with a more compact though still large area and a fleet of about 700 buses, giving a need for a new central works and headquarters building; land for this, at a site in Grange Road, Darlington, was purchased in 1931. The registered office moved from Kilburn House, York to the Grange Road address on 6th January 1932. Bishop Auckland continued as the centre for overhauls until the new works was ready in late 1933.

United followed a policy of modernising existing vehicles where appropriate. By 1931, the four-year-old F-class ADC 415 buses remaining in the fleet after the transfers to Lincolnshire and Eastern Counties were beginning to seem inadequate in passenger appeal - standards were changing rapidly at that time - yet were fit for long enough to make it economic to refurbish them. More comfortable seats were fitted, reducing the capacity to 32. Exteriors were rebuilt with full-width canopies. Later the relatively deep destination box showing both route number and place-name display by then becoming standard was incorporated, and the skirt panels were extended downwards to disguise the relatively high build.

The Coach Factory is recorded as having reseated and repainted 20 buses (F3, 7, 15, 21, 23, 33, 42, 55, 56, 57, 64, 70, 71, 86, 105, 107, 109, 112, 114, 115) in 1931, payments accordingly being made to Eastern Counties between October and December 1931. In the first half of 1932. W G Edmond in Middlesbrough carried out work listed as "body modified" on ten more (FA12, 19, 24, 25, 27, 28, 31, 38, 72 and 84) - by then the rebuilt vehicles were classified FA, this being applied to all 30. No new bodies are shown in the records for any of the F-class, etc., buses, nor is there any authorisation in the Board minutes, so that seems to be firmly ruled out. Some at least of the unrebuilt buses were given FL designations, the L signifying large-capacity.

United's practice of removing bodies at overhaul and quite often moving them to different chassis, usually of the same batch, meant that the rebuilt bodies often went on to other chassis. The distinctions made by the FA and FL designations were dropped in the course of the 1935 renumbering, when surviving buses were renumbered into a pruned AF series. Plaxton may have carried out some unspecified rebuilding work on F-class buses in 1935. A further exercise

The great changes of 1931, whereby United ceded territory to the Lincolnshire Road Car Company, gave up its East Anglian operation to the new Eastern Counties Omnibus Company and thereafter concentrated its efforts on its north-eastern activities, are recalled in these views of a former member of the E class, ex-E42 (PW 8231), running as Lincolnshire No. 139 at Skegness in July 1931 *(above)*, and ex-FD127 (PW 9927) in service with Eastern Counties at Cromer depot in 1932, complete with typical ECOC "bible" destination box. This was one of the Daimler-engined ADC 415D models, apparently still with higher-backed seats. *(G H F Atkins; E G P Masterman)*

involving this class was the conversion by July 1933 of ten (F13, 22, 29, 32, 46, 49, 50, 51, 67 and 78) for the Scarborough sea-front service. They were redesignated FT, apparently to signify "Toastrack", and replaced the surviving D-class Daimler CB or CK runabouts, although the conversion consisted of the installation of partially folding roofs, with canvas covers that could be rolled back in good weather, and not the open-sided body normally covered by the toast-rack description. They took the new numbers AFT1-10 in 1935; most were withdrawn soon thereafter.

For 1932, the new vehicle intake consisted of 25 Leyland Tiger coaches, AT168-92, delivered in the period April-July. The chassis model had moved on to the TS4 by then, with a slightly heavier-duty specification and a larger-bore 7.6-litre version of the six-cylinder petrol engine as standard, though still looking much like the TS1 to TS3 range of 1928-31. They formed the first delivery to United of bodies built under the Eastern Counties name, though made in the same plant at Lowestoft as previously; the 30-seat body design could be counted as a development of the United-built version on the four 1931 Tiger coaches, though with rear entrance. The last twelve had opening roof panels. Standards of interior comfort and finish had greatly improved over the previous few years and these were thoroughly civilised coaches in which to travel quite long distances. Their registration numbers, NG 2268-92, the last for United from the Norfolk tax office, had been booked well in advance to match the fleet numbers in the usual way. Many were impressed for military use in wartime, only a few returning to the company.

It seems logical to include here what were to be the final additions of new Leyland Titans to the fleet, a batch of eight TD2s, equivalent to the TS4, delivered in June-July 1933; they proved to be United's last new petrol-engined double-deckers. They also differed from the earlier Titans in the fleet in having what was becoming known as "highbridge" layout, with centre gangway on both decks, and by having bodywork built by Eastern Counties to an up-to-date style with sloping profile also being supplied to that concern's own fleet; they seated 54 passengers. They were numbered AH207-14 and registered HN 9007-14, the latter reflecting the change to Darlington as the company's headquarters in effect by then; HN registration marks or combinations thereof were to be characteristic of United buses until the reorganisation of local government in 1974 led to the closure of the Darlington motor taxation office. The choice of highbridge bodies for these buses was to prove exceptional, United reverting to the

lowbridge layout for all subsequent new double-deckers until 1950.

The A series of numbers used for new Leylands from late 1929 was being further augmented by examples from acquired businesses. A few of these were of pre-1926 types and the Lion PLSC era was quite well represented but there was a useful inflow of the family of more modern models which comprised the Tiger types from TS1 to TS4, the Lion LT1 to LT3 and LT5 and the Titan TD1 and TD2 over the period up to 1934; many of them were to have long careers in the fleet.

During this period there were several further instances of fleets of businesses becoming wholly owned United subsidiaries but retaining their existing legal identities and fleetnames for various reasons. With one exception to be mentioned later, these were given numbers in the appropriate United series, to which an appropriate prefix letter was added until the businesses and vehicles were fully absorbed. On the other hand, in cases where United did not have a controlling shareholding and the management remained separate - e.g. Redwing up to November 1931 and Blumer's until 1934 - the fleets were not numbered in United's series.

Smith's Safeway Services Ltd, of Middlesbrough, had become a significant competitor in that area, but United acquired it in October 1930, at first covertly, and it remained a separate entity until November 1932. In 1931 its fourteen Leylands were given A-series numbers immediately after United's four new Tiger coaches AT133-6 of that year, the type letters of some at least of the Safeway vehicles being prefixed S, even though not shown thus in official fleet records. Lions SAL 139, 144 and 150 were recorded as such by contemporary observers. Omitting the S for simplicity, AL137-40 and 150 were Lion PLSC models dating from 1928/9; AL141/2 were Lion LT1s of 1929; AL143/4 were LT2s of 1930; AT145/6 were Tiger TS2s of 1930;

Pictures of the 1933 TD2 Titans in service with their original bodies are very rare. This one of HN 9009, which originally had the fleet number AH209, shows it in 1947; at that time it was numbered LHO5, having been fitted with a Leyland oil engine in 1938. The view is at Percy Street, Newcastle, outside Haymarket bus station, where they were a familiar sight. *(Alan Townsin)*

The two open-staircase TD1s in the Safeway Services fleet, DC 9386 and DC 9447, photographed when brand new in 1929. These vehicles became United's A147/8 when the Safeway fleet was finally absorbed in 1932, but initially ran for a short time under United control with "S" prefixes as SA147/8. *(Senior Transport Archive courtesy BCVM)*

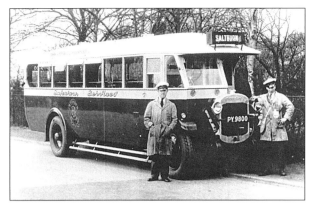

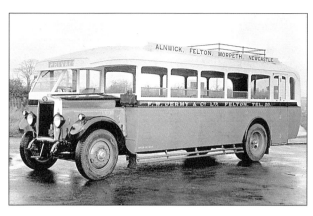

The immense variety of second-hand vehicles being acquired through takeovers of competitors at this time cannot be better illustrated than by comparing PY 9800, a Thornycroft BC *(above left)*, ex-J B Fraser, of Redcar, with bodywork by W G Edmond, of Middlesbrough, which became United's M38, and the canvas-roofed Albion TY 4633 *(left)*, acquired from Gray's Motor Service, of Alnwick, and numbered CM83. On the other hand, the Leyland Tiger TS3 *(above)* acquired from F W Jermy & Co Ltd, of Felton, fitted in well with United's contemporary new vehicle purchasing policy. In this view, the Tiger was in as-built condition on 10th November 1930. *(Edmond & Milburn Ltd; Robert Grieves Collection; STA courtesy BCVM)*

and A147-9 were Leyland-bodied lowbridge Titan TD1s, registered DC 9386 and 9447 in 1929 and DC 9953 in 1930; the two 1929 buses were built with open-staircases. The Lion LT-type and Titan buses all remained in service until 1950 and the last survivor from the Safeway fleet, Titan DC 9953 by then running as LLL10, ran until 1953. Other Safeway vehicles taken into stock included pairs of Albion PM28 and Gilford 166OT buses dating from 1929 and withdrawn by 1937, and a Tilling-Stevens B10A demonstrator, which remained in the fleet until 1940.

A similar pattern in regard to acquired Titans applied to those from Redwing Safety Services Ltd, of Coatham, near Redcar, which had been formed in March 1929 to take over a business run by Fleming and Nash. As mentioned earlier, the LNER had held a half share in this business via Thompson, McKay from March 1929, which was transferred to United in January 1930. The Redwing fleet was given numbers with R prefixes in the United series in November 1931 when the company came under full United control. In this case there were five TD1 models with open-stair Leyland bodies, two of which, PY 9416/7, were the oldest run by United, dating from December 1928: at that date there were only six examples of the type in the north-east of England, placed in service in July-August by Stockton Corporation. Three more, PY 9867 and VN 207/8, were new in April-June 1929. They were given fleet numbers RA163-7 but in the reverse order, as was apt to be United practice. In addition to Redwing's AEC Reliances with LNER background mentioned earlier, there were ten Tilling-Stevens single-deck buses and coaches, of B10A forward-control and B10B

normal-control types dating from 1927-9, which became RP20-9, six Reos (RB116-21) and two Guys (RG17/8). The fleet was absorbed by United in November 1932, by which time three of the Reos and the Guys had gone. The Tilling-Stevens faded from the fleet by 1937 but the Titans all soldiered on, rebuilt and re-engined in the manner described later, until at least 1950, with one, VN 208, by then LGL8, running until 1953.

Another fleet in the same area to contribute some long-lived Leylands, mostly with Leyland bodywork, was that of J B Fraser, of Redcar, who in late 1927 started joint operation with Smith's Safeway on the Stockton-Middlesbrough-Redcar-Saltburn service. Fraser adopted the Safeway name shortly afterwards but remained independent when Smith's came under United ownership in 1930 until itself taken over in August 1931. In this case, the Lion LT1 was the largest group, there being four, dating from 1929/30, which became AL152-5. In some other large fleets the pugnacious-looking LT1 models, with a different and simpler chassis design to that of the rest of the Leyland bus models of 1928-31, tended to have fairly short lives but United treated them as part of the family, the engines being as found in the LT2 and LT3, and the ex-Fraser ones were typical in all lasting to 1949/50. There was also a 20-seat Cub KP1, which became AN156, kept (latterly as LC1), until 1936, but AL157/8 were Lion LT2 models of 1931 with the well-rounded style of Leyland body by then current and they lasted until 1949/50. There were also a Reo, two Thornycroft BCs and a BAT, of which all but a Thornycroft went by 1932, the exception lasting until 1936.

A fleet of fourteen all-Leyland single-deckers, the

From the batch of 1932 TS4 Tigers, with Eastern Counties 30-seat bodies, AT179 (NG 2279) is seen at Lincoln in 1933 and, after renumbering to LT68, in Jesmond depot in 1936. *(G H F Atkins; Senior Transport Archive courtesy BCVM)*

These coaches had, by then, been slightly downgraded, in this case with blind for a short working on the Newcastle to Edinburgh service, but they were very comfortable, lively and smooth-running. They retained the half-and-half red and cream livery until wartime.

In this quartet of pictures we have further evidence of the remarkable diversity of chassis and body styles coming to United with acquired businesses in the early 1930s. Three 14-seat buses passed to United from Spowart Brothers, of Berwick-on-Tweed, in 1933, including this Chevrolet LQ registered TY 7951 *(top left)*. United did not use it as a passenger vehicle, but converted it to a parcels van with fleet number IL72. It was later renumbered PC46. John Young, of Norham-on-Tweed, ran TY 9490, a Gilford 168OT with Wycombe body, until taken over by United in October 1933. Five vehicles were transferred, of which this Gilford *(top right)* was the newest; it dated from April 1932. United numbered it B177, renumbered it SG8 in 1935 and ran it until 1939. Acquired by United from its Scarborough subsidiary, Robinson's Motors, in February 1933 and renumbered B141, this Maudslay ML4 registered PY 5369 *(above left)* was sold eighteen months later. The Ennis & Reed, of Crook, fleet of 13 vehicles of Daimler, Gilford, Leyland and Maudslay manufacture passed to United in early 1934. UP 5471 *(above right)* was a Maudslay ML6, numbered B160 by United, with a Willowbrook 32-seat body. It survived to be renumbered M6.6 in the 1935 scheme but its withdrawal date is not known. Nor is it known whether it had the remarkable, balloon-like roof extension in United ownership, for this - the only known picture of it - was taken after the vehicle's sale to a Middlesbrough independent, Buxton, of South Bank, in 1946. What was the roof-space for? Was it perhaps a brass band coach, with storage for the instruments provided in king-sized luggage racks? The vehicle alongside was also ex-United. Ex-SM1 (UP 6312) was a 1931 Morris-Commercial Dictator, acquired in 1936 from Charlton's Blue Safety Coaches, of Hebburn-on-Tyne. It had also been sold to Buxton. *(Fred Kennington Collection [2]; Alan Townsin Collection/G E Hutchinson; R C Davis)*

oldest just over three years old, came from the business of F W Jermy & Co, Felton, Northumberland in November 1932, taking numbers between AT193 and AT206. All but two were Tigers, the exceptions being another pair of LT2 Lions dating from 1931, which became AL200/1. There were examples of TS1, TS2 and TS3 Tigers, but the last three were TS4s dating from earlier in 1932. In this case, four were requisitioned for military use in 1940, two became parcel vans in 1939 and 1941 but the rest ran until 1949/50. The firm's Morpeth garage passed to United and in 2001 is still in use with Arriva Northumbria.

County Motor Services Ltd, of Stakeford, near Choppington, Northumberland, had a complex history in relation to United, parts of its fleet being taken over in three stages with different sections of

the business. In March 1933, the London-Scottish services were acquired jointly with SMT, United receiving three Lion PLSCs which became AL217-9, and a Tiger TS2 (AT216) which had originated with Link Lines of Glasgow and had bodywork by Midland of Airdrie; it was sold off in 1939. Two of the Lions, dating from 1928/9, proved to be the only PLSC buses in the United fleet to be rebodied, being included in a 1934 scheme described later. One, AL218 (TY 4671), later running as LL1, long outlived all the other PLSC models in the fleet by lasting until 1949. There was also a 1931 Regal coach with Burlingham body, KW 9397 (another case of a vehicle having been registered in Bradford by the supplier, Tillotson) which became R9, remaining in the fleet until 1950. Its twin, KW 9396, passed to SMT.

The second stage of the County take-over,

The four Leyland Titans - one TD1 and three TD2s - acquired from County Motor Services, of Stakeford, in early 1934, were all ex-demonstrators. The TD1 and one of the TD2s were lowbridge, the other pair of TD2s highbridge. All had Leyland bodywork. In order of the A-series fleet numbers allocated by United, they were registered TF 9947 (AH231), TF 7759 (A232), TF 7211 (AH233) and TF 5988 (A234). TF 5988 was built with two doors, but by the time of this October 1931 view *(top left)*, it had been rebuilt with a single forward entrance. TF 7211 *(top right)* was photographed in November 1932 in its "Leyland Hybridge" demonstrator livery. TF 7759 *(above left)* appears in a March 1951 photograph at Marlborough Crescent, Newcastle. By then it had been fitted with a Leyland diesel engine, the body rebuilt with modified cab as widely found in Tilling fleets and had been renumbered three times: as LD53, LDO55 and LLL5. TF 9947 had the first Leyland all-metal body. In this October 1932 shot it was also liveried as a "Hybridge" demonstrator. *(Senior Transport Archive courtesy BCVM [3]; Alan Cross)*

involving its local Newcastle-Forest Hall route, in March 1934, had an even longer-lasting impact. The four Titans concerned, all former Leyland demonstrators, remained in the United fleet, albeit rebuilt in varying ways, until 1951-4. All had Leyland bodies but two were non-standard prototypes. The oldest was a 1931 TD1, TF 5988, with an experimental front-entrance layout not put into production. The other three were TD2s, TF 7211 having the Hybridge version of the traditional piano-front body; TF 7759 was similar but lowbridge; the third, TF 9947, dating from October 1932, was noteworthy in having Leyland's first prototype metal-framed body, also of highbridge form. The arrival of these buses in United's fleet saw another case of the policy of backwards numbering in terms of age, the highbridge buses being given AH prefix letters, TF 9947 becoming AH231 and TF 7211 was AH233 whilst the others became A232 and A234. The third and final stage of the County take-over did not occur until 1937 and will be covered later.

Although acquired bus fleets in this period included some of very mixed types, often sold off quickly, there was one further major intake of Leylands, mostly with Leyland bodies. The fleet of Thomas Allen & Sons, of Blyth, was taken over in July 1934 (a Blyth-Whitley Bay service had been sold to United and Tynemouth jointly in November 1933 but no vehicles were then involved). There were twelve Lion PLSCs, which became AL238-48 and AL253; two Tiger TS2s (AT249/50); two Lion LT1s (AL251/2); and two TS1s (AT254/5). The five oldest PLSC buses and an Albion PJ26, the only non-Leyland acquired, all dating from 1927, were sold off almost immediately.

As it turned out, that was to be the full extent of the A series of Leylands, the 1935 renumbering intervening before any more of the make were taken into stock. Although there were to be some substantial batches of new Leyland Tigers and limited numbers of further acquisitions in later years, the total of 255 new and mostly quite modern used Leylands acquired in the period from December 1929 to May 1934 represented a major part of the fleet and remained so until well after the

1939-45 war. Several other acquired fleets contributed smaller numbers of Leylands to this total, usually surviving long after their former stablemates.

### A quiet debut for the diesel engine

Ennis & Reed Ltd, of Crook, Co. Durham, was acquired jointly with Northern in January 1934, though the latter took no vehicles. There was one Lion LT1 with Leyland body, which became AL220 and ran until 1950, although two 1927 Lionesses (AM222/3) went in 1934 and a PLSC (AL221) in 1936. There were also two Maudslays - one a six-cylinder ML6 - and a Gilford CP6 20-seater but that fleet was more readily remembered as contributing six Daimler CF6 buses, mostly ex-demonstrators with an assortment of bodies, which became N35-40. The last of these, new in January 1929, was a former Daimler demonstrator to Dundee Corporation, having been registered in that city as TS 7664. It had a Willowbrook body. This latter CF6 was sold to Ennis & Reed in July 1929 but its main claim to fame was that it was converted to diesel

power with a Gardner 5LW engine. It was the first diesel vehicle to join the United fleet, and was taken up with great interest by United's engineering department.

Interest in oil engines, as they were then almost always called, for bus use had been growing since about 1930. By 1934 several major operators had adopted them as standard but United was far from being alone among major English company fleets in not having pursued the possibilities at that stage. For a modest-sized independent operator to adopt this line of action at so early a date was very unusual. Gardner had introduced its LW series of engines in September 1931, and the 5 in the designation signified its five-cylinder form, the capacity being 7.0 litres. Doubtless it gave the outstanding fuel economy associated with this engine make and word of its merits might even have spread more widely among companies under Tilling control or influence. The bus was renumbered DO1 in the 1935 renumbering scheme but in 1936 the 5LW engine was removed to be included in a conversion programme using 25 more such engines applied to Leyland Titan double-deckers, as

*Above:* In this group picture at the former E Johnson & Sons Great Ayton depot are three 1928 Tilling-Stevens buses in the Blumer's fleet. The middle one is PY8702, clearly visible in reverse on the back window. It had been new to Johnson, and had passed with the business to Blumer's Motors on 1st May 1931. It had a Davidson, of Trafford Park, body. The other pair, UP1985 (left) and UP2024, had been new to Blumer's at Greatham. All three went into the United fleet on 1st March 1934. *(D Stainthorpe)*

*Left:* The Crossley Eagle chassis was designed as a single-decker, but Blumer's had two as double-deckers. The earlier, VR 88, was built as a demonstrator. It is seen at Greatham, probably in 1929 when still new to Blumer's. The possibly unique Roe body had many unusual features. VR 88 was numbered CD3 when it passed to United in 1934. *(W Woddy)*

described in the next chapter. The CF6 reverted to a petrol engine, becoming D1 before being broken up for spares in 1941.

The acquisition of independent operators continued to include many small concerns, most of whose vehicles made no lasting impact on the fleet. The company was becoming increasingly discerning in what was to be retained more than briefly or at all. William Rutherford, based in the fishing village of Craster, a few miles from Alnwick, whose business was taken over in November 1932, had a fairly typical mix: three Gilfords and two Stars of 1928/9 became B133-7 and two Guys of 1927/8 were numbered G19/20; all went in 1933. Arthur Howe, of Blyth, trading as Pride of Blyth had nine vehicles when acquired jointly by United and Tynemouth & District in 1933, but United took only three of them. A 1930 Daimler CF6 with Willowbrook bus body, TY 7395, was numbered N41, and later joined the ranks of this model that were to survive rebodied and latterly with AEC petrol engines, in this case as late as 1950. Two 1929 Gilfords, VN 536 (ex-Northallerton Omnibus Company) and TY 5783 became B171/2 and were sold the next year, while Howe's six other vehicles - two more Gilfords, a bonneted Daimler CF6 of 1929 and three Reos of 1926-8 - were apparently not taken into stock.

A more significant bus-operating business, which came under full United control in late 1933 and was merged into the United business in March 1934, was noteworthy as the last piece of the LNER jig-saw to be fitted into place. This was Blumer's Motors Ltd, of Greatham, near West Hartlepool, a concern by no means fitting the accepted pattern. T S Blumer had been running services linking West Hartlepool with other centres since the early 1920s but the company was formed as a 50/50 deal with Thompson, McKay in February 1929. At that point the fleet consisted largely of Reo and Tilling-Stevens buses but, contrary to the policy adopted for LNER-related fleets elsewhere, four Crossley Eagles were purchased. Crossley, well-known as a car maker, had only recently begun the manufacture of full-sized buses though there were many earlier examples of vehicles in the 14-seat class, mostly on ex-military chassis. The Eagle was a conventional four-cylinder petrol-engined model intended as a single-decker, but the first of Blumer's examples, registered in Manchester by the maker as VR 88, had a Roe lightweight 48-seat double-deck body. There were two more ex-demonstrator Eagles, VR 394 and VR 1660, but these were 32-seat single-deckers, also bodied by Roe. Finally, another 48-seat double-decker, this time with Crossley body and registered locally as UP 4089, was delivered in April 1930, three months after the Thompson, McKay shareholding passed to United.

Mr Blumer subscribed extra capital in May 1932 to finance the purchase of the business of A Dunning & Sons of Great Ayton, this causing United's holding to fall below 50%; it may be recalled that United acquired two vehicles from Robert Dunning, another of the above-named sons,

in August 1931. The A Dunning fleet taken over by Blumer's comprised one 1930 Crossley Alpha, a six-cylinder model having a Crossley body, an Albion PKA26 and a 32-seat Maudslay of similar age, three 1928 Leyland Lion PLSCs and two 1929 Lion LT1s. When United took Blumer's combined fleet into stock in 1934 there were 26 vehicles in all. The two Crossley double-deckers became CD2 and CD3 and the single-deckers C4 and 5 although lasting only until 1935 before sale. The taken-over fleet included eleven Tilling-Stevens which became P32-42, some surviving into the later 1930s. Blumer's had withdrawn the Maudslay but the other ex-Dunning vehicles became United's C1, CM89, AL227/8/30, and AL225/6. Although the PLSC models were sold by 1937, as usual the Leylands proved the longest lived, the two Leyland-bodied LT1 buses running until 1950.

### The earlier Great North Road and other coach fleet acquisitions

The operation of coaches along the Great North Road linking London with the north-east attracted several concerns and competition was fierce in the late 1920s and early 1930s. United had shown little interest in long-distance operation and its entry into this field came by chance. Blue Band Bus Services Ltd, of Normanby, abruptly ceased trading in March 1930 because of insurance difficulties and United stepped in the following month, taking over the fleet of Albion vehicles as already mentioned, together with two services, one local but the other a twice-daily Sunderland - Tees-side - London service. United made no attempt to expand this at first, perhaps waiting to see how the new route licensing procedure under the Road Traffic Act of 1930 settled down, but from 1932 a fairly aggressive policy of acquiring the competition was pursued. There were six such acquisitions in the 1932-4 period, one being the County service linking London and Scotland already mentioned as purchased jointly with SMT in 1933. Four of these were retained as subsidiaries so that the licences could be retained as a means of giving maximum advantage over firms who had not yet succumbed. Ultimately, by 1936 and at great expense - in round figures, £170,000 or the equivalent of about £8 million in today's money - United had obtained a monopoly.

The first of these acquisitions was that of the business of J Glenton Friars, based at Blaydon-on-Tyne, who had started operations with UP 632, an ADC 423 with full-fronted Short Bros 20-seat toilet-equipped coach body, which had been exhibited at the 1927 Commercial Motor Show and rebuilt to CF6 specification; it was later used by Daimler itself. It was followed in late 1928 by three bonneted Daimler CF6s with Hoyal bodywork, one of which, UP 1888, had the first CF6 chassis, number 7001L. These three were retained by Mr Friars when the Glenton Friars (Road Coaches) Ltd business passed to United control in March 1932, becoming absorbed in October that year. Six CF6 forward-control coaches with Hoyal bodies of 1929/30 were then in use - four with Durham registrations UP 3232/3 and 4215/6, plus HX 851 and GH 1736 with Middlesex and London marks. The first two were of more or less conventional form but the others were what were then usually called observation coaches with high-level floor line at the rear and luggage space below - they were to a design registered by Glenton Friars. They were given fleet numbers GN15-20 in the foregoing order during the period when Glenton Friars was being run as a subsidiary, filling in gaps in the N series left by NA-class buses that had been transferred to Eastern Counties - some records showed the observation vehicles as GNX17-20, but this latter version was not quoted on the vehicles. The prefix letters were altered to N15/6 and NX17-20 when the fleet was absorbed.

The next stage in this story was the take-over of Majestic Saloon Coaches (Newcastle and London) Ltd, based at Ebchester, Co. Durham, in which the leading figure was Robert Armstrong. The firm became a United subsidiary on 1st September 1932 and continued in this form until 30th September 1936. The fleet included six normal-control Gilford 166SD coaches with Duple bodies of 1929 which became MB123-8 but were sold in September 1933. There were three 1930 Daimler CF6s, one with Duple body, MY 1500, which became MN21 and two bodied by Weymann, GH 1955/6, which became MN22/3. The most modern coaches were six AEC Regals, four with Burlingham bodies, UP 5434/5 and 5574/5, dating from 1931, which

became MR3-6 and two bodied by Duple, GX 166 and 168, which became MR7/8. Disaster struck MR6 in January 1935, when it was burnt out.

National Coachways Ltd, of London, NW1, which had operated jointly with Glenton Friars, and in which Mr Friars held an interest, also used Daimler CF6 coaches, all with Hoyal observation-type bodies of the same pattern. This company was the subject of a purchase agreement dated 28th April 1932 though it was not taken over by United until 18th September that year; there was thus in this case no period of operation as a subsidiary. Of the nine National Coachways coaches, the 1931 vehicles registered GN 374-6 and GN 7157-9 took the fleet numbers NX24-9 while GH 9968-70 of 1930 became NX30, 31 and 34. The body of NX24 had been destroyed before the take-over, and the chassis was fitted with the Duple bus body removed from B86 (VN 537), a 1929 Gilford 166OT acquired from the Northallerton Omnibus Co, the last survivor of of 14 vehicles (B79-86 and H50-5), largely of American makes, acquired from that concern in 1930. The Daimler then became NA24, perhaps implying that the chassis had become similar to the ADC 423 vehicles as re-engined, although another possibility could be that of some confusion with the previous vehicle to bear this number.

The surviving London-service Daimlers and ex-Majestic AECs had long and quite complex lives with United. A quite different type of coach business was absorbed in February 1933, this being Robinson's Motors Ltd, whose address was

The most unusual vehicles to operate on the London services were the 1930/1 Hoyal-bodied 26-seat Daimler CF6 observation coaches of Glenton Friars (Road Coaches) Limited and of National Coachways Limited. HX 851 was numbered GN19 during the short period in 1932 when Glenton Friars was a subsidiary of United. These observation coaches were rebodied as service buses for United in 1934 by Northern Counties. HX 851 was parked at St Peter's Hill, Grantham, during a meal break on the London run. *(G H F Atkins)*

*Above:* A Glenton Friars Daimler CF6, either UP 3232 or UP 3233, with conventional coachwork, also by Hoyal, dating from 1929. The two gentlemen on the roof were demonstrating the covers to the luggage compartment. *(John Banks Collection)*

*Right and below:* Majestic AEC Regal UP5435 is seen after a substantial rebuild carried out at Grange Road Works, Darlington, typical of the type of work done to modernise appearance in the mid 1930s. The work included altering the destination screens to match United's standard layout. The fleet number MR4 had also been applied. *(Philip Battersby Collection)*

quoted as Railway Station Yard, Scarborough, although by then it was already entirely United-owned. The same proprietor's bus business had been acquired in March 1926, as mentioned earlier. There had been an agreement, initially with the North Eastern Railway, to operate excursions from the station and the LNER had taken a half shareholding in March 1929, but both this and the ex-Robinson holding passed to United in January 1930, although, unusually, United-style fleet numbers were not issued at that stage. There was a mainly elderly fleet, mostly recorded as charabancs, painted in a white livery. At the time of the take-over, eight Lancia 20- or 23-seaters dated from 1923-5, though two were rebodied by United as folding-roof all-weather coaches in May 1931, and four Maudslay, seating 20 to 28, dated from 1926/7. There were also two Austin 20hp 14-seaters of 1926/7, these being on the 3.6-litre four-cylinder chassis then also much favoured as an ambulance. The foregoing vehicles were given the numbers B138-51 in reverse order of date; an Austin and the two rebodied Lancias lasted until 1937/8. The only modern vehicle that had been built specifically for this fleet during the period when run as a subsidiary was a Leyland Tiger TS1

with United folding-roof coach body of June 1931, registered VY 2798; it became AT215. However, one of United's Tiger TS4 coaches, NG 2281, was diverted to the Robinson's fleet in white livery when new in May 1932 though joining the rest with its original intended number AT181 in February 1933.

A rather grand-sounding business taken over in August 1933 was that of the Leeds and Newcastle Omnibus Company Ltd, of Northallerton, which had operated with vehicles supplied by its members, one being Walters and Johnson of Ferryhill, though that firm was running a Durham-Darlington service when taken over by United in October 1932 - its four Gilfords became B129-32, and a Thornycroft A1 was numbered M40. Leeds and Newcastle had a Gateshead office in the premises of the local Gilford dealer. United initiated negotiations on the purchase of the business, on its own account for the local services, and on behalf of the Limited Stop Pool for the services from Newcastle and Middlesbrough to Leeds. Three Gilford vehicles of 1927-9 came into United ownership; one was sold the same day and the others became B157/8, though a month later the engineers reported them to be in extremely bad condition. Eight other Gilford coaches were sold on behalf of the Pool. However two TSM coaches with Roberts bodies dating from 1931 were numbered P30 and 31, becoming STS16/17 in 1935, the first surviving with United until 1949 though the second was taken for war service in 1939.

By far the most important London-service operator to come into association with United was the Orange Brothers concern, of Bedlington, which Thomas Tilling Ltd purchased in May 1933, but this began a new strand in United's involvement with express service operation and is covered in the next chapter.

This chapter has described the split between United and the new Eastern Counties Omnibus Company in 1931. One result was that United was no longer a coachbuilder. Before the split, bodywork produced carried an oval transfer incorporating the United scroll name as part of the phrase "United-built"; and on delivery the newly bodied vehicles carried a poster with the proud legend "Built by United". This one was an ADC 416 demonstrator. *(Senior Transport Archive)*

At the end of the five years covered by this chapter the scenes on this page, though less than a half-decade in the past, were already part of the pre-history - the folklore, almost - of the London express services. Majestic Saloon Coaches (Newcastle & London) Limited, of Ebchester, had a 1928 W & G Du Cros, scarcely a common make. It looked, even when new, decidedly eccentric, with its narrow radiator and bonnet. It did, however, have kitchen and toilet facilities and luxurious seating. In this wonderfully atmospheric shot on 8th May 1928 at Marlborough Crescent, Newcastle, the W & G is about to leave for London (despite the destination blind). It never left, however, because of mechanical problems, and 1928 Reo TY 1151 was

substituted. Its Robson 20-seat body with bus seating was hardly ideal for a London trip. Reo had quite a good name but here it is, later in the day, broken down near Catterick. The unfortunate passengers were transferred to a Liverpool-bound vehicle for a few miles and then to an Orange Bros coach to complete their journey to the Capital. *(Both: Robert Grieves Collection)*

As the 1930s progressed, the vehicles that had been taken into United's fleet with the businesses of acquired operators began to blend into the scenery until it was almost as if they had always been there. In the Stockton High Street panorama *(above)*, the former Smith's Safeway Services Leyland Titan TD1, A149 (DC 9953), was two or three years into its lengthy United career (it was to last until 1953). It is the third vehicle from the right. The second, which is comprehensively identifiable despite the police officer and the pedestrians, is Underwood, of Sunderland, Robson-bodied Albion BR 7052. This operator had no connection with W T Underwood, but long after the demise of this particular vehicle the direct Middlesbrough to Sunderland service did pass to United, whose buses F24 and L106 complete the row at the far end. The star of the show is Stockton Corporation's 1931 Daimler No. 4 (UP 6077), a Brush-bodied CH6. Photographs of ex-Scarborough District Albions in United livery are as rare as stardust, which makes this view *(below)* of CM52 (VN 453) doubly welcome. The occasion was the race meeting, advertised on the window bill, at Hamilton Park on Saturday, 7th July 1934. The hardy passengers had travelled from somewhere in Northumberland, and the bus, a PMA28, one of five dating from July 1929, was parked at Lanarkshire Traction's former tram depot in Hamilton Road, Motherwell. Late the following year it returned to Scotland permanently upon sale to W Alexander & Sons. *(Both: Robert Grieves Collection)*

# 5 Progress Towards Standardisation 1933-1940

## Bristol buses - a new beginning

The United Board Minutes of 29th November 1932 had authorised the ordering of eight Titans and 20 single-deck vehicles, indicating that the latter's make had not been settled. The Titans were the TD2 batch with highbridge Eastern Counties bodies mentioned in the previous chapter and the single-deckers also duly arrived in mid-1933. On the basis of United policy since late 1929, there was reason to expect that they too would be Leylands, and since at that date four-cylinder models were evidently preferred for bus work, the Lion LT5 would have been the logical choice, but this line of action was not pursued. There had been the precedent of the 130 Bristol B-type buses of 1929, and it could be argued that, as United had reduced that order from 150 to 130, there was an ongoing obligation, although the contract had been for the latter figure. On the other hand, this was a legacy from the days when United had been an independent company, and at that stage, the Tilling-managed companies had never chosen the Bristol make.

Yet a complex chain of events was changing the picture. Amid the swirl of railway investment in bus companies around 1929, the Great Western Railway was keen to take a 50% holding in the Bristol Tramways & Carriage Co Ltd but held back, not having powers to engage in the manufacture of motor vehicles, nor operate tramways or taxicabs, in all of which BTCC was involved. In December 1931, a solution was found when it was agreed that a holding which had been taken up after being offered to GWR, then of 50%, would be transferred to the Western National Omnibus Co Ltd, which itself had been associated with the GWR since its formation from part of the National Omnibus & Transport Co Ltd, with headquarters in Exeter, from January 1929.

A further, and key, layer to the new situation was that a controlling interest in NOTC had been acquired by Thomas Tilling Ltd in February 1931. The deal was not completed until March 1932, but the effect of it was that Tilling thus had an indirect interest in BTCC, though not at that stage appointing its Chairman. The manufacturing side of the business was going through a difficult time, hit by the depression, with annual output down to 72 Bristol chassis in 1932; its future remained very uncertain.

However, the new alliances opened up fresh possibilities, and two of the newly associated companies took batches of the Bristol H single-deck model. One, naturally enough, was Western National, now nominally BTCC's parent company,

although in fact a somewhat smaller concern, taking an initial batch of 39 buses of the type. The other purchaser was indeed United, taking 20 with Eastern Counties bodies; it seems likely that the firm's experience with the B-type buses and perhaps B V Smith's reported role in their choice as Chief Engineer, had at least some continuing influence. The new buses were numbered LH131-50 and were registered HN 9031-50. The first was taken into stock on 16th May 1933, the remainder following in June-July.

The H model had a four-cylinder 6-litre side-valve petrol engine, very similar to the GW unit used in the B-type, though improved in detail and designated LW. The appearance was more modern, with a taller, slimmer radiator, although a similar style had been introduced on the final version of the B-type from 1931. Bristol had introduced new models to suit the new regulations governing overall length in effect from 1st January 1932, the H four-cylinder and the J six-cylinder types, as they were initially, both having 17ft 6ins wheelbase to suit the 27ft 6ins overall length limit - there was also an equivalent G-type six-cylinder double-decker model.

The bodywork on the batch for United was to a new design providing the basis for the company's standard bus styles for the next five years. It had resemblances to the Eastern Counties standard coach designs of the day, and indeed there were traces of the 1931 batch of United-bodied Tiger coaches, such as the slender moulded waistband. Although finished in bus livery, in some respects they belonged to the category of that time best described as a 'saloon', with such features as full-length interior luggage racks and glass louvres over all side windows. At the front, the windscreen was quite strongly raked, with the roof projecting slightly forward of its upper edge in the manner then still usual. There was enough depth in the well-rounded roof panels to allow the relatively deep single roller-blind destination box henceforth adopted as United's new bus standard to be incorporated neatly at the front - it was also provided on the TD2 buses, AH207-14. Alternative mock-up destination box layouts were used to arrive at this design, which was similar in general form to that on the 1930 Tiger saloons but noticeably deeper. All these 1933 deliveries also had rear destination boxes.

A departure for United was the choice of rear-entrance layout, although the form of folding entrance door was much as used since the mid-1920s. A roof-mounted luggage carrier was provided in the manner then usual for coaches, suggesting that possible use on express service

*Above:* The second of the 1933 Bristol Hs, photographed in June 1933. LH132 (HN 9032) was in spotless original condition. The roof-mounted luggage compartment with its small mounting platform is shown, as are the five rather small fold-down steps running up the centre of the rear panel and between the rear windows. *(Alan Townsin Collection)*

*Below:* By the time of this June 1937 photograph at Cayton Bay, HN 9049, the former LH149, renumbered BH19 in 1935, had lost its roofrack. This alteration was an early example in a programme which removed the racks from this batch over a period of several years. *(G H F Atkins)*

duplication may have been in mind. The seating capacity was 36, with all but the pairs of seats over each rear wheel-arch facing forward, with a bench seat for five at the rear and a row of three immediately in front of it. Although A T Evans was at that date still Secretary and Traffic Manager, effectively he had been put in charge of the company under the authority of the Board - his official appointment as General Manager was made on 24th July 1934, a position that he was to hold until 1st August 1959. He was a strong believer in the merits of the 36-seat, or a little later, 35-seat single-decker for the overwhelming majority of United's services and the large numbers of such vehicles added to the fleet in the period up to 1950 reflected this.

The 1934 delivery of new buses comprised a further fifteen Bristol H models with Eastern Counties 36-seat bodies, LH151-65 (HN 9751-65) placed in service in July-August. The basic design and body structure were similar to the earlier batch, though the windows were slightly deeper and the appearance was modernised significantly by several detail changes. At the front, the roof no longer projected forward of the windscreen, of which the bottom edge now curved gently downwards towards the offside. The rear dome panel was given a slightly more rounded look and advertisement panels with neatly shaped ends were added above the side windows. In passing, it is noteworthy that these, standard on United single-deckers from then until 1940, were normally used for United's own advertising, from simple slogans urging travel by United or use of the company's parcel services to more specific wording about, for example, the London service. This batch had a sliding entrance door and omitted the roof-mounted luggage carrier, although the few rear view photographs available to us suggest that there was no rear luggage boot to compensate.

At that stage, Bristol as a chassis maker was still on quite limited trial as far as Tilling-managed companies in general were concerned. The only other customer from the group taking substantial numbers of vehicles at that stage was again Western National, with a further 24 H-types delivered in 1933/4. Indeed, the future of Bristol as a manufacturer was far from assured. In May 1933, just as United's first H-types were being delivered, there had been a joint approach from Leyland and AEC (despite the fact that they were themselves then unconnected rival concerns) for the acquisition of what was always called the Motor Constructional Works from BTCC. Negotiations dragged on for almost exactly a year but then fell through. Similarly, Eastern Counties entered into negotiations on the possible sale of the Coach Factory to Charles Roberts & Co Ltd of Wakefield in the summer of 1933, but this also fell through.

### More London-service influence on the fleet

An important step in the build-up of United's involvement in the services linking London and the

The 1934 batch of Bristol Hs had a significantly more modern style of body; one is seen in a postwar view at the Company's Grange Road Central Works, Darlington, in the late 1940s. By then towards the end of its life (it may, indeed, have been "not under maintenance", i.e. withdrawn from the operational fleet), BHO26 (HN 9756) had long been a Gardner 5LW-engined bus, hence the BHO prefix to its number - it had previously been BH26 and originally LH156. This view confirms the apparent lack of doors for a luggage boot, despite the absence from new of roof-mounted luggage-carriers on these 1934 machines. The wide rear pillar is a legacy of the steps for such a fitment on the previous batch. *(R C Davis)*

north-east came on 27th May 1933 with the purchase by Thomas Tilling Ltd - although using United's money - of a £72,500 majority interest in the business of Orange Brothers, based in Bedlington, Northumberland. This was the strongest of the independent operators involved and operated through to Edinburgh and Glasgow, a total distance of about 440 miles. A new company, Orange Brothers Ltd, was formed as a direct Tilling subsidiary on 12th June and it was arranged that the dividends from this shareholding were also to be remitted via Tilling to United. The three Orange brothers remained as minor shareholders and were given appointments with the company.

A significant aspect, thought to be the reason for the apparently clumsy indirect purchase, which was kept secret and seems not to have been disclosed even in later years, was that E B Hutchinson took a minority shareholding and acted as Managing Director. It seems to have been thought desirable to use EBH's knowlege and skills but he was barred from acting for United under the terms of his 1929 severance. The appearance of a quite separate business was maintained, Orange services not being shown in United's timetable books while those of Majestic were.

This arrangement continued until August 1934, when - following the signing of an agreement for the mangement of Orange Bros Ltd by United - Hutchinson gave up his connection, the nominally direct Tilling control ceased and United became the majority shareholder in its own name. Orange Bros was to remain a separate subsidiary until 1950. The Orange brothers subsequently gave up their shares and in 1935/6 their employment ceased. The opportunity was taken to make extensive changes in Orange's activities and organisation. It no longer had any employees, henceforth using United staff, and the Newcastle to Edinburgh and Glasgow section was passed to SMT with five vehicles, also in August 1934. In practice this traffic passed to the existing United-SMT joint services, suitably strengthened.

There were 34 coaches in the Orange Bros fleet at the time of the 1933 agreement. Gilford chassis had been chosen in the 1927-30 period, at first various bonneted types of which eight remained, but this era ended with three forward-control 168OT models (TY 7076-8). Two AEC Reliance coaches (TY 6470/1) came in 1929, followed by four AEC Regals (TY 7079-82) in 1930 - the latter were noteworthy in being among the first AECs to be built with the larger-bore (110mm) version of the standard petrol engine for this model, increasing the capacity from 6.1 to 7.4 litres - at that stage it was an option, later becoming standard. The Maudslay ML6, having a six-cylinder petrol engine of quite elaborate twin-camshaft design, was chosen for eleven coaches in 1931/2 (TY 8092-7, 8885 and 9402-5), together with one more Gilford, of the rare 168MOT type with Meadows engine (TY 8886), before a return to the Regal was made with five supplied in 1932 (TY 9605-8, 9654), two more on order at the time of the agreement (JR 468/9),

arriving in June 1933. Weymann had been the main bodybuilder from 1930, though Strachans had bodied the Reliances and three of the 1932 Regals. The Gilford 168MOT had proved unsatisfactory and was sold immediately after the May 1933 agreement, followed by five older Gilfords in February 1934, while Maudslay TY 9402 was lost by fire in May 1934.

In the August 1934 reorganisation, the five coaches transferred to the Scottish Motor Traction Co Ltd were a Gilford 168OT (TY 7076), a Maudslay ML6 (TY 9403) and three AEC Regals (TY 7081, TY 9607, and JR 468); three of these coaches moved again to the Western SMT Co Ltd in 1935. There were thus 24 coaches remaining to be brought into the United fleet numbering system, using the usual device of adding a prefix letter to distinguish them from United's own vehicles. The two Reliances became OK62 and 63, eight of the Regals became OR11-8, nine of the Maudslay ML6s became OB186-94, three Gilford 166SDs became OB195-7 and the two Gilford 168OTs became OB198/9.

Almost immediately after this, in September 1934, United took control of a further London service operator, Phillipson's Motor Coaches Ltd, of London, N1. Again the device of adding an appropriate prefix to the fleet numbers was used, so five Gilfords (four 168OT and one 168SD) dating from 1930 became PB200-4, and five AEC Regals took PR-prefix fleet numbers. Two of the Gilfords were sold in 1935 to West Yorkshire Road Car, who took over the company's Scarborough service, the others being sold off soon afterwards. Four of the Regals, VY 2551/2 and 2784/5, (respectively given the numbers PR21/19/20/22) had been new in 1931 to London & East Coast Motor Service Ltd, of York. Of them, VY 2551 is reported as having bodywork by London Lorries, this firm also possibly having bodied the others, but a photograph of VY 2552 in Phillipson's livery as AR1, evidently taken in the summer of 1935, shows a body design appearing to be Burlingham's standard of 1931, very like the Majestic ones of that date. The archives reveal no evidence that this body was not the original on this chassis. These coaches passed to Phillipson's in October 1932, but AGH 405, with Duple body, was new to Phillipson's in March 1933 and became PR23. All five Regals were to have long careers with United.

Thus quite a substantial fleet of acquired coaches was built up from the London-service operators' fleets brought into the United empire in 1932-4, latterly with a marked increase in the number of AEC Regals - all but four of the 23 of that model operated were in the Majestic, Orange and Phillipson's fleets. Most had 110mm bore engines and those delivered from 1932 to these operators had the "high-power head" version giving 120bhp, so were lively as well as refined coaches. Indeed, bearing in mind the 25 Leyland Tiger TS4 coaches of similar refinement and performance bought new in 1932, there was now a surplus of older coaches, the Gilfords generally being sold off quite quickly, and the Daimlers no longer being

Two Orange Bros coaches that were retained under United control are shown in their original condition on this page. Orange No. 22 (TY 7078), a 1930 Gilford 168OT with Weymann 26-seat coachwork *(above)*, was numbered in United's B-series as OB199, and renumbered SG5 in the 1935 scheme. Orange No. 39 (TY 9605) had been new in June 1932. It was an AEC Regal bodied as a 28-seater, again by Weymann, which became OR14 in the United system. *(Both: Robert Grieves Collection)*

When Phillipson's became a United subsidiary in 1934, this 1932 AEC Regal, VY 2552, was numbered PR19 and then became AR1 in the 1935 renumbering, as seen in this view taken in London that year. The body, as explained in the text, was possibly by London Lorries, or perhaps Burlingham, to whose style it conformed. In 1936 it was transferred to the ownership of Orange Bros Ltd, but in 1937, along with three other ex-Phillipson Regals, it was rebodied by Eastern Coach Works as a service bus in United livery and re-engined with an AEC oil engine. *(J F Higham)*

needed on coach duties. In the economic climate of the time, the market value of models such as the Daimler CF6 coaches was low and yet the chassis were still in good order.

The outcome was the rebodying in 1934 of seventeen existing chassis as buses to a broadly similar design to what was beginning to emerge as United's standard style of the period, as chosen for the Bristol H-types. The bodies were built by Northern Counties Motor & Engineering Co Ltd, Wigan, not normally a supplier to United but also carrying out some rebodying work for the West Yorkshire company that year, in that case on Albion chassis. Of the United batch, fifteen, supplied in July, were on Daimler CF6 chassis dating from 1929-31, all but one previously having coach bodywork. It is noteworthy, after the earlier bad experience with Daimler sleeve-valve engines, that examples of this model had their lives extended in this way. Yet enough experience had been built up with the CF6 model for it to be considered suitably reliable - certainly it was a smooth-running model from the passengers' viewpoint and evidently the heavy use of lubricating oil was considered acceptable - also the low value of the chassis made it possible to produce some modern-looking buses at low overall cost. The concept of rebodying as a means of helping to update the fleet was not new, but it had clear

appeal at a time when fare revenue was being hit by the depression.

The vehicles chosen included all six of the ex-Glenton Friars coaches and eight of the nine from National Coachways (the exception being NA24, which had received a second-hand bus body on acquisition, as already mentioned), plus one further vehicle, N41 (TY 7395) that had been taken over from A Howe of Blyth in August 1933, this having had a Willowbrook bus body.

There were alternative versions of these new bodies, depending on whether the chassis were of short- or long-wheelbase type, the former, applying to five of the ex-National Coachways vehicles and the ex-Howe bus, having a short bay amidships and seating for 32 passengers, while the others, with even pillar spacing, seated 36. The body outline largely resembled the 1933 version of the Eastern Counties bodies on Bristol H chassis except at the front, where the profile, with the top of the windscreen mounted flush with the roof canopy, was closer to the 1934 version.

The other two new bodies of the Northern Counties batch, dating from August 1934, were of similar style, fitted on Leyland Lion PLSC models that had been acquired from County Motor Services in 1933, AL217/8 (TY 5982 and 4671) dating from 1929 and 1928 respectively - the latter was a short-wheelbase PLSC1 model and seated 31 as rebodied;

*Above:* Ex-Glenton Friars 1930 Daimler CF6 UP 4216, seen circa 1947 at Polam Lane, Darlington with United's headquarters building in the background, displays the 36-seat version of the 1934 Northern Counties replacement body. Numbered GN18 when first under United control, it became D36 in 1935 and, after the war, DR36 after fitment of an AEC six-cylinder petrol engine. *(Alan Townsin)*

*Below and right:* A direct comparison between the longer and the shorter Northern Counties body is possible in these views of former D34 (GH 9970) *(left)* and what was apparently ex-D40 (GN 376) *(right)*, both originally with National Coachways. GH 9970 was rebodied as a 36-seater and the other vehicle was one of those with 32 seats; the short centre bay is quite clearly shown. GH 9970 was doing duty as a static caravan at Happy Valley, Hart Station, in the mid 1950s. An interesting souvenir and a rare survival *(right)* is its 1942 wartime Defence Permit. The vehicle thought to have been GN 376 was photographed at West View Estate, Hartlepool, circa 1954 in use as a building contractor's site hut. *(David Burnicle [2]; Ron Maybray Collection)*

There was snow on the ground in Bishop Auckland Market Place when this unique photograph was taken in the very early postwar period. It shows the two ex-Orange AEC Reliances, AK31/2 (TY 6470/1), carrying their 1935 replacement Burlingham 32-seat service bus bodies. *(Alan Townsin)*

the other seated 32. They were to remain the only examples of this model in the fleet to be given new bodies.

Although not completed until May 1935, it seems appropriate to mention here that five more bodies to the same style were built by Burlingham, which concern built the bodies on that year's new United coaches. Three were fitted on the Majestic Daimler CF6 chassis MY 1500 and GN 1955/6, which had been running as MN21-3 though re-entering service as D21-3 under that year's renumbering scheme (the retention of the same numbers being coincidental). Their seating capacity was 32, these being on the short chassis.

The two other Burlingham bodies of this design, also 32-seat and with the same short bay amidships as used for the short-wheelbase CF6, were fitted on the 1929 AEC Reliance chassis from the Orange Brothers fleet which had run as OK62/3 and here too they then received the new-series numbers AK31 and 32 they carried in later years. All five at first remained in the ownership of the respective subsidiary companies though now in United bus colours and with United fleetnames - they were sold to United in 1936; the temporary continuation of the former ownership was to gain obsolescence tax relief that would have been lost if there was a break in ownership.

Another group of vehicles which received special attention was that operated from Scarborough under the Robinson fleetname in a distinctive white livery. By the mid-1930s, this was composed largely

of the Albion Viking Six coaches dating from 1929 that had been taken over from Blue Band of Normanby. United records show that four of these went to Edmond for rebuild to "all weather coaches" in 1934 - CM78 in May and CM71/3/7 in July. Three more from the same group of coaches, CM74-6, went on what was probably a similar basis to Plaxton, of Scarborough, then a relatively modest-sized bodybuilder, in March 1935.

A notable exercise carried out during 1934 was the conversion of the seven open-staircase Leyland bodies on the Titan TD1 buses dating from 1928/9, taken over from Redwing (A163-7) and Smith's Safeway (A147/8), to give them enclosed staircases, thus bringing them into line with the later buses of the type. The work, giving an appearance quite close to the Leyland enclosed-staircase style for this model, is understood to have been carried out in the Darlington body overhaul workshops and is a good example of United's policy of modernising vehicles where this proved practicable. Although some other operators carried out similar conversions, this might well have been the earliest such case applied to the TD1.

Another manifestation of United's policy of modernising vehicles related to to destination displays. The existing provision on many older buses was beginning to look old-fashioned as well as impractical. The deep though narrow destination board fitted on the nearside of the front bulkhead as adopted for single-deckers in the late 1920s was not as readily visible as a display centrally placed at roof level, and the shrouded lamp above the board gave but limited and patchy readability at night.

The Leyland Titan TD1 buses had introduced roller-blind destination display to United's fleet, of the rather shallow kind standard on that model. The first AT class Leyland Tigers had introduced a deeper roller blind, neatly built into the front canopy, at first in addition to the illuminated board. The latter was then discarded and the B-types, as well as many other vehicles, were fitted with similar though slightly deeper roller blind boxes much like those on the new Bristol H single-deckers, giving both service number and brief route details, during the mid-1930s. For acquired coaches, the equivalent procedure during this period was to adopt the side-by-side arrangement of destination boxes shaped to match the roof contours as introduced on the 1931 TS3 coaches. Apart from the practical benefits, this feature, applied to some of the acquired AEC Regals and the Orange Bros Maudslays, helped to modernise the appearance quite significantly.

### The diesel challenge

Meanwhile, another strand of development was under way as the potential of the Gardner oil engine had engaged the attention of the Bristol Tramways & Carriage Co's engineers. In November 1933, a new single-decker with the 5LW 7-litre five-cylinder engine was exhibited on the Bristol stand at the Commercial Motor Show for service in BTCC's own fleet. It was given the designation JO5G although it had been built as an H-type and indeed had been the first example of that model - the chassis of the two types were almost identical except for the engine.

Bristol had decided to standardise on the G double-deck and J single-deck chassis, both henceforth offered with alternative engines. The next step was to construct two G-types with 5LW engines, these thus becoming the first of the GO5G model, supplied to the West Yorkshire Road Car Co Ltd in April 1934. The outcome was the gradually widening use of 5LW-engined Bristol vehicles within Tilling-managed companies and in 1935 United received batches of ten GO5G and five JO5G models, as well as of the Leyland Tiger TS7 model by then current and with Leyland oil engines - it was to be an historic year for the company's fleet.

Fleet numbers LG166-75 were reserved for the ten Bristol GO5G buses which were the first due, followed by LN176-225 for 50 Bristol J.NW petrol-engined buses, both of the foregoing ordered in September 1934, and LJ226-30 for the five JO5G models ordered in December 1934 at the same time as five oil-engined Leyland Tigers - the registration numbers AHN 366-435 were also booked, with the intention of matching the fleet numbers as far as the Bristols were concerned. The Bristol NW engine was again a four-cylinder 6-litre side-valve unit, the latest in the family of engines of basically similar design already familiar in the United fleet in the B and H model chassis.

*Upper and centre:* In July 1934, former Blue Band Albion Viking Six CM73 (DC 9384) was substantially rebuilt with a full-length sliding canvas roof for use on tour work at Scarborough. In these views the work had just been completed by W G Edmond, of Middlesbrough; the livery was mostly white with Robinson's, of Scarborough, fleetnames. *(Edmond & Milburn Ltd)*

*Lower:* LGL1 (PY9417), one of the ex-Redwing (fleet number 34) Leyland TD1 Titans of 1928, seen at West Hartlepool depot in March 1951. It had been running with a Gardner 5LW oil engine as LDO1 since April 1936 and the enclosed staircase conversion, done in 1934, can be seen. *(Alan Cross)*

The existing numbering system was making it difficult to cope in a logical way with the increasing variety of models, notably the extra variations created by the introduction of oil engines, coming into service. This led to the adoption of a new numbering system for the whole fleet - its

**115**

*Above:* The 1935 petrol-engined Bristol J.NW in original condition is epitomised by BJ41 (AHN 416) at Valley Bridge bus station, Scarborough, soon after entering service, waiting to leave on the 20-mile run down the coast to Bridlington on service 111. The general appearance of United's Bristol single-deckers altered little from 1934 to 1937, the 190 buses of this general style dominating the fleet until outnumbered by the L types. Two of United's Morris Cowley inspection cars, IC6 (left) and IC4 (VF 7236 and 7232) are also visible. IC6 was sold in October 1935; the photograph must therefore date from that year. *(Ron Maybray Collection)*

*Below left:* The five Bristol Js which were oil-engined from new were thus of type JO5G. This postwar view in Thirsk shows the first of them, BJO1 (AHN 426). *(Philip Battersby Collection)*

*Below right:* The 1935 LTO-class Leyland Tiger TS7 buses which were delivered with oil engines are also represented in a postwar, circa 1948, view in which LTO5 (AHN 435) is at Marlborough Crescent, Newcastle, waiting to leave for Carlisle on service 34. *(Alan Townsin)*

application to existing vehicles from around May 1935 will be examined later, but the first manifestations were on the new deliveries described here. A combination of two or three prefix letters was now used to describe the vehicle type, using appropriate initial letters, and in general each type so defined had its own numbering series beginning at 1.

Thus the ten GO5G double-deckers first registered in February-March 1935 were numbered BDO1-10, the prefix indicating Bristol, Double-deck, Oil-engine; they retained the registration numbers already booked for them, AHN 366-75. They had Eastern Counties bodywork to a rather

plain five-bay lowbridge design - similar buses were also supplied to the West Yorkshire fleet. They were shown in United records as seating 52 and were allocated to Darlington, Middlesbrough and Redcar depots.

The 50 Bristol J.NW buses received 36-seat Eastern Counties bodywork almost identical to that on the 1934 batch of buses on H-type chassis, although a detail change was the introduction of a small curved extension of the side panelling to disguise the gap behind the nearside front mudguard. The differences between the H and the J.NW models were very slight and a blindfolded passenger would have been hard put to tell the

The celebrated J.NW oddity, with the Bristol registration AHY 239, by then rebuilt bodily with postwar-style rubber-mounted glazing, fitted with a Gardner 5LW engine, renumbered BJO210 and again to BJ133, was photographed in Park Street, Middlesbrough, on 29th July 1954. *(David Burnicle)*

difference, both being quite comfortable and reasonably smooth but hardly exciting in terms of performance - my recollection is of admittedly quite full buses making quite heavy going of the moderate gradients encountered in the more southerly parts of Durham. They were to prove the last new petrol-engined buses supplied to the fleet, and were delivered from the bodybuilders between March and May 1935 - though some did not enter service until June - being given the fleet numbers BJ1-50, though again the registrations booked for them, AHN 376-425, were retained, except for one.

This was BJ10, of which the chassis was allegedly "borrowed" by BTCC, being given the Bristol registration AHY 239 for use as a demonstrator; it retained this number when placed in service by United. This is strange, as BTCC is reported to have borrowed only the chassis, straight off the production line, in September 1934 yet selling it to United on 1st October. It was standard practice for manufacturers to use trade plates for any use of chassis on public roads, including for demonstration or press road tests, registration only being necessary if it was to carry fare-paying passengers and hence being bodied. Yet bodying at ECOC, to the same design as the others of the batch, proceeded quite normally and delivery of the completed vehicle was made with the others in March 1935. A possible explanation is that it was temporarily given a stock body by BTCC for some purpose involving use in service. The five JO5G buses became BJO1-5 (AHN 426-30).

AHN 370 was BDO5 when new and became BGL5 in the 1951 renumbering. In this 1953 view at Grange Road Works it had recently been withdrawn from service. *(J Dawson)*

The five oil-engined Leyland Tiger TS7s were numbered LTO1-5 (AHN 431-5), and these ten buses, delivered in June 1935, all had basically the same type of 36-seat Eastern Counties body as the BJ class buses, except in respects related to the differences in the two makes of chassis.

The Leylands, as well as not having the unusually high bonnet line of the Bristol chassis, also had a lower frame level, giving a slightly lower build to the vehicle as a whole, differences which applied to successive batches of vehicles for United on the two chassis makes up to the war period. The Leyland six-cylinder oil engine as offered in the

**117**

TS7, and also the subsequent TS8 and TS11 chassis, was an 8.6-litre unit, fitting neatly into the more compact front-end as compared to the TS1 to TS4. It gave a lively performance with less noise or vibration than almost any other oil engine of the day, although there was a rather agreeable and characteristic roar, quite different from the clattering bark of the Gardner 5LW; on the other hand, the latter was exceptionally economical. Bristol had developed a five-speed overdrive gearbox both to help this economy - at 30mph in overdrive the engine ran at about 1,100rpm - and to suit Gardner's governed speed, sharply cut off at 1,700rpm, this gearbox soon becoming standard on JO5G models unless operating purely in urban areas. Some comparative testing in service is suggested by the fact that both BJO1-5 and LTO1-5 were allocated to Northumberland Area by January 1936; in March there were examples of each at Ashington, Blyth, Morpeth and Newcastle.

Another landmark in the development of United rolling stock was the arrival of the first LTO-class coaches. Burlingham had introduced a new coach design as its 1935 season standard, having the side windows grouped alternately in singles and pairs, the idea doubtless being partly intended to allow the same basic design to be offered with front, centre or rear entrance. United chose its usual rear-entrance layout of that time, with very comfortable seating for 30 passengers. Even so, the result had a distinctive appearance and some of its features, notably the style of waistline, with a swaged section from which mouldings were swept down in graceful curves at front and rear, were to have an influence on United coach design extending well after the original style had ceased its long run in the fleet. By largely reversing the layout of the main colours from that used on existing United coaches, so that the main side panels were cream and much of the upperworks red, though the roof remained cream, together with mudguards painted red instead of the black used on buses, a new and distinctive appearance was created.

Although United was roughly in line with most English company operators in not venturing into the operation of diesel buses until 1935, it was among the first major concerns south of the Scottish border to use diesel-engined chassis for coaches. There may have been some influence from the Scottish Motor Traction Co Ltd, which had been running oil-engined AEC Regal coaches on its London-Edinburgh service since 1933. As well as these running through United territory, there was the continued presence on the the United Board of Sir William J Thomson, Chairman and Managing Director of SMT, who could report on experience and passenger reaction. The logic of taking this step was quite strong for a long-distance express service, particularly along a route like the Great North Road. Even though coaches, like all public service vehicles, were supposed to keep down to 30mph, in practice there were long stretches where they could cruise steadily at 40mph or so, the oil-engined TS7 or TS8 being almost as refined as the petrol version at such speeds even if the difference was rather more marked when idling or running at slower speeds. Indeed it is noteworthy that United actually referred directly to its "new Leyland Tiger coaches" in advertising for the London services of the period - it was most unusual to refer to a specific make of vehicle in such a way in publicity at that time.

The first batch of coaches comprised five vehicles, numbered LTO6-10, also taken into stock together with the bus versions in June 1935. As ordered there were two separate batches of five chassis numbers, evidently ordered some months apart, presumably for the buses and coaches respectively, but they became intermingled, so what were numerically the first two chassis of the first batch became the first pair of coaches. In addition, LTO6, which was allocated to Majestic to replace fire-victim MR6, remaining its property until taken into United stock in June 1936, received the unused registration number AHN 385 intended for BJ10; the rest of the batch, delivered directly to United became AHN 811-4.

The supply in December 1935 of a further five Tiger TS7 coaches with the same style of Burlingham 30-seat body suggests encouraging reaction. They were numbered LTO11-5, of which LTO15 was new to Orange and in that company's livery. They had registration numbers BHN 261-5 drawn from a block of which the bulk were used for further JO5G and TS7 buses delivered from February 1936 and described later.

For LTO11-4, a new style of United fleetname for use on coaches was introduced, using lower- case lettering with a curved scroll running from the large U, below the first letters and swinging above the later ones. Similar styles had been used since about 1934 on Orange, Majestic and Phillipson's coaches, but the United version was larger: about 4ft long rather than 3ft. From this time, the Orange version was similarly enlarged. This form of lettering, which was to remain standard for coaches until the NBC corporate image era, bore some similarity to the version used briefly in 1920 and it seems quite probable that E B Hutchinson's influence may have been at work.

The year 1935 was also to have major implications for the Bristol Tramways & Carriage Co Ltd, for in October John F Heaton added the Chairmanship of it to his existing extensive hold over Tilling activities, reflecting more direct Tilling influence, and arrangements for expanding chassis production with the opening of the Chatsworth Road works to augment the Brislington premises soon followed. Eastern Counties was already the main bodybuilder for the group at its ex-United Lowestoft factory and the combination of Bristol chassis and Lowestoft-built bodywork was set for a long run, not least for the United fleet.

### The 1935 renumbering

The general renumbering, formally dating from 1st May 1935 though it is not known how promptly it was applied in practice, provides a convenient snapshot of the fleet content at the time, although some vehicles due for early withdrawal were not included. The accompanying table gives an indication of the new prefix letters, their previous equivalents, the types of vehicle in each group and the quantities of vehicles that were renumbered. Prefix letters indicating ownership by subsidiary companies were discontinued.

The 'S' prefix used for most of the smaller categories signified 'sundry'. The letter 'D', when indicating vehicles which were double-deckers, implied 'lowbridge' except where accompanied by 'H' signifying 'highbridge', although 'H' was later used on its own in this context. The letter 'O' normally signified 'oil-engined' though this seems to have been forgotten in regard to the single Commer in the fleet, SCO1 (TY 7365), a 1930 20-seater of unspecified type acquired from J E Allan, of Chatton, in June 1934 and at first numbered B181 - it was sold in September 1936. Another oddity was that the single Crossley Alpha, SC3, a six-cylinder bus, was also referred to as SC6.3 but it is not known if this was displayed on the vehicle.

Overall, the system worked very well, having the virtue of being readily understood by staff, not to mention inquisitive schoolboys: the author began to figure out what the codes meant at about the age of 11; they played no little part in setting off his interest in buses.

Adding the 75 vehicles supplied new in the earlier part of 1935, a combined fleet total of 819 (of which 40 were owned by subsidiaries, including Majestic's new LTO6) is reached, ignoring a few survivors of the previous numbering system which lingered on briefly, retaining their old numbers; some of these may well have been in store pending disposal; only two survived beyond the end of the year. Ignoring such exceptions, the composition of the combined fleet of United and its subsidiaries, as it stood in mid 1935, can be summarised in descending order of quantities as follows (vehicles were petrol-engined unless otherwise stated):-

73 DOUBLE-DECKERS:-
    63 Leyland Titan (53 lowbridge, 10 highbridge)
    10 Bristol GO5G oil-engined lowbridge

746 SINGLE-DECKERS:-
    220 Bristol (130 B-type, 50 J.NW and 35 H, plus
        5 JO5G oil-engined)
    184 ADC (95 425, 75 415, 12 426 and 2 423)
    138 Leyland (84 Tiger, 23 Lion PLSC, 20 Lion LT
        and 1 Cub, plus 10 Tiger oil engined)
    81 AEC (59 Reliance and 22 Regal)
    41 Daimler (40 CF6 plus 1 CF6 oil-engined)
    24 Albion (16 four-cylinder, 8 Viking Six)
    17 Tilling-Stevens (B10)
    15 Maudslay (5 four-cylinder, 10 ML6)
    8 Gilford
    6 Thornycroft
    4 Bedford
    3 Crossley
    2 Lancia

    1 Austin
    1 Commer
    1 Dennis

The balance had already swung towards Bristol as the most numerous make overall with 230 vehicles - at that stage, United was the only operator other than BTCC itself where that was so - with Leyland in second place at 201, and ADC third at 184, although that last total was soon set to drop, as were most of the less numerous groups, particularly the smaller types of vehicle.

Indeed, when it is recalled how frequently small buses had been acquired with taken-over businesses over the previous half-dozen years or so, remarkably few remained in service. Admittedly, there were a number of instances of acquired vehicles of this type which had quite long lives in the fleet, but the numbers in use at any one time were very small. The company's policy was based on A T Evans's view, continued by his successors, that a vehicle of about 35-seat capacity was a better overall purchase because of its earning capacity at busy times even if it ran relatively empty for much of the day.

United's two business acquisitions in 1935 had no effect on the bus fleet, although that of Trutime Deliveries Ltd in February brought in 29 parcel lorries and vans, plus five trailers expanding what was to remain an important activity. At the time of acquisition, the vehicles were given the fleet numbers IL80-108. As already noted, IL was a subdivision of the inspection car class IC. Under the 1935 renumbering scheme, the IC class remained for cars and small vans (though these were now renumbered from 1 upwards), and a new PV class was started for parcels vans. The "V" was soon replaced by a letter indicating make: A for Albion, C for Chevrolet, F for Ford and M for Morris-Commercial; plus, later, B for Bedford and L for Leyland. Vehicles used by the Engineer's Department were put into a new ED class, and for the period up to the war there was also to be a small PD class for Publicity Department vans.

A significant final event of 1935 was the resignation, with effect from 31st December, of B V Smith, from the post of Chief Engineer, which he had held under slightly varying titles since 1st October 1924. He left to become General Manager and Chief Engineer of the Southern National and Western National companies, where he was to remain General Manager until he died in office in 1957. His influence on United through a period of great changes was considerable, not least in the planning of the maintenance methods and facilities needed to keep so large and widely spread a fleet in good order and coping with the amazingly mixed influx of acquired vehicles.

Appointed as his successor as United's Chief Engineer was Percy S Pelling, who continued in

>> *Following page:* A tabulated survey of the buses and coaches renumbered at the introduction of the 1935 numbering scheme.

| NEW CLASS | OLD CLASS | TYPE OF VEHICLE | QUANTITY RENUMBERED | COMMENTS |
|---|---|---|---|---|
| AF | F etc | ADC 415 | 75 | Included former FA, FL, FT types |
| AJ | J | ADC 425 | 95 | |
| AJA | JA | ADC 426 etc | 12 | One ADC 417 later AJ96 |
| AK | K | AEC Reliance | 59 | |
| AL4 | CM | Albion (four-cylinder) | 16 | |
| AL6 | CM | Albion (six-cylinder) | 8 | Numbered AL6.17-24. Robinson's livery on AL6.17/19-24 |
| AR | R | AEC Regal | 22 | |
| B | L | Bristol B | 130 | |
| BH | LH | Bristol LH | 35 | |
| D | N etc | Daimler CF6 etc | 42 | Included two ADC 423s with 5.7-litre engines, formerly NA32-3, becoming D2-3 |
| DO | N | Daimler CF6/5LW | 1 | Became D1 when petrol engine refitted circa 1936 |
| LC | AN | Leyland Cub | 1 | |
| LD | A | Leyland Titan | 53 | |
| LDH | AH | Leyland Titan (highbridge) | 10 | Numbered LDH54-63 |
| LL | AL | Leyland Lion | 43 | Included both PLSC and LT (In 1936, LL24-43, which were LT types, became LT4.1-20) |
| LT | AT | Leyland Tiger | 84 | Robinson's livery on LT50 and 70 |
| M4 | B | Maudslay (four cylinder) | 5 | |
| M6 | B | Maudslay (six cylinder) | 10 | Numbered M6.6-15 |
| SA | B | Austin 20hp | 1 | Robinson's livery |
| SB | B | Bedford WLB and WHG | 4 | |
| SC | C | Crossley Eagle and Alpha | 3 | |
| SCO | B | Commer 20-seat | 1 | |
| SD | B | Dennis Dart | 1 | |
| SG | B | Gilford 166SD and 168OT | 8 | |
| SL | B | Lancia | 2 | Robinson's livery (rebodied) |
| ST | M | Thornycroft BC and A2 | 6 | |
| STS | P | Tilling-Stevens B10A etc | 17 | |

| Total Renumbered Vehicles | 744 |
|---|---|

Of the foregoing, the following 39 vehicles were owned at that time by subsidiary companies, taking new-series numbers as follows:-

| Orange Bros | Majestic | | Phillipsons |
|---|---|---|---|
| AK31-32 | | | United bus livery |
| AR11-18 | AR6-10 | | AR1-5 |
| | D21-3 | | United bus livery |
| M6.7-15 | | | |
| SG1-5 | | | SG6-7 |

| 24 vehicles | 8 vehicles | 7 vehicles |
|---|---|---|

*Above:* The first batch of Leyland Tiger TS7 coaches of June 1935 began a dynasty of United coach designs, even though their Burlingham bodies were to that coachbuilder's standard design for that year; they were also the first oil-engined coaches in the fleet. The livery was in the standard colours of the day, though with more cream and less red. The registration number of LTO9 should have read AHN 813 rather than the ANH 813 shown. *(United)*

*Below:* The next five TS7 coaches, LTO11-5, were also bodied by Burlingham, and had the new-style coach fleetname. LTO11 (BHN261) was dressed as a travelling advertising bureau for United's tours and holidays programme. Potential customers were invited to "inspect this United luxury coach, one of the recent additions to the United fleet". *(United)*

office until 1941, and who had been Chief Engineer of Hants & Dorset Motor Services Ltd since 1931. That concern then had a predominantly Leyland fleet, favouring Brush and Beadle as bodybuilders.

### The BJO in volume

When first considering the following year's requirements for new single-deckers in July 1935,

the Board had only very brief experience of the initial batches of five oil-engined Bristol and Leyland buses and at that stage it was resolved to purchase 80 single-deckers of unspecified type, registrations BHN 201-80 being booked accordingly. Five of the allocation were used for the urgently-needed coaches LTO11-5 as already described. In the event, the decision went mainly to the JO5G and thus United began the large-scale use of Bristol chassis with Gardner five-cylinder engines as its single-deck standard, a choice that was to continue not only to the end of front-engined models but almost to the end of the era of standardisation on mid-engined types in 1962. The

five JO5G buses of 1935 were followed by 60 more in 1936 and the same number in 1937, all having rear-entrance bodywork of basically similar design, giving the complete class of 125 buses a unity, as well as a level of familiarity across most of United's territory, reminiscent of the big deliveries of ADC models and then the Bristol B fleet of 1929.

The 1936 buses, BJO6-65, delivered between early March and the end of May, took the registrations BHN 201-60, the usual tidy matching of fleet and registration numbers having been lost. The five-speed overdrive gearbox was standard by then and Bristol's early design included helical gears for both third and fifth gears, giving very quiet operation, although the benefit of this was largely lost because of the level of engine noise. The earlier JO5G models did have rubber engine mountings to moderate internal noise and vibration. They were fairly effective at running speed but had the unfortunate side-effect of magnifying the vibration at idling speeds, setting up irritating rattles in such items as half-drop windows.

The Eastern Counties bodywork was again of 36-seat rear-entrance layout but there were detail changes to the appearance. Perhaps most noticeable was the adoption of outswept skirt

*Above:* On 1st February 1935 the parcels business of Trutime Deliveries, of Newcastle, was taken over. One of the vans transferred to United ownership was this Morris-Commercial Courier, TY 8964. It was at first given the fleet number IL97, but later in 1935 was renumbered PV44, then PM44 and finally, from 13th March 1943, it became ED7 in the Engineer's Department. It was photographed at Grange Road, Darlington, on 13th June 1954, apparently in the course of a repaint, though it was sold four months later. Never common, the type was very rare by then. *(David Burnicle)*

*Below:* The 60 Bristol JO5Gs of 1936, with their Eastern Counties rear-entrance 36-seat bodies looked like this when new. BJO11 (BHN 206) was on service 22 from Alston to Carlisle. The photograph is believed to have been taken at the Alston terminus of the service. The illuminated fleetname panel on the cab front can be clearly seen. *(C F Klapper)*

*Above:* This wonderful picture, taken in Carlisle bus station, illustrates one of the 1936 Leyland Tiger TS7 service buses with roof-mounted luggage carriers, LTO16 (BHN 266) *(second from the left)*, as well as two Bristol Bs, including B45 (VF 5145), and one of the Lions *(far right)* that were rebodied by Northern Counties in August 1934. TY 4671 was a PLSC1 ex-County Motor Services, of Stakeford, first numbered AL218 by United. It was subsequently renumbered twice: to LL11 in 1935, and in 1937 to LL1. Note the style of uniform then in use and the provision of new destination boxes on the B types *(C F Klapper)*

*Below:* The first of the 1936 "high" lowbridge Bristol GO5Gs with ECW bodies was BDO11 (CHN 101), seen here after renumbering to BOH1 as an acknowledgement of the overall height. The redoubtable Charlie Bullock, a Scarborough depot stalwart for many years, and happily still with us as these words are written in 2001, was in charge. *(Charlie Bullock)*

panels, a feature by then coming into favour on coach bodywork. The foremost side windows at the front of the passenger saloon were now of shaped outline and, on the nearside, the cream-painted roof panelling was swept downwards, emphasising this feature. The idea of extending the panelling forward to hide the gap behind the front nearside mudguard was developed further, there now being a hinged panel at that point so as to allow the outline of the panel to continue the curve of the canopy valance more strongly. The nearside sidelamp was attached at its tip, the whole being designed to swing out of the way to give access to the engine when needed.

Another feature to be characteristic of United vehicles for the rest of the 1930s also made its appearance on this BHN-registered batch, this being the illuminated name sign incorporated in the cab front panel. With plenty of independent operators still to be found in United's territory, quite apart from situations where municipal or other company buses shared parts of the same routes, it was an imaginative move, and in the dark its shape, size and position allowed identification of an oncoming bus as "a United" some time before the destination blind could be read.

Almost identical bodywork was built for fifteen more Leyland Tiger TS7 oil-engined chassis, LTO16-30, with, in this case, partially matching registration numbers BHN 266-80. A clue to their intended purpose may have been given by the

provision of a built-in roof-mounted luggage carrier, not fitted on the BJO-class vehicles and, incidentally, a feature that was subsequently removed from the BH-class buses. Although the JO5G had become the main type, United continued to include orders for a significant minority of Tiger buses used largely in the Northumberland area, which included Carlisle. From the passengers' viewpoint, they were well suited to longer routes, especially over fairly hilly terrain, although doubtless inferior to the JO5G in fuel economy.

Additions to the double-deck fleet were very modest during the later 1930s. A batch of six GO5G models originally numbered BDO11-6 (CHN 101-6), delivered in October 1936, completed United's total of sixteen of the type. By then, the Lowestoft Coach Factory had been transferred to Eastern Coach Works Ltd, a newly created subsidiary of ECOC formed on 1st July, 1936. These buses had 53-seat bodies to a rather stylised design peculiar to United, with sunken side-gangway lowbridge layout but of slightly greater overall height than usual for such a design, although less than a highbridge bus - the author recalls perhaps an extra 4 or 5ins of internal headroom over the upper-deck seats compared to usual lowbrige types. No record of the exact height has been found but it is estimated as about 13ft 9ins, and by no means the 14ft 3ins that has been suggested, which would have made them as tall as a London STL or RT. It seems possible that 14ft 3ins was the minimum bridge headroom under which they were allowed to run. At first all were in the Northumberland area, though BDO11

was transferred to Scarborough by March 1937. There was some unease about their height - it is known that a bridge near Saltburn was tight even for the BDO1-10 batch - and circa mid-1939 BDO11-6 were reclassified, becoming BOH1-6, evidently to reduce the risk of them being used on an unsuitable route.

Completing the 1936 deliveries of new vehicles, and authorised at the same Board meeting, were a further nine Leyland Tiger TS7 coaches, LTO32-40 (taking registrations CHN 107-15, following on from the double-deckers) dating from December; the number LTO31 was issued to an acquired vehicle, as mentioned later. They had 30-seat rear-entrance bodies of almost identical design to the 1935 Burlingham batch, but built by Brush. This concern had not hitherto been a supplier to United, having been more associated with companies in or managed by the BET group. Although it developed its own styles, a major part of its output was built to operator specification and the reproduction of existing designs was something of a speciality, apt to be publicised quite shamelessly even when based on another maker's standard. It seems possible that Percy Pelling, the new Chief Engineer may have influenced the choice of bodybuilder - Brush had copied Hants & Dorset's style of coach body for TS7 chassis, hitherto built by Beadle, for a 1935 Show vehicle, shortly before he left to join United.

The only significant departure from the Burlingham outline on the CHN-registered coaches was the addition of the illuminated name sign, basically as introduced on that year's buses but

The Brush-bodied Tyne-Tees-Thames coaches of 1936 on Leyland Tiger TS7 chassis were a shameless copy of the 1935 Burlingham design, although given a distinctive look by the high-mounted name sign over the destination boxes. They served the Company long and well. This is a postwar view of LTO32 (CHN 107) taken, it is thought, at Gallowgate, Newcastle. This was a posed view for United's publicity, and the passengers were a group of press-ganged office staff. *(United)*

positioned centrally above the two-panel destination display, the front dome of the roof being reshaped to suit. This simple change had quite a striking effect on the frontal appearance and the feature was to be repeated on further batches of London-service coaches, becoming characteristic of both United and Orange vehicles well into the postwar years.

At first it had been intended that three of these coaches, LTO36-8, were to be owned by Orange Bros Ltd, but the arrangements for this were cancelled even though they were supplied in the Orange Bros brown livery and with Orange fleetname, the others being in the United cream and red style of the time. It is noteworthy that the Minute authorising these CHN-registered batches, and also 60 Bristol single-deckers to be described later, recorded that the bodies were to be of types approved by the Chairman, thus making clear J F Heaton's direct involvement in such matters.

### Rebuilds for practical and visual effect

Development of existing vehicles to improve efficiency or passenger appeal was also engaging the attention of United's engineers. Perhaps the most important development, forming a key step in the rapid swing from standardising on petrol engines to wider adoption of diesel power, was the conversion of existing LD-class Leyland Titan TD1 buses from petrol, using Gardner 5LW engines. The purchase of 25 such engines was authorised by the United Board on 25th February 1936 - in addition the 5LW unit in the ex-Ennis & Reed Daimler CF6, DO1, was removed, bringing the engine total to 26, all of which were fitted to TD1 buses, creating a new LDO class, separately numbered from the LD class from which they were drawn.

In the 1935 renumbering, the opportunity had been taken to issue the new numbers in the various classes broadly in date order and the way in which the converted vehicles were drawn, mainly in twos and threes, but again largely in correct order, from the LD class, suggests most were selected at the beginning of the exercise, perhaps on a depot allocation basis, although the actual order of conversion was doubtless related to availability and when buses were in the workshops for other reasons. The work began in March 1936, when four buses were converted, including LD2, one of the oldest pair of Titans in the fleet, PY 9416, ex-Redwing, together with three of the 1930 batch with VF 76xx registrations, becoming respectively LDO2, 13, 14 and 16. Six, including LD1 (PY 9417) which became LDO1, followed in April, with a similar total in May, the pace then slowing a little; the exercise ended in January 1937 with the conversion of LD46 to become numerically the final bus in this set of vehicles, LDO26. The ex-Ennis & Reed engine went into LD45 which thereby became LDO24 in June 1936, although it doubtless moved to other vehicles in the course of subsequent overhauls. At the end of the exercise, all of the ex-Redwing Titans and the two older of the three from Smith's Safeway

were among the conversions, the remainder being made up by VF 76xx and 85xx buses new to United.

Thus, exactly half the 52 Titan TD1s then in the fleet were converted with 5LW engines in this period. They were to run far longer in this form than as built and withdrawals did not begin until 1949. United, like other Tilling-managed companies, may not have been particularly quick off the mark in adopting the diesel engine, but once begun the policy was pursued with enthusiasm. The resulting vehicles no doubt gave very substantial fuel savings, and the performance was still reasonably lively, aided by the modest weight of that model, barely 6 tons even as converted. However, both passengers and passers-by were made acutely aware of the conversions by the staccato bark of the Gardner five-cylinder engine, simply bolted into the chassis in place of the original ultra-smooth six-cylinder petrol engine, even the exhaust taking on a new resonance. The investment probably paid off several times over, and what had always been good reliable if rather thirsty buses now became very efficient. With hindsight, it is perhaps surprising that the policy was not then pursued further, yet it may have been judged that further investment in what were doubtless then seen as quite old buses was not justified - some operators were beginning to withdraw early Titans and at that stage no-one could forsee that the TD1 fleet as a whole had over a dozen years ahead of it because of the war and its after-effects. In the event, further conversions were

VF 8503, one of the 1930 TD1s, originally numbered A60, and renumbered LD43 in 1935, was one of those which were fitted with Gardner 5LW engines, thus being renumbered again, as LDO23. It was allocated yet another fleet number, LGL17, in the 1951 renumbering. This is a postwar view taken at Grange Road Central Works, Darlington, which shows the rebuilt cab then standard. *(R C Davis)*

carried out in 1946/7, though using the Leyland 8.6-litre engine.

Other reconstruction was based on the quite different perspective of passenger appeal. In the 1930s there was intense rivalry for business between seaside resorts. Blackpool had created quite a stir with its new fleet of streamlined trams introduced in 1934 and quickly becoming part of that resort's sea-front scene. Clearly there was a wish that Scarborough should have something of an equivalent nature. Accordingly a new AS class of ten buses with fully fronted centre-entrance bodywork was created, the body contract being given to F W Plaxton & Sons Ltd, of Scarborough. In this case the body architecture had much in common with United's standard single-deckers of the day, save for the special features. In addition to those already mentioned, the cantrail panels were glazed and the section of the roof between them was arranged to fold open. There was even a hint of the Blackpool tram trolley tower base in the built-up structure carrying a destination box on each side and housing the folded sections of the roof when open. The then current coach livery of cream and red was applied, but with the service bus style of fleetname transfer rather than the scroll type introduced for true coaches some months previously.

The chassis selected to carry these quite glamorous bodies might have seemed rather an anti-climax, being ADC 425 models dating from 1928, suitably reconditioned, rescued from the AJ class by then in course of withdrawal. They were renumbered AS1-10, re-entering service in this form between March and July 1936 and, in those days, there weren't too many enthusiasts around to notice that the registration numbers VF 2705, 2719, etc., identified what they really were. The original radiators were retained but with a central dividing strip to hint at later AEC types. It was doubtless reasoned that ambling along the sea-front at rarely more than 12 to 15mph or so was well within their capabilities and indeed they carried on until the 1949 season. Alan Townsin recalls sampling the service, probably in the summer of 1947, and the only opportunity to judge normal performance was at the end of the route when the driver accelerated briefly to reach the turning point, and the engine was revealed as rather rough when thus exerted. By that date they may well have been the only buses still in revenue-earning service with the AEC 4-type four-cylinder side-valve petrol engine, basically a 1920 design first used in the LGOC's S-type buses.

Another development was the rebodying of a further four Daimler CF6 models with new bus bodies. This time the work was given to Lowestoft, and the four vehicles in question were in fact the first received by United after the changeover to ECW came into effect, being delivered from there on

The Plaxton bodies of 1936, mounted on 1928 ADC 425 chassis, became part of the fabric of Scarborough. Visits to the resort in the early postwar years remain in the memory - forged in the brain of a very small John Banks at the most impressionable age - and include the ADCs gliding almost silently (they were petrol-engined, of course) at little more than walking pace past the milling throngs around the cockle and whelk stalls at Sandside or at a dignified canter along Marine Drive and Royal Albert Drive. AS8 (VF 2778) features in an official photograph taken in the early postwar period. *(United)*

30th July 1936. The body design in this case was almost exactly as on the new JO5G buses, noticeably more stylish than the 1934/5 rebodyings within this class, though shortened to suit the short-wheelbase CF6 chassis and seating 33 - this latter was quite a rare seating capacity in the prewar period because steps in the road fund licence rates of those days made 32 much more common. The vehicles chosen included the one former National Coachways vehicle that had been running since take-over with a second-hand ex-Gilford body, GN 374, by then renumbered D38, though originally NX24.

The other three CF6 vehicles rebodied were three acquired with the business of Bolton Bros, of Embleton, in May 1936. The Bolton fleet, all dating from 1928-31, consisted of three Leyland Tigers, (two TS1s and a TS2 which became LT91-3), two Lion PLSCs (LL24/5), four Daimler CF6s (D44-7) and a W&G Du Cros, which was sold off unnumbered. The PLSC buses formed a rare instance of the reuse of fleet numbers, LL24/5 previously being carried by a pair of Lion LT1 buses from the Smith's Safeway fleet which had been renumbered LT4.1/2 when it was decided to split the PLSC and LT types of Lion into separate series. Three of the four CF6s had come from the large fleet of this model operated by the Lanarkshire Traction Company, many of which found new owners in north-east England, and it was these three, D45-7 (SC 6902, VD 75 and VD 409) that received the new ECW bodies. This completed the process of rebodying D-class CF6s as buses conforming to United's mid-1930s styles. A total of 22 such vehicles had been created. The ex-Gilford body removed from D38 as mentioned above was moved

on again, to D44 (VC 174) from the Bolton Bros fleet.

Also carried out in August 1936 was the rebodying by Beadle, as 33-seat rear-entrance buses, of three Leyland Tigers, LT51 and 52 (TY 8670/1), which were late examples of the TS1 model dating from 1931 taken over from the Allen fleet, and LT93 (CK 4337), a TS2 newly taken over from Bolton Bros, although new in 1930 to Scout of Preston - its old body, a coach, was by Spicer. Beadle was a major supplier of bodywork to TBAT companies based further south, including Hants & Dorset and thus well-known to Mr Pelling, but less familiar in the north. Of the three, only LT93 survived into the postwar period, the other two having been taken for military use.

By this time there had been some consolidation in the operation of the London services. The Phillipson's licence had been revoked by the Metropolitan Traffic Commissioner in January 1936 on something of a technicality concerning interavailability of tickets, and the fleet, by then down to five Regals, was consequently divided between United (AR2 and 5) and Orange (AR1, 3 and 4).

The last remaining competitor for the Newcastle-London traffic, Charlton's Blue Safety Coaches Ltd, of Hebburn-on-Tyne, was taken over in March, with eight vehicles; the agreement to sell had been negotiated as long before as August 1935. Charlton's, based in Northern General Transport territory, also had a local bus service but that went with the remainder of the business to Northern in July 1937 together with 26 vehicles.

In mid 1935 Charlton's had received two new coaches, APT 784 and 785, oil-engined Leyland

The vehicle on the right of this quiet, damp scene in Bishop Auckland Market Place, very soon after the end of the Second World War, is ex-Bolton Bros D45 (SC 6902). The body was by Eastern Coach Works, fitted in 1936. D36 (UP 4216), ex-Glenton Friars in 1932, had also been rebodied in 1934 to a plainer style by Northern Counties. *(R C Davis)*

*Top row:* One of the rarest vehicles in the United fleet must have been SM1, a 1932 Morris-Commercial Dictator, with Caffyns body, registered UP 6312. The two pictures show it as Charlton's Blue Safety Coaches fleet No. 31 in London working on Charlton's express service between the Capital and Newcastle. *(J F Higham)*

*Bottom row:* The two impressive Leyland coach-bodied Tiger TS4s delivered to Charlton's in 1932 and 1933 were Nos 35/6 (UP 7220/895) They became LT89/90 in the United fleet. *(Senior Transport Archive courtesy BCVM)*

Tiger TS7 models with 32-seat bodies built by Wycombe, among the last produced by the firm which had been the bodybuilding arm of the Gilford concern. Of these, APT 784 became United LTO31, though its chassis was not to have a long career, as explained later, while APT 785 was retained by Charlton's, later passing to Northern. There were two Tiger TS4s with Leyland bodies built to a rare 30-seat full-coach design in 1932 and 1933, UP 7220 and UP 7895, which became LT89 and 90. Four Tiger TS2 models of 1930 with Leyland bus bodies, UP 3986-9, became LT85-8. The most unusual of the eight was a 1931 Morris-Commercial Dictator, UP 6312, this being a full-sized forward-control six-cylinder model briefly in production in the early 1930s; it had bodywork by Caffyns Ltd of Eastbourne, later better known as a major car dealer, to a 30-seat coach design known as the "Coastguard", and became SM1 in the United fleet. The body was rebuilt incorporating a standard United destination box and extended roof luggage carrier, the vehicle remaining in this form until sold in September 1946 *(see p.98)*.

With the acquisition of the Charlton's business, the advantage to United of having a large number of licences for the London services was greatly reduced, and so Majestic ceased to trade on 30th September 1936. Majestic's current fleet, AEC Regals AR6-10 and the Daimler CF6 service buses with United fleetnames, D21-3, were transferred into United ownership; the Leyland Tiger LTO6 had already been transferred in June. The Majestic and Phillipson's companies, the latter already dormant,

were both put into liquidation, and from this time onwards only Orange Brothers Ltd continued in being alongside United on the London services.

A series of acquisitions of small businesses occurred in 1936, bringing interesting additions to the fleet. In May, two Leyland Cub KP3 buses came from E Pashley, of Billy Row, becoming LC2 and 3 and lasting to 1946; a Bedford WTL from John Walker, of Crook, became SB5, while Chas Harman, of Sunniside, contributed a Leyland Lion LT7, the only example in the fleet, which became LT4.21, both these latter dating from 1935 and lasting until 1950. Also ex-Harman was ST7, a 1930 Thornycroft A6 24-seater, but that was withdrawn the same year. A Reo Gold Crown from Harman and a Ford BB from Walker were sold in September 1936 without being numbered in the fleet. There seemed to be some confusion in regard to the fleet number prefix system as two small Bean buses acquired from T W Smith of Hesleden in October 1936, RP 8506 and UP 4194, were given the numbers SB6 and SB7 respectively though sold within weeks; the numbers were used again for Bedfords.

Bristol was the sole supplier of new buses in 1937, with the final 60 JO5G buses, BJO66-125 (CHN 266-325) delivered between mid-March and mid-June *(see p.142)*. They were outwardly almost identical to the previous batch, though with ECW rather than ECOC bodies, a minor change being a reduction in seating capacity to 35, the row of three seats by the rear entrance doorway proving to give too little room for easy passenger movement. By

Bedford WTL with Robson, of Consett, 24-seat body SB5 (APT 980), new in 1935, came from John Walker, of Crook, in 1936. It was photographed in Durham on 24th July 1948. It lasted until 1950. *(C F Klapper)*

then, the early attempt at flexible engine mounting had been abandoned and although steadier idling resulted, the internal noise level when on the move for passengers seated near the front was enough to make conversation difficult. Yet in terms of serviceability, United's JO5G buses had a good record, only two being withdrawn (because of fire or accident) before 1951 and some of the class lasting until 1955. As in other Tilling fleets, a rehabilitation programme on this generation of Bristol buses was carried out in the immediate postwar period, covering both chassis and bodywork, which helped to extend their lives.

### An AEC episode

Despite the emphasis on Bristol and, to a lesser degree, Leyland as suppliers of new buses in the later 1930s, there was a rather surprising undercurrent of AEC involvement in developments relating to United's fleet around that time. AEC had been one of the leading British pioneers in the development of diesel engines for road vehicles, beginning in 1930, but had favoured indirect injection, which gave good power output and smooth running but was inferior to the direct injection of fuel into the engine's cylinders in regard to fuel economy and thus could not match Leyland and, especially, Gardner in this respect. In 1934, the six-cylinder engine usually known as the 7.7 litre (even though its true swept volume was 7.58 litres) had been put into production, at first in A171 indirect-injection form and becoming standard for most new AEC chassis from early 1935.

A direct-injection version of the 7.7-litre type was put into limited production as type A173 in 1936, the engine bearing the first production number, A173-1, going into an existing demonstrator AEC Regal bus registered AML 774. AEC was keen to interest companies under Tilling management and this bus is known to have visited United before

being sold to County Motor Services of Stakeford in February 1937; it was sold on to OK Motor Services Ltd later the same month, thereby missing being acquired by United later in the year when the last part of the County business was taken over, as described later.

The next step was the fitting of quite an early A173 engine to one of the Orange Bros AEC Regals, AR17 (TY 9654) on 4th December 1936, the vehicle being renumbered ARO1. This 1932 vehicle had received a new Burlingham rear-entrance coach body to the same pattern as the 1935 Tiger TS7 coaches in June 1935. It continued on the London service and indeed briefly became ostensibly the most modern coach in the Orange fleet. Soon afterwards, AR5 (AGH 405), a 1933 Regal coach ex-Phillipson, also received an A173 engine, becoming ARO2 in February 1937 though in that case retaining its original Duple body, still quite modern-looking.

Although older AEC Regal coaches had continued to be mildly updated, for example by adding shaped display panels over the side windows, it was decided to rebody seven AEC Regals dating from 1930/1, formerly coaches, as buses in much the same way as had been done with Daimler CF6 models. This had been agreed at the same United Board meeting in September 1936 as that confirming the last four rebodyings of CF6s and that of the three Leyland Tigers, as already mentioned - the latter two sets of vehicles had, in fact, just been delivered.

The rebodied Regals did not appear in service in their new form until July 1937, evidently because it was also decided to fit them with new AEC oil engines, these again being early direct-injection 7.7-litre units of the A173 type, the vehicles becoming ARO3-9. The new ECW bodies were to the latest 35-seat specification and painted in standard bus livery with United fleetnames. The vehicles in question were, in order, VY 2552, 2784, 2551 and 2785, previously AR1-4 and acquired with the Phillipsons business, and TY 7079, 7082 and 7080, previously AR11-3 and of the Orange fleet. Both AEC and United records show these latter three vehicles as having received their new oil engines in mid to late May but the old bodies were sold off during May and June - indeed it is known that the old body from TY 7080 was on another chassis by 27th June, as will be explained later. This confirms that the vehicles did not re-enter service until both the re-engining and rebodying processes were completed. Only one of these vehicles was at this stage owned by United - this being ARO4 (VY 2784) - the remainder all being owned by Orange Bros Ltd, the other three ex-Phillipsons vehicles having been transferred to Orange in January 1936 as already mentioned. Official documents show this Orange Bros ownership, which seems to have been

*Above:* United's only AEC Regent, AOH1 (AML 664), a Park Royal-bodied fluid-transmission former demonstrator new in 1933, came with the final part of the County Motor Services, of Stakeford, acquisition in August 1937. It was photographed in Newcastle circa 1947, soon after a major body overhaul. *(R A Mills)*

*Below:* Brush-bodied AEC Regal ARO14 (DHN 254) with Orange brown livery and fleetname , and United's Tyne-Tees-Thames slogan above the windows. This was the last of the batch of five new in 1937, and the only one thus turned out. It was owned by United and not, as might have been thought, by Orange Bros. *(G H F Atkins Collection)*

Another rebuild on an ex-County bus was the changing of the special Leyland body on the former TD1 front-entrance demonstrator, TF 5988 *(see p.99)*, acquired in 1934, to rear-entrance layout. It is thought this was done in 1935, the bus having become LD49 in the renumbering that year. Though the design had been derived from the standard Leyland piano-front style, the pillar spacing was non-standard - such reconstruction would have been well within the capabilities of the body shops at Darlington. Even so, the body structure evidently lacked the rigidity of the standard version due to the additional doorway and special emergency exit openings and a second-hand standard Leyland body was purchased from Eastern Coach Works in June 1939 (thought to have come from Eastern Counties, then rebodying many of its TD1 buses) and fitted to this chassis, the bus then becoming virtually standard.

In line with earlier County tradition, the other three buses taken over in 1937 were all ex-demonstrators. There were two Daimlers with fluid flywheel transmission, initially given the fleet numbers DDO1/2, it probably not being realised at first that they were highbridge. The first, given the fleet number DOH1 by about 1938, had been displayed at the 1931 Commercial Motor Show with Brush body in West Hartlepool Corporation livery but was registered in 1932 by Daimler as KV 1396 for demonstration duty, being at one stage in Westcliff livery. It was originally of type CH6, having a sleeve-valve petrol engine, but was fitted with a Gardner 5LW engine to become a prototype for the COG5 and demonstrated to Birmingham Corporation, leading that undertaking to standardise on the type, before being sold to County. KV 1396 resembled the Stockton Daimler shown on page 106.

The second Daimler was also an ex-demonstrator but was registered JR 1891, evidently on sale to County in May 1934, at which date it appears in Daimler sales records as a CP6. It had a Park Royal body, and when acquired by United is said to have received - or was possibly in the process of being fitted with - a Leyland oil engine, allegedly becoming of type COL6. There is some evidence that this may have been removed or the conversion not completed, and the vehicle run with petrol engine, the fleet number DD2 being quoted for it in October 1937. United records indicate that it was converted to oil as DDO2 in 1940, though the fleet number was quoted as DOH2 by 1942. The make of engine used was not stated but at that stage it might well have been a Gardner 5LW.

Also taken over from County was an AEC Regent, at first quoted as ADO1 but becoming AOH1 by 1938, United's only example of the model, registered AML 664 in 1933 and also with Park Royal body. It also had fluid flywheel transmission and had received an early example of the 7.7-litre oil engine, an indirect-injection A171, in November 1934 in place of the original 8.8-litre unit it had had when new. Almost certainly the A171 engine was converted to direct-injection, thus becoming similar to the A173 engines in the ARO-class single-deckers.

By 1938 and until post-war, AOH1 and DOH1 were regular performers on the Whitley Bay-Newcastle service 17. In 1947 the two Daimlers - DOH2 having been moved to Richmond quite soon after take-over - were withdrawn, but at about the end of the war the body of AOH1 was overhauled, and it soldiered on until 1951.

Other businesses taken over in 1937 were small - though a consortium of five in the Coundon area of County Durham taken over in July trading jointly as Service Cars had nine vehicles altogether - and few vehicles were added to United's fleet more than briefly. Notable among the exceptions was a 1929 Bristol B with London Lorries coach body acquired from F G Cowey, one of this group. It began life as a demonstrator, registered HW 3864, but was soon sold to the Merseyside Touring Co Ltd, passing to Ribble Motor Services Ltd before sale to Cowey. It became B131 in the United fleet, remaining in service until 1949, quite soon receiving a United bus body of the standard type for the class, in place of the original, sold off in June 1938. The building of two spare bodies of this type had been authorised in August 1929, presumably to create an overhaul 'float', as also done for some earlier classes, but it seems that lengthening the chassis would have been needed in this case. Other noteworthy vehicles from the Service Cars members included a Reo Gold Crown, UP 4375, ex-Mrs M Allan, which briefly created a new class as SR1, though it was sold the following October. Much longer-lived were two Leyland Lion LT1s with Brush 30-seat bus bodies, originally in the Yorkshire (Woollen District) fleet, HD 3764 and 3769, which came from H Hutchinson and T W Teasdale respectively, becoming LT4.22/3, both surviving until 1950. Another long-term survivor from that consortium was AUP 75, a 1936 Thornycroft Handy with Grose 20-seat coach body from Ellen Wheatley, which became ST9 and ran until 1950 as one of the "Robinson's" white coaches operated from Scarborough.

It seems logical at this point to mention the conversion of the BH-class Bristol H single-deckers of 1933/4 to diesel, using Gardner 5LW engines, carried out between October 1937 and June 1938. In that case the general principle followed was that buses would switch the prefix code while retaining their original numbers, and with most of them that was done.

However BH19 and 20 were Scarborough Town cars and were excluded, evidently because the Corporation of that town had agreed to pay for the depreciation of buses in the town fleet as part of the tram replacement deal and this had already caused disagreements - another factor might have been council opposition to the noisier buses. The two 5LW engines intended for them were fitted in BJ6 and 7 instead, these being renumbered BJO126 and 127 accordingly in December 1937. To avoid a gap in the BHO class, the numbers BHO19 and 20 were taken by the former BH34 and 35, although belatedly BH19 and 20 were, after all, converted in 1942/3, becoming BHO34 and 35, and the class thus became entirely oil-engined, although for some unknown reason, BHO15 and 21 reverted to petrol as BH15 and 21 in 1947. United accounts for the month ending 30th September 1938 show that engines from six of the BH buses were dismantled and used for spares, this also applying also to various Leyland engines, with specific references to instances of engines being moved from one bus to another in terms suggesting that engine transfers at overhaul may not have been normal practice at that date.

There was also a conversion programme for the highbridge Leyland Titan TD2 buses to oil engines between December 1937 and March 1938, this covering the two earlier ex-County acquisitions as well as the eight with Eastern Counties bodies dating from 1933. This time the engine chosen was the Leyland 8.6-litre unit and as the 1933 buses had the later-type "silent-third" gearbox introduced that year, as converted they sounded just like contemporary oil-engined Titans. They were renumbered from LDH54-63 to LHO1-10. There was thus an inconsistency with the use of AOH, BOH and DOH to signify highbridge (or simply "high") oil-engined buses of other makes, but it may have been thought preferable to be consistent with LDO.

New fleet additions for 1938 were modest in number, but not lacking in interest. There were 24 Leyland Tigers, based on the TS8 model chassis with minor design revisions by then current. Nine were coaches, numbered LTO41-9 (DHN 441-9), with what were described as "Brush special coach bodies" to a new 30-seat design. This retained the rear entrance and had a front-end and much of the side mouldings similar to the CHN series, but with higher-built bodywork having a stepped waistrail, allowing a fairly spacious boot to replace the roof-mounted luggage carrier of previous designs. They were designed for the London services, being painted in a distinctive new olive green and cream livery to remain familiar on such duty for over 30 years. Two of the batch, LTO43/4, carried Orange fleetnames despite being United property. The DHN-registered coaches were to prove highly successful, remaining a familiar sight on that route, even if latterly duplicating more modern types, until shortly before their withdrawal in 1956, a remarkably long career on such duty.

They replaced nine Orange Bros Maudslays - thus there was a considerable, but not total, shift in the balance between the United and Orange components of the London services. Over the next year or two the earlier vehicles used on these services were repainted into the new livery, so it is likely that by the time the Orange operation ceased in 1941, as described later, the traditional Orange livery had gone, and a more unified appearance was presented to the public. By 1938, six United coaches carried the Orange name (LTO36-8/43/44 and ARO34, formerly ARO14). These balanced the six Orange Bros-owned vehicles rebodied as service buses in United livery (by then numbered ARO21-3/5-7), suggesting that book-keeping was an important consideration. In addition, six older coaches with Orange fleetnames remained (now numbered AR13-6, ARO28 and LTO15).

The nearest to routine additions that year were the balance of fifteen Leyland Tiger TS8s but with 35-seat ECW rear-entrance bus bodies, looking very like the 1936 Eastern Counties-bodied TS7 batch, but without the luggage carriers. They were numbered LTO50-64 (DHN 450-64) and, in May and June, entered service in the Northumberland area, as usual for LTO buses.

### Arrival of the Bristol L5G

Bristol had introduced two new models at the 1937 Commercial Motor Show, the K double-decker and L single-decker, both with the Gardner 5LW engine as standard and signified by '5G' as previously, though the 'O' for oil engine was now omitted. The chassis had been quite extensively redesigned yet most of the characteristic Bristol features remained. The most obvious mechanical difference was that the gearbox was now directly attached behind the engine instead of mounted mid-chassis as on the G, H and J.

There was a slightly more solid appearance, with a new radiator, though this was still taller than average, as with the J; internally, the sound effects were much the same, the tones of the new gearbox, with overdrive standard for L models, barely detectable under the usual 5LW staccato bark. United took only 20 of the L type for its first delivery and these had ECW rear-entrance 35-seat bodies almost identical to those on the final CHN-registered batch of JO5G buses. They were numbered BLO1-20 (DHN 465-484), and were delivered in March-April 1938, though all entered service on 1st May, allocated to garages in the south of the company's area. These vehicles, and later Bristols, were supplied without rings on the front wheels, although United generally did not retain such embellishments in any case.

Another new vehicle that year was more in the nature of a rebuild. The ex-Charlton's Leyland Tiger TS7 coach, LTO31 (APT 784), had been involved in an accident, suffering severe front-end damage to the chassis, recorded as being dismantled in February 1938. The Wycombe body proved to be repairable and was transferred to a new Tiger TS8 chassis, which was given the registration number DHN 810; the resulting ensemble retained the fleet number LTO31, re-entering service in this form in June 1938. This vehicle was unique among United's Leyland Tigers in having an overdrive gearbox, a fact confirmed by a driver who drove it in post-war years on the Newcastle-Scarborough service; the coach survived until 1954. It seems possible that the gearbox might have been transferred from APT 784, perhaps together with other undamaged units, assembled into a new TS8-type frame. For several years in this period Leyland offered what was described as a fifth speed

*Above:* The nine 1938 Leyland Tiger TS8 coaches, LTO41-9 (DHN 441-9), marked a major step in the evolution of the distinctive United coach for the Tyne-Tees-Thames services, that phrase itself given fresh prominence by the illuminated panels above the side windows. The bodies were built by Brush to a unique design, with sufficient continuity in appearance from the 1935-7 coaches to give the fleet a sense of unity, yet with fresh improvements and an attractive new olive green and cream livery, the latter remaining associated with these services until 1972. They were higher-built, allowing the 30 comfortable seats to be ramped slightly to improve comfort over the rear wheel-arches. The first of the batch is seen in Darlington when brand new - its cream-painted upper waist gave way to green on the rest of the batch. *(United)*

*Below:* LTO47 (DHN 447) was not very old in this early 1939 picture and was being used as an advertising vehicle for United's extended coach tours for the 1939 season. It was photographed at South Park, Darlington. The reduced size of fleetname transfer, introduced in 1939, is now carried. Note the almost completely blanked-off radiator - United provided these neat aluminium plates for its oil-engined vehicles and this was a typical "winter" version. *(Senior Transport Archive)*

135

*Above:* A line of eight Tyne-Tees-Thames Leyland Tigers assembled for the photographer on the occasion of the reintroduction, in 1946, of the London services. The 2nd, 4th, 7th and 8th are DHN-registered examples dating from 1938, recognisable by the absence of a forward entrance on their Brush bodywork; the others, thus equipped, were 1939 Harrington-bodied examples. Nine of the coaches, including all the 1939 batch, had been transferred to the Orange Bros company for the reopened service; the Orange fleetname shown here is thus now a true indication of ownership. *(United)*

*Below:* The renumbering to more closely identify the type of work for which these coaches were intended had brought them into a new LOC class in 1941. LOC6 (DHN446) was parked in the exit from Samuelson's coach garage, opposite Victoria Coach Station, in the late 1940s. The "United" plate at the top of the radiator reveals the vehicle's previous ownership.  By then these coaches were building up big mileages, but were still well cared-for and very smart.*(C F Klapper)*

attachment giving a ratio of 0.77 to 1, fitted at the rear of the gearbox but controlled by the main gear lever and thus directly equivalent to the Bristol overspeed fifth ratio, but it was extremely rare. In retrospect, it seems rather surprising that United, so familiar with the Bristol version, did not specify it at least for the London-service coaches. The 8.6-litre Leyland oil engine ran particularly smoothly towards the top end of its speed range and in this sense provision of an overdrive ratio might have been thought unnecessary, but fuel savings could have repaid its cost.

Agreement that United should take over the Branch End group of services of Newcastle Corporation led to the transfer in April 1938 to United of ten Daimler single-deckers purchased in 1935 for the routes. At the time of their construction Armstrong-Saurer commercial vehicles were being built in Newcastle and Saurer four-cylinder oil engines were specified for these buses, designated as type COS4. The 34-seat bodies of the first five were by Metro-Cammell and

the others, to very similar style, were by Northern Coachbuilders; the batch of ten became United's DSO1-10 (registered BTN 104-13).

In October 1938, the businesses of five small operators trading as Deerness Motor Services, plus two others based in the same Esh Winning area, were taken over, most vehicles acquired soon being sold off. However, there were a few exceptions, one being CUP 491, from Oliver Bros, an almost new Bedford WTB with Duple 26-seat bus body, which became SB15 and was kept in service until 1949 and in 1950 converted as a United service vehicle, fleet number ED1 *(see p.148)*. Another, slightly older, Bedford from this operator became a service vehicle in 1939. Kelly & Briggs contributed a further ex-Lanarkshire Daimler CP6, VD 1538, which in June 1939 joined the Bell's Services collection of the type as its No. 26, replacing the CF6, VD 400, which previously had this fleet number but which reverted to being United D53.

Earlier in 1939, the crisis atmosphere relating to prospects of war that had built up in 1938 had largely subsided in regard to most aspects of life and normal developments continued. The Bristol K5G made its first appearance in the fleet with a modest batch of five examples with basically standard ECW lowbridge bodywork, to the neat design as already built for various other Tilling-managed fleets since the autumn of 1937, often in greater numbers. They are recorded as having 54-seat capacity, an unusual total for a lowbridge bus; official ECW photographs show 28 seats in the lower saloon and 26 upstairs. They had the standard front destination box and a small one on the nearside above the platform, though this was later removed. They continued the BDO series of fleet numbers begun by the GO5Gs, being given the numbers BDO17-21 (EHN 617-21) and were

A grim, dank north-eastern day as LOC1 (DHN441) heads into Newcastle across the Tyne. A long run from London lies behind it in an era when motorways - and even dual-carriageways to some extent - were still some way in the future. The aura peculiar to the Tyne-Tees-Thames vehicles working these services was marked: there was "a certain something"; hard to put into words, but it existed, and it lasted into the 1960s and the 43-seat Bristol RELH6Gs on the same runs. The Newcastle tram was still in wartime grey and the Northern bus was another TS8 Tiger, albeit very different from the United vehicle. *(Alan Townsin Collection)*

The 1938 Tiger TS8 service buses had identical bodies from Eastern Coach Works to those on the first Bristol L5Gs, which appeared in the fleet at the sme time. These views are of DHN 453, originally LTO53, by then renumbered as LL33, though looking much as it had when new, save for the quick-action radiator filler-cap by then standard across Tilling fleets, and the former LTO64, running as LL37 (DHN 464), at Marlborough Crescent in 1954. In the latter case the original moulded waistline had vanished in the course of a body overhaul. The buses were standing in more or less the same spot and were working the 34 service from Newcastle to Carlisle, served by similar buses since 1936 - see page 123. *(S N J White; David Burnicle)*

The only photograph known to the authors of the mysterious LTO31 in any of its incarnations is this view taken at Prudhoe Place, Newcastle, on 26th June 1954. By then the 1938 replacement chassis, DHN810, had been renumbered LL31. It had lost the Wycombe body which it had inherited from the ex-Charlton's chassis registered APT 784, in favour of an Eastern Counties 36-seat service bus body with roof-mounted luggage carrier. As on most prewar bodies by that date, the vulnerable individual glass louvres over the side windows had given way to a continuous metal louvre. The body can only have come from one of the 1936 batch of Leyland Tiger buses registered BHN 266-80, which had the only bodies of this exact description to have been bought by United and which were rebodied in 1949. The photographer was only just in time, for this fascinating vehicle was withdrawn later in 1954 and sold - in the September - to a dealer. *(David Burnicle)*

purchased in January-March 1939; they are thought to have been allocated to Darlington and Bishop Auckland initially.

As far as the single-deck fleet was concerned, the big news was the appearance of a new standard style of bus body. That year's batch of Bristol L5G models amounted to some 70 vehicles, BLO21- 90 (EHN 521-90), and for them, a fresh body style had been evolved, doubtless as a joint exercise between United and ECW; evidence of the latter's design work could be seen in the characteristic outlines common to its products for various other operators even though the basic design and such items as the fairly narrow pillar spacing were peculiar to United.

The most obvious change was a reversion to front entrance layout but there was also a slightly higher build with a mildly ramped seating layout, making it possible to arrange all 35 seats to face forwards. The higher waist lined up neatly with the L-type's high bonnet line and well-executed detail

features included a particularly neat treatment of the front destination box, which was set in a panel upswept from the cantrail, and an attractively shaped single rear window. The overall effect was of an elegant and neatly-finished design - the writer retains a vivid recollection of the sense of a marked improvement in appearance on seeing one of these buses when newly delivered.

As for their riding qualities, it has to be said that they did not live up to the impression created by the appearance. Although the interiors were well finished, the noise level continued to be noticeably higher than in AEC, Daimler or Leyland models of the time. Even for a passenger of medium height, sitting in the seat just behind the wheelarch became barely tolerable as one's legs were forced into an awkward angle and taller people found the seat spacing too tight, though part of the problem was the shaping of the back of the seat, convex where it needed to be concave. Even so, they were

The Saurer- (later AEC six-cylinder petrol-) engined Daimlers, which came from Newcastle Corporation in 1938 along with the Branch End group of services, were seldom seen anywhere else in United's territory, although DA2/5-7 were at Northallerton for a while during the war, and DA2 (special reserve) and DA5 had previously been briefly at Darlington depot. DA6 (BTN109) *(above)* was the first of the Northern Coachbuilders batch, and DA5 (BTN 108) *(left)* was the last of those with Metro-Cammell bodies. It was at Marlborough Crescent, Newcastle, on 4th August 1948, as was DA6 on an unknown date. *(Roy Marshall Collection; Peter Robson)*

solid, dependable and economical buses, virtues soon to become even more important. None of this batch was withdrawn until 1955 and some lasted until 1959.

Another detail change introduced on the EHN-registered buses, both K5G and L5G, was a reduction in the size of the fleetname to about 4ft 6ins compared to the previous 6ft. A similar reduction applied to the scroll-type coach version, also from 1939 deliveries, reducing from about 4ft to 3ft, and in the case of Orange, reverting to the 1934 size.

Just before the last of the 1939 L5Gs arrived, delivery began of a Leyland equivalent. In one sense this was a repeat of United's practice in most years since 1935 in that ECW built to a basically similar body outline on Tiger TS8 chassis, complete with bus-style destination display to the latest standard. However, this time the 20 vehicles, numbered LTO65-84 (EHN 965-84), dating from May-June 1939, were finished as coaches, with more luxurious seats for 32 passengers, the awkward position directly over the wheel-arch being omitted by using single seats at that location. They were in the olive green and cream livery, with what had become the United standard style of coach side mouldings. Again, a sharply-focussed personal recollection comes back of the first sight of a pair when brand new, looking very handsome. Tour or hire work was the intended function of at least some of them, for ten were fitted with sliding roofs. They were still regarded as sufficiently appealing for the whole class to be sent for body rebuild (eight were despatched to Willowbrook and twelve went back to ECW for this work) as late as 1951 for further service as coaches, becoming LLE9-28, though not in the same order; some ran until 1957.

There were five more TS8 coaches that summer, LTO85-9 (EHN 985-9), delivered in June; these were 30-seat London-service vehicles, this time with bodywork by Harrington - a fresh choice for

*Above:* United celebrated the arrival of its first Bristol L5G by taking an official photograph of it. BLO1 (DHN 465) shows the smart, lined-out Tilling red and cream livery, to which the finishing touch was added by a cream roof, a luxury that disappeared, as did so many others, during the war, never to reappear. *(United)*

*Below:* DHN 478, the former BLO14, was renumbered BG28 in the 1951 renumbering scheme. This Marlborough Crescent bus station, Newcastle, shot of it was taken on 24th November 1956. It soldiered on for a further three years and was withdrawn as a 21-year old in 1959. *(Geoffrey Holt)*

From this angle there was very little to distinguish the new Bristol L5Gs from the JO5Gs that had preceded them. BLO15 (DHN 479) again displays *(above)* the carefully thought-out livery, with its lining out and cream roof. The panel above the windows, so avidly used for commercial advertising after the war, looked so much smarter and in-keeping with the rest of the ensemble when used for in-house advertising as shown here. The message on the other side was different; it read "London - Day or Night - UNITED". The JO5G for comparison is 1937's BJO68 (CHN 268) which had yet another variation of the advertising message; on its other side was "UNITED To London - Day or Night" as a variation on a theme. *(Alan Townsin Collection)*

The 1939 EHN-registered Bristol L5Gs had front entrances and revised styling around the front destination indicator. The first of the batch, BLO21 when new, had been renumbered BG35 (EHN 521) when photographed *(above)* in Middlesbrough depot yard circa 1954. Another comparison with a 1937 JO5G is afforded by BJ111 (CHN 313) alongside. The rear view of BG104 *(below)* reveals some of the differences over the 1938 DHNs, most obviously the one-piece rear window, though the higher build and ramped seating layout, with all seats facing forward, are evident when compared with the views opposite. BG104 was registered EHN590 but, in a rare mistake on the part of the signwriter, it had been turned out as FHN590. It was at Haymarket bus station, Newcastle, circa 1955. *(Ron Maybray; David Burnicle)*

United or its offshoots in terms of vehicles ordered from new. They were of front-entrance layout though retaining much of the general look of the previous year's batch, allied to a touch of Harrington flair in respects such as the more graceful rear end; again, they were impressive vehicles.

As additions to the United London-service fleet, they had the effect of further tipping the balance in terms of age of vehicles and numbers from Orange to United. No reason for this policy has been discovered, but it is interesting to speculate where it might have led had the war not intervened. They were to have long careers, albeit soon to be interrupted by the war.

In July 1939, three Leyland Titan TD1 buses with Leyland 48-seat bodies, CK 4237/41/75, were purchased from Milburn Garages, a dealer, having originated with Ribble Motor Services Ltd. They dated from 1930 and were almost identical to United's own examples of that year. Ribble tended to sell its vehicles at a life of 8 to 9 years at that time; they had been well-maintained and in the already uncertain circumstances of the summer of 1939 many were purchased for further short-term use by various operators, but in the event then often remained in service longer than with their original owners, as in this case. Several other major Tilling-managed operators purchased second-hand TD1 buses in the months before the outbreak of war in 1939, in some cases initially to provide transport for workers on military establishments. These three were numbered LD65-7, at least on paper, though the first two were immediately resold to Bell's Services Ltd and it seems likely that, at the outset, the same had been in mind for LD67. Like the Daimlers before them, they entered the Bell's fleet without having operated for United, so neither their colour nor their registration numbers would reveal the then hidden connection between Bell's and United. Just why they passed through United's books before going to Bell's is not clear but there seems likely to have been an accountancy reason.

### The outbreak of war

When the German invasion of Poland led to Britain's involvement in what came to be known as the Second Word War, on 3rd September 1939, many aspects of life in Britain changed almost immediately but others were at first little affected. For a while, most bus chassis and body makers were able to continue with orders in hand, even if delivery dates slipped somewhat as priority was given to war work. Chassis manufacture by Bristol, where the whole of United's order for 1940 had been placed, was at first even less affected than with most makers, as there was no involvement with military vehicle production even though the machine shops were busy with aero-engine work.

While work on this new rolling stock was in hand, the business of Chamberlain Brothers, who traded as "Elite", of St Helen Auckland, was acquired in November 1939, together with four vehicles. Two, numbered AL4.26 and 27, were Albion Victor PK115 models dating from 1937, one with a Barnaby bus body, the other unidentified. The others were Bedford WTB models of 1937/8 which became SB16 and 17, with Plaxton and Robson bodies respectively - both of these and one of the Albions remained in the fleet until 1950. This was the last take-over of an operating concern until after the war - the pace of such acquisitions had been slowing, and even though there were still numerous independent operators running services within United's area, including several substantial concerns, the era of expansion by this means was all but over.

Meanwhile the chassis for a further 50 L5G and five K5G buses ordered to meet United's requirements for 1940 were being built. As it turned out, Britain was involved in far less military activity than had been expected in the winter of 1939/40, this period sometimes being referred to as "the phoney war", and at that stage ECW was also able to continue almost normally. The bodies for the L5G chassis were to be front-entrance 35-seat buses of almost identical design to the 1939 batch of EHN-registered vehicles, a style not built for any other operator. The numbers of the 1940 batch - BLO91-140 - followed on and it was evidently intended that they were to have the partially matching registration number sequence FHN 791-840; in the event BLO92 and 93 were registered as FHN 892 and 893, probably because the intended numbers had been unintentionally released - such departures from normal arrangements were quite common at that time.

For these single-deckers, United had decided to adopt a two-box destination display, with separate route number and a shallower route indicator panel and this made the FHN-registered batch instantly identifiable even from a considerable distance although in later years there were a number of swaps of bodies with earlier BLO-class buses to confuse the issue. A few of these buses were running with four-speed gearboxes rather than the usual five-speed type, at any rate towards the end of their working lives. It has been suggested that this may have been specified for those originally allocated to Scarborough depot but no firm evidence has been found to confirm this.

The K5G lowbridge bodies were again much as being built for other Tilling-managed companies, though retaining the single-aperture front destination box and small side box, as on the previous batch. They also are recorded as having the 54-seat capacity when new, but by 1946 had been rebuilt as 55-seaters: 29 upstairs and 26 down. They were numbered BDO 22-6, with registrations FHN 922-6.

Before any of these vehicles were delivered, the war situation rapidly became much more ominous. The German invasion of Denmark and Norway in April 1940 acting as a prelude to the westward onslaught that was to follow. By the time the first three of the L5G buses were delivered to United on 22nd May, Holland, only 100 miles across the

Only five double-deckers were delivered during 1939: a batch of Bristol K5Gs with Eastern Coach Works 54-seat lowbridge bodywork. BDO17-21 were registered EHN 617-21. BDO17 (EHN 617) *(above)* appears in an early postwar view at Marlborough Crescent bus station, Newcastle. At that time it was fitted with a prototype Bristol six-cylinder oil engine and had run in this form on the service to Throckley since September 1945. On the following page is EHN 619, by then renumbered BGL19, at Park Street, Middlesbrough, in 1955. This was the only one of the five to retain its original body throughout its United service; the other four were rebodied by Charles H Roe in 1950. *(Philip Battersby Collection; David Burnicle)*

North Sea from Lowestoft, had fallen. The German army was sweeping into France, having even reached the English Channel at Boulogne, and the rapidity of advance caused the risk of invasion to be judged far more serious.

Five days later, the military authorities ordered the immediate closure of ECW's factory and the clearance from it of all vehicles in course of body construction, regardless of what stage they had reached, a circumstance not suffered by any other major British bus bodybuilder. Remarkably, this was achieved in a 24-hour period from 28th May. ECW delivery records show BLO91, 94 and 95 as delivered on 22nd May, evidently normal deliveries. Then BLO93/6/7, 100/4/5/12/8/9/20 are shown as delivered on 29th and 30th May, and the five K5Gs all on 31st May. These were to be the last recorded ECW deliveries to United until August, all but one of these being licensed on 1st June, also the recorded date of purchase of both chassis and bodies; the exception, BLO120, was not purchased and licensed until 1st October, suggesting that it may have been incomplete to quite a major degree.

Associated operating companies co-operated in the evacuation of ECW, many of the part-built vehicles being stored at various operating garages of group companies in or not far from East Anglia. It proved possible for ECW to have the use of

premises at Irthlingborough, Northamptonshire, which had been a depot of the United Counties Omnibus Co Ltd and steps were taken to set up a smaller-scale bodybuilding works there. Much of the stock of materials or parts, including seasoned timber, went to Irthlingborough once ECW was established there. Some of the group's operators with suitable bodybuilding facilities took delivery of part-completed vehicles and finished the work themselves. One was United, though it has not been possible to establish which vehicles were involved. In addition to BLO120, two others with a significant gap between delivery and first registration were BLO123 and 127, both recorded as delivered in November 1940 but first registered on 1st May 1941. One source has reported that a stock of machined timber for bodies in hand was sent to United's Barnard Castle depot, but this was small and seems unlikely to have had space for more than a limited quantity, perhaps for those to be completed at Darlington.

After the May 1940 deliveries, there were 37 L5G buses outstanding for United. An official note in August, just after supply resumed, listed 34 as then having incomplete bodies: BLO92/8/9, 101-3/6/8/10/1/3/4/6/7/20/2-40. ECW's record of 'deliveries', which may have meant the dates when they were regarded as complete and no longer

ECW's responsibility (which does not necessarily exclude completion work carried out by United), show two in August, two in September, five in October, thirteen in November (all 1940), two in January 1941, one in February, two in March, five in April, and a final three in May of 1941, with a further two for which no dates are known.

It is perhaps appropriate to mention the two L5G chassis supplied to United as such and never bodied. These were numbers 50097 and 54088, which implies construction circa late 1939 or 1940,

the former coming between the EHN and FHN series, and the latter following immediately after the end of the FHN batch. It is understood that they were dismantled for use as spares soon after delivery, a very strange phenomenon bearing in mind the close co-operation between BTCC and group operators.

Eventually, the FHN batch was completed, joining the earlier L5G buses, soon to become a familiar sight in almost all parts of the company's territory. The combination of Bristol chassis and

Gardner 5LW engine found in the 140 BLO, 125 BJO and 35 conversions (33 BHO and the two further BJO buses converted from BJ at that stage) brought the total of such single-deckers, built new or converted, to 300. They were to serve the company well, forming the main front-line strength of the fleet for the next five years until they began to be augmented by post-war models, initially of almost unchanged mechanical design even if very different appearance.

The equivalent BDO and BOH class double-deck fleet, at that date totalling 26 buses on GO5G and K5G chassis, was much more modest, reflecting A T Evans's preference for single-deckers. Backing them up were the Leyland Titan TD1s converted with Gardner 5LW engines in 1936/7, also totalling 26 vehicles, and indeed those retaining their petrol engines, still in everyday use as was to remain so until well into post-war years. If the staccato bark of a Gardner 5LW engine was the most familiar sound of a United bus of that time, remaining so for many years, the deep roar of a Leyland 8.6-litre oil engine took quite a strong second place among the more modern vehicles in the fleet, especially in Northumberland, where most were based. There were 89 LTO-class Leyland Tigers at that stage, although some of the London service coaches were stored for much of the war, as explained below. In addition there were the ten highbridge LHO-class Titan TD2 double-deckers which had been converted with similar engines in 1938.

In the early stages of the war, the normal pattern of withdrawal of older vehicles gave way to one where buses were taken for military or civil defence use, sometimes to be returned, sometimes not. A note of 25th November 1940 shows that 102 buses were "out with the military", these including 29 AK-class AEC Reliances, 25 LT-class Leyland Tigers, 16 B-class Bristol Bs, 12 D-class Daimler CF6s and ten AR-class AEC Regals. The cutting-back of services to save fuel meant that fewer buses were needed in the operational fleet; those delicensed were largely drawn from the petrol-engined types. Recorded overall fleet strength did not dip far from the 915 mark applicable at 30th September 1939, dropping a little to 894 a year later and then recovering slightly to 901 at the same date in 1941. However this latter figure, at least, included numbers of requisitioned buses not officially written off until 30th June 1942 - by then it had become clear that many of those taken would not return to the fleet. Other types temporarily little seen for a while did reappear later in the war, when all the surviving petrol Tigers, well down in numbers, and most of the petrol Regals, back almost to full strength, were converted to operate on producer gas, but that and other stories will be told more fully in the next volume.

The United Board minutes of 22nd April 1941 noted that, upon instructions from the Ministry of Transport, the Orange Brothers service between Newcastle and London was to be discontinued on 30th April. The wording suggests that United's own service had already ceased, although some other operators of long-distance services were allowed to continue for a time. In connection with this, the vehicles in Orange ownership (six coaches and six buses) were passed over to United with effect from 30th April, and the Orange company entered a dormant period. United's last two batches of coaches bought for the London services, LTO41-9 and 85-9, were renumbered shortly after this, becoming LOC1-14, possibly to emphasize their unsuitability for use as buses in emergencies, and were put into storage; some, at least, of the 1939 Harrington-bodied batch were in Berwick depot, sheeted over and with engines removed circa 1943.

When a rather basic London service restarted, in 1946, nine of these, LOC3, 4, 6 and 9-14, were transferred into Orange ownership, with Orange fleetnames, which LOC3 and 4 had presumably retained from prewar days through the period of storage. When Orange Brothers Ltd was wound up in 1950, the vehicles reverted to United ownership. In the 1951 renumbering LOC1-14 became LLT1-14, the "T" standing for Tyne-Tees-Thames, the brand name used for the London services since 1935. The vehicles lasted until 1956: a remarkably long career on such duty.

**CK 4237 was one of the trio of ex-Ribble Leyland TD1 Titans acquired in 1939 and was in the ownership of the Bell's Services subsidiary until the end of 1944. In this picture outside West Hartlepool bus station on 28th July 1953, after withdrawal, and by then with a Leyland 8.6-litre oil engine and the fleet number LLL6, it was being tow-started prior to being driven to store at Normanby. (David Burnicle)**

*Above:* In what must be one of the most atmospheric of bus photographs, taken on 22nd April 1954, the ex-Ribble Titan, LLL6 (CK 4237), had been incarcerated, pending disposal, in United's Normanby store shed, the former Blue Band Bus Services garage. Alongside was BGL10 (AHN 375), one of the 1935 batch of ten Bristol GO5Gs. In 1943, when still numbered BDO10, AHN 375 had been badly damaged by fire, as a consequence of which it was rebodied by Eastern Coach Works to the same design as the 1940 FHN-registered K5Gs. On the right of the picture is Gardner-engined Titan LGL18 (VF 8505). The radiator and cab in the immediate foreground belonged to another Leyland Titan TD1, LLL10 (DC 9953), which had been acquired from Smith's Safeway Services in 1931. All were sold for scrap later that year. *(David Burnicle)*

*Below:* One of the last second-hand vehicles of the prewar period was a 1938 Bedford WTB with Duple 26-seat bus bodywork which came from Oliver Brothers, of Esh Winning, in October 1938. Numbered SB15, CUP 491 ran as a bus until 1949. It was then converted to a lorry by removing the seats, side windows and central roof section. As ED1, the Bedford was photographed at Scarborough depot circa 1953. *(J S Cockshott)*

*Above:* The 20 Leyland Tiger TS8 models with ECW bodies of May-June 1939 followed previous practice in having bodies of the same outline and layout as on the contemporary Bristol buses but this time were finished as coaches with 32 comfortable seats. They were finished in the olive green and cream livery, complete with side mouldings resembling those on the London-service coaches, giving a distinctive appearance. Some, at least, were intended for tour and private hire work and LTO80 (EHN 980), seen soon after entering service, was one of the ten with sliding roof. *(Alan Townsin Collection)*

*Below:* The five TS8 coaches for the Tyne-Tees-Thames services delivered in June 1939 marked a change of bodybuilder to Harrington. Here too, there was a change to the front entrance position, but the front-end design otherwise retained a general resemblance to the Brush-bodied 1938 batch, although with more flowing lines at the rear. This picture dates from June 1946, taken at the same time as the line-up shown on page 136 and shows EHN 988, originally LTO88 but renumbered LOC13 in 1941 and with Orange fleetnames, as explained in the text. It was still in smart condition, even though having a dark-painted roof as a legacy from wartime, and lacking its front wheel-nut guard rings in usual United manner. Next in line is LOC3 (DHN443) of the 1938 batch. *(United)*

*Above:* A sign of the times: United's Bristol L5G BLO95 (FHN 795) was delivered from ECW on 22nd May 1940, just before the Lowestoft Coach Factory was shut down by the military because of the risk of invasion. It was complete with wartime additions to its livery in the shape of white wing tips and side valances. Masked headlamps and sidelamps would follow before it entered service. Apart from the livery modifications, the major difference in comparison with the EHN-registered L5Gs was the shallower two-piece destination screen. *(Alan Townsin Collection)*

*Below:* The first of the batch, FHN 791, seen in its postwar guise as BG105. The 1951 renumbering system made BLO1 into BG15, and all prewar BLOs advanced by 14. BG105 was photographed in Park Street, Middlesbrough, on 11th January 1958, still looking very sound; it was withdrawn later that year. *(Geoffrey Holt)*

United's final batch of five Bristol K5G buses with bodywork to prewar standards was delivered from Lowestoft on 31st May 1940, just after the shut-down imposed on the ECW factory at Lowestoft by the military authorities because of the sudden threat of invasion. Yet they were virtually identical to the previous five, supplied early in 1939, even to the illuminated name panel on the cab front. Normal bus output was being disrupted but the process of ordering and manufacture had begun under peacetime conditions. These pictures taken at Feethams, Darlington, on two occasions in 1955, both show FHN 923, originally BDO23, by then running as BGL23, little changed by 15 years' service though the livery by then omitted the lower-deck cream band. In the lower view, one of the later wartime buses with "utility" bodywork has drawn up behind. *(David Burnicle)*

An interesting feature of the prewar Bristol L5Gs was the occasional example of body swapping among the three different batches. The original BLO3, by then BG17 (DHN467), had acquired a body from one of the 1940 FHN-registered vehicles. It was seen *(above)* at Grange Road Works, Darlington, on 19th May 1957. There has been a suggestion that these "wrong-bodied" vehicles were simply the complete original chassis/body combination given a new identity on overhaul, much as London Transport did with the RT class at Aldenham; there is no official evidence in support of this theory. In 1947, BLO39 (EHN 539), a 1939 chassis, received a body from one of the 1938 vehicles, BLO11 (DHN475). In the view below, in its later guise as BG53, EHN 539 was at Scarborough bus station on 24th May 1958. This vehicle has survived in preservation, but has not, at the time of writing, been restored, and it has been given the identity of DHN 475. *(Both: Geoffrey Holt)*

*Above:* An exchange of bodies in the opposite direction saw the chassis of 1939's BLO82 (EHN 582) matched with a 1940 body from the FHN-registered series. The date of the body swap and the identity of the vehicle from which the 1940 body came remain for the moment unknown. Once again we are indebted to Geoffrey Holt for an illustration of the hybrid EHN 582. With its later fleet number, BG96, it was outside Scarborough railway station circa 1957.

*Below:* In another 1947 swap, 1940's BLO132 (FHN832) acquired the body from 1939's BLO77 (EHN 577). When photographed in United's West Hartlepool depot yard on 9th April 1955, it had its 1951 identity of BG146. The Shell tanker was present on that occasion, delivering fuel to keep United's wheels turning. *(David Burnicle)*

# INDEX